W9-CSS-115

Jackson & Perkins®

BEAUTIFUL
ROSES
MADE EASY

Copyright 2003 Teri Dunn, Bruce Asakawa, and Sharon Asakawa

All rights reserved. No part of this book may be reproduced or transmitted in any form, or by any means, electronic or mechanical, including photocopying, recording, or by any information storage and retrieval system, without permission in writing from the publisher.

Published by Cool Springs Press, a Division of Thomas Nelson, Inc.
P.O. Box 141000, Nashville, Tennessee 37214.

Dunn, Teri.
Jackson & Perkins beautiful roses made easy : Southwestern edition /
Teri Dunn, Bruce Asakawa, Sharon Asakawa.
p. cm.
ISBN: 1-591860-71-7 (pbk. : alk paper)
1. Rose culture—Southwest, New. 2. Roses—Southwest, New.
I. Title: Jackson and Perkins beautiful roses made easy.
II. Asakawa, Bruce. III. Asakawa, Sharon. IV. Title.
SB411.D8624 2004
635.9'33734'0979--dc22
2003026744

First printing 2004
Printed in the United States of America
10 9 8 7 6 5 4 3 2 1

Managing Editor: Jenny Andrews
Designer: Bruce Gore
Production Artists: Bill Kersey and S.E. Anderson

Visit the Thomas Nelson website at www.ThomasNelson.com

Jackson & Perkins®

BEAUTIFUL
ROSES
MADE EASY

• SOUTHWESTERN EDITION •

TERI DUNN &
BRUCE & SHARON ASAKAWA

COOL
SPRINGS
PRESS

Nashville, Tennessee

A DIVISION OF THOMAS NELSON, INC.

www.thomasnelson.com

Acknowledgements

With thanks to Jim Shearer, Jenny Andrews, Donna Mello, Chuck Prophet . . .
y los tres amigos.

—Teri Dunn

Thank you to the photographers and illustrator who contributed to this book, and to the staff of Jackson & Perkins® for their participation and assistance in this project.

Illustrations: Elayne Sears

Photos: Unless otherwise indicated below, rose photos are courtesy of Jackson & Perkins®.

Jerry Pavia: 15A, 16A, 17B, 18, 21B, 28CDE, 32E, 34B, 35A, 36AC, 37AB, 40AB, 47A, 50B, 52, 57, 59A, 61A, 62A, 63A, 67, 83B, 102, 103B, 108A, 113B, 122, 125A, 127AB, 128, 134, 144B, 148A, 166B, 170B, 171B, 177AB, 179A, 180B, 185A, 188A, 189B, 190B

Neil Soderstrom: 33A, 36D, 49B, 58, 68, 71, 72A, 77A, 84, 85, 86, 89, 90AB, 91AB, 92, 94, 95, 99, 104, 109, 113A, 115AB, 116B, 117, 119, 129AB, 131, 132B, 133AB, 155A, 160A, 168B, 185B

Thomas Eltzroth: 12BC, 13, 16B, 17A, 20B, 28B, 32CD, 34ACD, 35BC, 36B, 37CD, 54, 60A, 63B, 66, 82, 124AB, 137, 147B, 162A, 166A, 175A, 178B, 181A, 184AB, 187AB, 200

Charles Mann: 12A, 42A, 43, 48A, 56, 59B, 61B, 62B, 83A, 97, 141, 195, 198

Heirloom Roses, Inc. (www.heirloomroses.com): 74, 164B, 170A, 178A, 182AB, 183A, 189A, 203

Liz Ball: 60B, 143

Felder Rushing: 121, 132A

Laura Coit: 186A

Lorenzo Gunn: 12D

Dency Kane: 44A

Ralph Snodsmith: 103A

Corbis®: 14BC, 24AB

Getty Images™: 25B, 27A, 101, 140

Key: from top to bottom of page and left to right, A=first photo, B=second, C=third, D=fourth, E=fifth

Chapter introduction photos: 'Bella'roma' (page 6), 'Fame' (10), 'Our Lady of Guadalupe' (22), 'Wildberry Breeze' (38), 'Gemini' (64), 'Disneyland® Rose' (96), 'Grand Prize' (142), 'Sultry' (194)

TABLE OF CONTENTS

INTRODUCTION

WHETHER IT'S LOVE, FRIENDSHIP, OR DESIRE, the rose has long spoken for us, making it one of the greatest and most powerful flowers to ever grace our gardens. Is there another flower on earth that holds us so completely in its power? If we see a rose in passing—driving or walking by someone's garden or even an old churchyard—our eye goes to it, our spirit cleaves to it, drinking in a brief "ahhh" of desire and admiration. If we draw near—in our own garden or in a bouquet—time stands still as the rose's luscious beauty envelops our attention and bewitches our senses.

Indeed, the rose is unique among all the flowers of the world for its long and captivating history with people. Once upon a time, it was a wildling, a thorny little bush studded with pretty little single-form flowers. It adorned hillsides on the island of Crete thousands of years before the birth of Christ. Centuries later, it had been successfully coaxed into gardens. The Chinese and the Egyptians were probably the first to begin selecting plants on the basis of flower color. By the time of the Roman Empire, roses were widely grown and exalted: crowns of rose-buds were worn at feasts and banquet floors were carpeted with their fragrant petals. Spurred by the importation of Asian species, nineteenth-century Europe at last brought the rose into full and glorious cultivation. The amazing variety we find in roses today fulfills all their early promise—even as modern rose breeders continue to provide us with better and more beautiful ones.

Luscious colors and diverse forms are not the only reasons the world loves the rose. Along the way, its enchanting scents have been distilled into perfumed oils. The flowers have always been a favorite in bouquets, with one another or in combination with other flowers or greens. The sweet petals have been added to salads and pastries, fresh or candied, or made into jelly. One rose in particular, *Rosa gallica*, dubbed "the Apothecaries' Rose," was long touted in various medicines and as a tonic. Vitamin-C-rich rose hips have been used in teas, desserts, and remedies. The showy flowers have been featured in paintings and inspired architects designing windows for great cathedrals; their forms and colors have been incorporated into fabrics for clothing and decoration; and many poets and writers have praised the rose's incomparable appeal.

'Purple Tiger'

'Sun Sprinkles'

Mankind's romance with the rose is deep, passionate, and primal, going beyond the plant's long and fascinating history. Other flowers may appeal to our eyes, but the rose, in its many forms, from small sweetheart blossoms to big, commanding showpieces, from simple five-petal ones to plush, petal-laden beauties, is undeniably lovely to look at. Roses also excite our senses of smell and even taste, drawing us near to inhale scents so varied and sweet as to make us abandon our reliance on vision and get lost in that heady, delicious fragrance. Even the texture of roses invites admiration—unlike the tough petals of tulips or the fleeting wands of gaura or delphinium—these blossoms are silky and soft to the touch.

And while rose flowers appear so pretty, so seductive, so feminine, they are carried on stout, thorn-lined stems that can be said to possess a muscular, masculine vigor. And so the rose we love to love is both yin and yang, a little bit bitter with the sweet, and—

ultimately—irresistible. Like perhaps no other flower on earth, we savor its many pleasures and lessons while it lasts. In the words of the poet William Blake, this exceptional flower invites us to "kiss the joy as it flies."

'High Society'

Song of the Rose

*"If Zeus chose us a King of the
flowers in his mirth,
He would call to the rose, and
would royally crown it;
For the rose, ho, the rose! is the
grace of the earth,
Is the light of the plants that are
growing upon it!"*

Sappho, Greek Poet, 600 B.C.

pests and their control—noting safe solutions. A directory of 100 recommended roses shows you just a hint of the many beautiful rose options, from reliable classics to the latest introductions.

With the many possibilities of wonderful roses for every situation, and the ease of care, every gardener should include roses in their landscape, to enjoy for many years to come.

'Simplicity'

The following chapters will show that you, too, can include this paragon of flowers in your own garden, to enjoy its glorious blooms and enticing fragrance. Selecting the right rose for your needs and landscape situation is the first, very important step. There are a multitude of options available today, with varying sizes, colors, hardiness, and heat tolerance. The selection seems infinite! And rose breeders continue to make advances to bring us ever more lovely (and tough) roses for every garden.

There are chapters on planting and care, offering guidance on easy, reliable maintenance practices. Study your particular site, and be attuned to your local climate and soils. At the back of the book is a chapter pertaining to your region that will provide you with a wealth of information on weather, soils, rose selections, maintenance, and resources. There is also information on

OUR ROMANCE WITH ROSES

The Rise of the Rose

In the oft-quoted words of the poet, "a rose is a rose is a rose." And despite all the wondrous variation in the world of roses, this is quite true. Roses have been found or grown in many diverse places throughout history, from ancient Persia to China to Madagascar to the American prairies, making for a complex family tree. Even the experts have trouble sorting it all out! But unlike, say, dahlias, which have some family members that would fool you into thinking that they are mums or even zinnias, the fact remains that roses are clearly recognizable as such.

The rose's journey through history is a colorful one, one that tells us much about our own human love of beauty. It's possible that no other flower has been so widely grown and admired, or captivated the intense efforts of plant breeders, like the ever-beautiful, versatile rose.

'Wildfire'

11

Potentilla	Pyracantha	Yoshino Cherry	Apple
(*Potentilla fruticosa*)	(*Pyracantha* species)	(*Prunus* × *yedoensis*)	(*Malus sylvestris*)

A number of familiar plants belong to the rose family, with signature five-petaled flowers in the species or wild forms. Members of the Rosaceae can also have attractive, even edible, fruits. It's no coincidence that rose fruits, called "hips," look like tiny apples since roses and apple trees are kin.

The Rose Family

Roses belong to and dominate the plant family Rosaceae. This group includes many other familiar plants: apple and crabapple trees, firethorn *(Pyracantha),* ornamental quince *(Chaenomeles),* strawberries and blackberries, spirea, and potentilla, to name only a few. All members, in unimproved or wild species, generally sport five petals. When the petals fall and the tiny seeds begin to develop, they are encased in various types of fruits; the seed-containing structure (fruit) on a rosebush is called a "hip." Though other members of the Rosaceae have fragrant flowers, develop colorful fruit, and have thorns, none have fired the imagination through the centuries as has the rose.

Ancient Roses

When we look at the fossil record or ancient art and artifacts, we find astoundingly early evidence of roses. They appear to have been growing as far back as 30 million years ago! There is also evidence of roses on nearly every continent, from Asia to Europe to North America. People in cultures around the world have been excited to "discover" and grow roses for thousands of years, setting the stage for the incredible diversity we admire today.

Among the earliest mentions of the rose are the poems of the 600 B.C. Greek poet Sappho, who praised it as "the queen of flowers," and the scholar Confucius, who described roses growing in the imperial gardens of the Chou Dynasty (1122-221 B.C.).

Let him
Who was love's teacher teach you
*   too love's cure;*
Let the same hand that wounded
*   bring the balm.*
Healing and poisonous herbs the
*   same soil bears,*
And rose and nettle oft grow side
*   by side.*

Ovid (Publius Ovidius Naso)
(43 B.C.-A.D. 18), Roman poet
Remedia Amoris (Cures for Love)

After the start of the first century A.D., the rose clearly appears to have gained popularity as cultures mixed and trade routes expanded. Its earliest heyday was during the height of the Roman Empire, when roses were imported from Egypt. They were revered as a source and symbol of beauty and luxury. Bridal couples wore crowns of roses. At civic celebrations and private parties, rose petals were strewn on the ground to beautify the setting as well as scent the air. Sometimes nets suspended from ceilings released fragrant showers of petals onto the revelers below. Petals were also added to bathwater, to cosmetics, even to food.

India, or more properly the ancient kingdom of Kashmir, is credited with cultivating roses as well. Indeed, there is an old story that an emperor and empress boating on a canal on the rose-landscaped palace grounds noticed fragrant oil floating on the water's surface; finding this naturally-occurring oil led to sophisticated distilling processes for the prized perfume known as "attar of roses."

The deliciously scented rose that supplied that oil, possibly *Rosa × damascena* 'Triginti-petala', eventually made its way from Asia Minor to the Middle East, where it was grown in the hills above the holy city of Mecca. Vials of Arabian attar of roses (in various grades, depending on the "pressing," like olive oil) were eagerly sought after in the ancient world and command high praise and high prices to this day.

The Crusades, beginning in the 12th century, dramatically increased trade with the East, bringing more plant species, including roses, into cultivation. Around this time, roses began to appear in paintings, murals, fabrics, and even architecture. As horticultural knowledge and techniques advanced, some rose-lovers began tinkering with improving existing varieties and creating new ones.

The damask rose, *Rosa × damascena*, has been in cultivation for hundreds of years and is the source of the perfume attar of roses. Tradition has it that this rose was brought back to Europe by the Crusaders from the city of Damascus (hence the name) in the thirteenth century. It is the parent of Portland roses, and the York and Lancaster rose, made famous by England's Wars of the Roses.

The shape of the rose flower, with its numerous overlapping petals, is the source of the word *rosette*, and is the inspiration for the names "rosette window" and the navigational device called a "compass rose."

ROSES AND LANGUAGE—A COLORFUL HISTORY

Roses have been popular for so long that they have acquired various meanings. Here are some interesting tidbits:

- **The word:** Despite all its evocative connotations in poem and song, the word "rose" apparently has no specific or historical meaning. In English, French, Danish, German, and Norwegian, it is *rose*. In Spanish, Portuguese, Italian, and Russian, it is *rosa*. In Dutch, it is *roos*. In Hungarian, it is *rozsa*. In Latin it was *rosa*, and in Greek, it has always been *rhodon*. Over time, however, the old names also came to designate the colors red and pink.

- **The shape:** From the shape of the rose flower came the word "rosette," which botanists have used widely, to describe not only blossom form but also an arrangement of leaves radiating from a center or crown (as with lettuce or ajuga, for instance). In architecture, there are "rosette windows," round, stylized patterns of the rose flower, with stained glass in radiating traceries. Rosary beads were originally meant to represent the Virgin Mary's crown of roses, *rosary* being the Latin word for "rose garden." A navigational compass, with its concentric circles, was even called a "compass rose."

- **The colors:** As roses became more domesticated and cherished in bouquets, during Victorian times the colors were assigned sentimental meanings. The gift of a red rose meant romantic love or desire; pink signified affection and friendship; white symbolized purity or virtuousness; yellow indicated either jealousy or congratulations on a perfect achievement.

In the "language of flowers" the gift of a red rose signifies love, a pink rose affection, a white rose purity, and a yellow rose congratulations.

China Rose, *Rosa chinensis* 'Semperflorens'

> *The red rose whispers of passion*
>
> *And the white rose breathes of love;*
>
> *O, the red rose is a falcon,*
>
> *And the white rose is a dove.*
>
> John Boyle O'Reilly

The Rose's Triumph in Europe

While roses continued to be domesticated, distributed, and enjoyed in places like France, Italy, and England, it was trade with Asia that brought a flood of important new rose species into Europe. These wildlings became the ancestors of practically every modern rose, and include: *Rosa gallica, Rosa × damascena, Rosa rugosa, Rosa odorata, Rosa foetida, Rosa moschata, Rosa multiflora, Rosa wichuriana,* and *Rosa chinensis.*

This last one, the China rose, arrived around 1789 and inspired rose breeders because it repeat-flowered. Enthusiasts collected pollen and crossed species and cultivated varieties with abandon, leading to an explosion of new roses. The lineage of the crosses was not always clear, or recorded, but the results were undeniable: Desirable new qualities such as extended bloom time, new colors (especially yellow), and new forms (climbers, in particular) entered gardens to great adulation.

Roses were also considered useful in herbal medicine. Dried petals of the apothecaries' rose, *Rosa gallica* 'Officinalis', were used to make tonics and purgatives. Even before people knew that rose hips were high in vitamin C, their astringent pulp was being

The bourbon rose 'Souvenir de la Malmaison' (1843), originally called 'Queen of Beauty and Fragrance', was grown in the rose garden of the Empress Josephine at her chateau outside Paris. It was given its current name after a Grand Duke of Russia acquired a plant for the Imperial Garden in St. Petersburg.

used in various drinks, remedies, and poultices. Roses were touted as helpful for everything from relieving headaches to providing aphrodisiacs.

Publicity, as ever, helped. Perhaps the most famous promoter of roses was the wife of Napoleon Bonaparte, the Empress Josephine. She was fanatical in her love for roses and assembled perhaps the largest and most complete rose collection of her day at Malmaison, her chateau outside Paris. At one time, it boasted several plants each of over 210 types of roses, including gallicas, centifolias, damasks, albas, and species roses. She employed top botanists and they worked

Rosa gallica 'Officinalis', known as the apothecaries' rose, has been used in various herbal remedies since medieval times.

to develop new, improved roses. This garden is still in existence, and a popular tourist attraction. It is said that you can smell its heady fragrances on the breeze many miles before you arrive at its gates.

Roses in America

In our country's relatively short history, the rose has won hearts and played important roles. What many people may not realize, however, is that few roses are actually native to North America.

During the Civil War, grieving families and comrades honored fallen soldiers by planting a rose on their graves. The rose of choice was a fragrant, single-flowered white rambler with prickly stems called the Cherokee rose (*Rosa laevigata*). Despite its common name, this species is actually a Chinese import. (The so-called "Confederate rose" is not a rose at all, but a bright-pink-flowered hibiscus relative also called rose mallow, or *Hibiscus mutabilis*.)

The state flower of the District of Columbia, the seat of our country's federal government, is the rose, though, again not a native rose, but rather an old French-bred tea rose called 'Mme Ferdinand Jamin'.

'Kathleen'

Spicily fragrant, rampantly growing wild beach roses grace the coastline of New England and the Mid-Atlantic, beautifying places where few other plants will thrive. Yet this species, *Rosa rugosa,* is of Oriental origin. Its virtues of toughness, disease-resistance, and spicy fragrance have been capitalized on by rose breeders, of course. Nowadays there are many fine cultivated, named varieties.

Another import, hailing from Japan, is cluster-blooming, tough little *Rosa multiflora,* which can be found growing wild throughout much of the United States. Introduced in the late 1800s as a rootstock for grafted roses, the multiflora rose was at one time promoted for erosion control, as a "living fence" for livestock and snow barriers along highways, and wildlife habitat, but has become a noxious weed in many areas of the eastern U.S., and is even illegal to grow or sell in some states. Enterprising rose breeders have also tried to corral its durability and hardiness in their breeding projects.

The Cherokee rose, *Rosa laevigata,* well-known in America during Civil War times, is actually native to China despite its common name.

Native American roses do exist. However, none have become popular garden choices, though they have been admired in their natural settings and occasionally brought into cultivation. These include the Carolina or pasture rose *(Rosa carolina),* the prairie rose *(Rosa setigera),* the swamp rose *(Rosa palustris),* and the Nootka rose *(Rosa nutkana).*

Also in the American mix are many old-fashioned roses brought to our shores by immigrants and taken west by pioneers. Some of these hardy beauties survive to this

There are several roses native to the United States, including *Rosa carolina,* the Carolina or pasture rose.

day in abandoned fields and homesteads, old churchyards, and the like. Identifying, or for that matter rescuing them, is often a trick, though there are historical-rose enthusiasts like the Texas Rose Rustlers who enjoy getting to know them better and saving them for future generations.

There is no doubt, however, that modern hybridized roses—from hybrid teas to cluster-blooming floribundas to climbers and minis—are the most popular and the ones we love best. They grow everywhere in our land of diverse climates and soils, in every sort of garden. That some Americans take roses for granted or mistakenly believe that they are native is actually a testament to their remarkable success in our country.

The qualities that have made *Rosa multiflora* a nuisance have also made it useful in the rose industry. It has become a noxious weed in many areas, but has also been used as a durable, cold-hardy rootstock for grafted plants.

The Birth of Modern Roses and Hybridization

The roses we grow and enjoy today emerged from and owe a great debt to a long, complex, and intriguing history. Drawing on an extensive gene pool and using ever-more-refined techniques, present-day breeders are able to bring us roses of astounding quality and beauty.

The Ascent of Hybrid Tea Roses

The story of the modern rose and its tremendous hold on us can be said to begin with the development of the first hybrid tea roses. When we think of roses, the form we picture is the hybrid tea. Historians cite France as the origin of this relatively new class of roses. A deeply fragrant, pink flower with silvery undertones called 'La France' is credited as the very first. The breeder was a Frenchman named Jean-Baptiste Guillot, and the year was 1867. He crossed a "hybrid perpetual" with an old-fashioned "tea rose," and the result was a unique and strikingly beautiful flower form. The shapely blooms featured petals unfurling slowly from an urn-shaped bud to reveal an elegant blossom with a high, pointed center.

Guillot enthusiastically publicized his achievement. When other breeders began to dabble in the same gene pool, they were able to duplicate his impressive results and more hybrid teas were introduced. 'Lady Mary Fitzwilliam', a light pink, richly fragrant one from an English hybridizer named Henry Bennett accelerated the class. 'Lady Mary Fitzwilliam', for whatever complex genetic

Hybrid Perpetual Rose, 'Baronne Prevost' (1842)
The development of the popular hybrid tea rose is a result of crossing a hybrid perpetual with a tea rose in the 1800s, which combined a beautiful flower form with a long bloom period.

reasons, was very fertile (unlike 'La France') and many more hybrid teas followed. In 1892, the National Rose Society gave its first-ever gold medal to another pink-flowered beauty, 'Mrs. W.J. Grant' (bred by Alexander Dickson of Northern Ireland), and the gates were flung open.

Americans became involved by the turn of the twentieth century. One breeder, E. Gurney Hill of Richmond, Indiana, issued dozens of hybrid teas before World War I. The American public was eager to acquire them and his roses began to appear in gardens from coast to coast.

Rose breeding then went on a hiatus during both World Wars, due at least in part to the need for greenhouses and growing fields for raising food rather than ornamental flowers. Then, at the close of World War II, a French breeder issued 'Peace', the most enduringly popular hybrid tea of all time—and with that introduction, ushered in a new era for hybrid teas both here and abroad. Many talented and persistent hybridizers not only developed but were able to market hybrid teas far and wide. Among them were Wilhelm Kordes and Mathias Tantau in Germany, the Meilland and Delbard nurseries in France, and Dines Poulsen in Denmark. In the United States, particularly in the mild, sunny, rose-friendly climate of California, several key players emerged: Fred Howard in Los Angeles, Herbert Swim and Ollie Weeks of Armstrong Roses, and the prolific Eugene Boerner of Jackson & Perkins. In their hands, hybrid teas became the most popular roses on earth.

Hybrid teas are deservedly popular. They represent the culmination of knowledge and expertise available to modern hybridizers. The color range for roses has never been wider or more exciting. In hybrid teas, we also enjoy

THE DOROTHY PERKINS ROSE

When Charles Perkins and his father-in-law A.E. Jackson started Jackson & Perkins in 1872 they sold a wide variety of plants, including roses. That changed in 1901 when hybridizer and foreman E. Alvin Miller crossed a wild trailing rose (Rosa wichuriana) with a French hybrid ('Mme Gabriel Luizet') and created 'Dorothy Perkins'.

Named for Perkins's granddaughter, it became one of the most popular roses of all time. Winning the British National Rose Society award for hybridizing, no garden in the early twentieth century was complete without 'Dorothy Perkins'. It was the first pink rambler to be hardy in colder areas and was widely planted to cover pergolas, arbors, pillars, and walls with its twenty-foot canes and abundance of small, light pink, highly fragrant blooms.

Hybrid Tea, 'Memorial Day'

The Advent of Floribundas

Around the turn of the twentieth century, in search of a more cold-tolerant rose for his chilly Danish winters, the aforementioned breeder Dines Poulsen successfully crossed a polyantha with an attractive rambler to yield a tough little cluster-blooming rose, pink 'Ellen Poulsen'. He called it a "hybrid polyantha." A flurry of other similar roses, all from the Poulsens, followed.

However it was not until Gene Boerner from the American firm of Jackson & Perkins and Wilhelm Kordes became involved that hybrid polyanthas were crossed with hybrid teas to create a new class of cluster-blooming roses, named "floribunda" by Charles Perkins's cousin, C.H. Perkins. Jackson & Perkins introduced a perky red one, dubbed 'World's Fair', at that 1939 event and the public's attention was secured. Back in the test fields, company hybridizers worked to refine the flower form to more closely resemble a hybrid tea blossom, as well as to bring improvements

regularity of bloom cycles unimagined a century ago, not to mention improved vigor and disease resistance. Their flowers, borne singly on long, strong stems, are gorgeous and long lasting, both in the garden and in a vase.

These days, with vast resources of parent plants, refined breeding techniques, ample space, plus creativity and good luck, rose breeders enjoy nearly limitless possibilities. Creating better and more beautiful hybrid teas remains a worthy project.

THE PEACE ROSE

Originally bred in 1935 by French hybridizer Francis Meilland, bud eyes of a promising new rose, then designated only as #3-35-40, were given to Germany, Italy, and the Conard-Pyle Company in the U.S. in 1939, just months before the start of World War II. The rose was given several names: Germany introduced the rose as 'Gloria Dei', Italy as 'Gioia', and Meilland called it 'Mme A. Meilland', after his late mother. At the close of the war, on April 29, 1945, the date of the fall of Berlin, Conard-Pyle formally introduced the rose as 'Peace', to commemorate the end of the conflict.

An early floribunda, 'Betty Prior' (left) was introduced in 1938. 'Lavender Lace' (right) is a 2004 introduction. Hybrid polyanthas were bred with hybrid teas to create a new type of rose, named "floribundas" by Jackson & Perkins.

in color and bloom size. Bloom time was successfully extended, and more compact growth habits encouraged. As color-laden shrubs, floribundas are without peer—and it has been through the concentrated efforts of Jackson & Perkins at improving and developing this group that these outstanding, cluster-blooming roses were brought to the level of popularity they continue to enjoy.

Back to the Future—English Roses

Another breakthrough in rose breeding in recent years is the so-called English roses, primarily developed by Englishman David Austin. With great skill and persistence, he succeeded in mixing the best of the old with the best of the new. His roses have the appearance of old-fashioned roses (with full loads of petals often on large bushes), they have the same scent (he retained the heady, intense fragrances of the old damasks and bourbons), and yet they are repeat-bloomers. Some are larger plants, while others are more compact. Many are quite cold hardy, some are disease-resistant. His first ones debuted in the 1970s, and as a group they are outstanding— and show great promise for Austin and other ambitious breeders who continue to work with this rose group in the future.

'Constance Spry' (foreground), an English rose introduced in 1961, was the result of early hybridizing efforts by Englishman David Austin. While it had nearly all of the qualities he was trying to achieve, it only bloomed once. Subsequent breeding work led to repeat blooming roses with an old rose look. Many pastel-colored English roses are descended from 'Constance Spry'.

WHAT'S IN A ROSE?

Uses of Roses

Like perhaps no other flower on earth, we savor the rose and its many pleasures. Our romance with roses owes a lot to the fact that they offer so much! It's a great delight to have them growing in a garden, but there are other ways to enjoy them as well.

Fragrances

Perfumes and fragrant oils have been derived from roses for centuries. The wonderful scents are generated by various aromatic chemicals and fatty acids embedded in the petals. Capturing them and bottling them is an ancient art, perfected over time, but based on simple techniques. Ideally, a blossom is picked at its peak scented moment, early in the morning as it is just opening. It is then confined or bottled for the oil to condense so it can be collected. A more productive variation on the process is to simmer or boil freshly-harvested blossoms and collect the distillate as it accumulates on the lid of the pot. Precious rose oil can also be carefully syringed off the surface of water mixed with rose petals. (For more on the concentrate known as attar of roses, see page 13 above.)

Yet another method of harvesting rose fragrance is to immerse freshly picked petals in a non-metal container of oil (olive oil or safflower oil are good choices). Since oil attracts oil, as the petals collapse, the oil gains their scent. Soaking petals in undenatured ethyl alcohol yields similar results. Either of these products can then be used as a base for perfumes or even homemade candles.

Because the scents of different rose varieties vary—from rich, old-rose damask to citrus to spice, just to name a few possibilities—so, too, do the waters, essences, and perfumes vary. The French in particular, following a long tradition of perfumery, not to mention a long love affair with the rose itself, are considered the producers of the finest rose-based cosmetics. But any nice soap shop or toiletries vendor around the world may have rose-derived perfume, shampoo, lotion, or soap.

The lavender rose 'Moon Shadow' has a strong antique rose fragrance.

Food

Rose petals are safe to eat (assuming, of course, that you have not been spraying them recently with garden chemicals). Indeed, it can be tempting to nibble on one when you are savoring its splendid fragrance out in the garden! They have gone in and out of fashion over the years in cuisine, but seem most enduringly popular in desserts. Rose petals have been strewn over the icing on cakes, or pressed between their layers. They've been candied, which preserves their color and shape. They've been added to jams and jellies, and even homemade sweet cheeses, for an extra element of unique, subtle sweetness. Creative chefs have sprinkled them over mixed salad greens, tossed them into fruit salads, and used them as garnishes.

Indian and Middle Eastern cooks have long used rose water in food and drink. A delicious Indian drink is "sweet lassi," which consists of cool plain yogurt blended with rose water. The famously rich, sticky candy "Turkish Delight" has rose water in it as well.

Last but not least, vitamin-C-rich rose hips are also widely used. They're naturally tart, like cranberries. Cooks have added them to syrups, jellies, pies, and even soups (especially in Scandinavian countries). Rose hip tea is available in many countries and is valued as an excellent source of the vitamin.

Fresh Flowers

Fresh-picked roses, especially those from your own garden, are a great joy. Very fragrant ones can scent a room with a single stem. But it's rewarding to pick bountiful bouquets, mix and match colors, and experiment with combining roses and greenery or other flowers in your own arrangements. It is also a pleasure to give away some of your bounty to those not lucky enough to have their own homegrown source of roses!

To keep your bouquet roses looking good as long as possible, borrow a few tricks from the experts—professional florists. Here are their classic tips; follow most or all of them to get maximum time and delight out of the bouquets you pick yourself. First, the cutting advice:

- Cut flowers late in the day, or early in the morning when they have the most starch reserves.

Rose petals and hips are edible—not surprising since roses are related to apples, pears, peaches, strawberries, blackberries, and cherries. They have been used to flavor such foods as desserts, jellies, and teas.

- Cut dry flowers, not damp.
- Cut flowers that are not fully open. Ones that are still in bud, however, should already be starting to open or you may not be able to coax them into opening indoors.
- Use very sharp pruners/clippers. Scissors tend to mash the stems. There are even tools made especially for cutting flowers that hold the stem as they cut.
- Bring along a bucket of water (warm, if possible) and immerse the stems as you go.

When you get your flowers indoors:

- Recut the stems. Use a sharp knife and cut at a 45-degree angle so there will be maximum surface area for the stems to drink water through. Some florists advise recutting the stems underwater, but this can be an awkward project, particularly if your sink is not large. Try this technique if you wish, or invest in an inexpensive gadget called an "underwater stem cutter." This is a jar with a lid that has a hole to insert the stem into for slicing, and a sharp cutting blade.

Most roses make excellent cut flowers, especially hybrid teas such as 'Sheer Bliss', a popular choice for floral arrangements and wedding bouquets.

WAYS TO PROLONG A BOUQUET'S LIFE

- Add a packet of flower preservative to the water (available from any florist). To increase the life of your cut flowers, fill the vase with a solution of one-half lemon lime soda and one-half water. A few drops of bleach will help keep the water clear and fresh.
- Change the vase water daily.
- Don't display the bouquet in a hot room or in direct sunlight. Or, if you must, make a habit of moving it to a cooler spot, or even into the refrigerator each night, or whenever nobody is around to admire the arrangement.

To improve the vase life of cut roses, immerse their stems in warm water immediately after cutting.

- Strip off any leaves that would otherwise be immersed in the vase water. They'll only cloud the water as they age.

- Put the recut stems back into a bucket or jar of water as you go. Let them stand for several hours or overnight, so they can draw up plenty of water.

Dried Flowers

Another way to enjoy rose flowers indoors, and for a longer period of time, is to dry them. The petals are substantial enough not to shatter easily, and the form holds up beautifully if the blossoms are handled with care. You can dry one long-stemmed rose, an entire bouquet, or even petals or small buds for potpourri, by using very simple methods.

But first, the picking advice:

- Relatively dry roses are ideal. Cut what you need in the morning, but after the dew has dried, or later in the day.

- Pick buds or blooms that are at exactly the point you want them to be when you display them—partially open, in bud but showing color, fully open, or whatever appeals to you. Decide now, because you are going to suspend them in that state (that is, they will develop no further as they dry).

Now, to preserve them. There are two ways, one low-tech, one that requires special supplies and more time. You can easily dry roses the same way herb-lovers dry their harvest. Bundle the stems with a string or rubber band and hang them upside down in a cool, dark, dry location like a shed or garage. Be especially sure that the chosen place is dry;

ROSE TIP

The best roses for drying

Not all roses dry equally well. For the most satisfying results, try bright pink roses—they tend to hold their color best. Red roses often dry black. Oddly, orange roses often dry bright red. Pastels, yellows, and whites, alas, fade. Blended, striped, and bicolor roses dry well also.

'Crackling Fire'
While red roses often dry to black, orange roses typically dry bright red. Large roses don't always keep their color or form, but miniature roses hold up well in the drying process.

even a little humidity will cause them to spoil.

For the best drying results you should:

- Get a drying box or container that has an airtight fitted lid (to prevent moisture from the air being absorbed by the crystals).

- Spread a layer of silica crystals/gel (an inexpensive white powder, available from hobby/craft stores) on the bottom.

- Lay your roses on top of the silica. Remember to strip off the leaves (they

don't dry well anyway), and don't let plant parts touch one another.

- Shake more gel over the roses to cover them completely. Seal the lid, and put the container aside in a cool, dark place.

- Check the results every few days. Depending on what and how much you are drying, the drying process may take up to two weeks. When it's time to remove the roses, handle with care and gently shake and blow off the silica gel. A small paintbrush can whisk off any excess powder.

How Many Petals?

The number of petals varies in rose varieties, but it is hard to generalize. All "single" roses are not necessarily old or in any way inferior to the plush "fully double ones," which could be anything from an old-fashioned damask to a modern English rose. It's hard to imagine someone actually hovering over a blossom, counting each petal one by one, though it might be pleasant work! Here's what terms mean when referring to petal quantities:

- *Single:* Having five petals.

- *Semi-double:* Having a petal count of between twelve to sixteen.

- *Double:* Any rose having a petal count of over seventeen; more typically, it's those full-flowered ones with twenty-six to forty petals per blossom.

- *Fully double or very double:* A rose with a petal count of over forty, and possibly as high as 100.

PETAL PUSHERS

'Purple Simplicity'

'White Lightnin'

'Geoff Hamilton'

Roses are often classified by their petal count. 'Purple Simplicity' is at the lower end with a count of 12 to 16 petals, 'White Lightnin' is mid-range with 30 petals, and 'Geoff Hamilton' has a high petal count of 108 petals.

Single Flower Form: 'Nearly Wild'

Semi-double: 'Penelope'

Double: 'Ards Rover'

Very Double: 'Mary Rose'

This single-form rose, 'Dainty Bess' (below), shows the five petals typical of most members of the rose family, including species roses, with a pincushion of stamens (the male part of a flower, which produces pollen) and a cluster of pistils in the center (the female part of the flower, which receives pollen and forms seeds).

Types of Roses

These days, roses are divided into—and sold under—various categories, or types. There are significant differences, including characteristics that will affect your decision when you go shopping, such as mature plant size and frequency of bloom. In truth, although roses are more alike than different, you'll want to familiarize yourself with the different types so you can acquire a rose that meets your garden's needs and your own taste and vision. Here are the categories you are most likely to see:

Hybrid Teas

These are the nobility of the rose world. They're medium-to-tall bushes, generally with a vase-shaped profile. The big, gorgeous, refined flowers are one-to-a-stem and often bred with long cutting stems, so hybrid teas are a great choice for bouquet lovers. Hybrid teas bloom continuously throughout the growing season.

Grandifloras

A grandiflora is a big, upright plant with large blossoms—but the flowers appear in clusters, like a floribunda. Grandifloras

Hybrid Tea, 'Pearl Essence'

Floribunda, 'Citrus Tease'

Floribunda

Grandiflora,
'Tournament of Roses'

Polyantha,
'Crystal Fairy'

bloom continuously throughout their growing season. A subclass of the hybrid tea.

Floribundas

These are outstanding landscaping roses. Floribundas are shorter, more compact plants, nice in groupings and suitable for smaller gardens or mixed flower beds. The flowers appear in clusters, and often some are in bud while others are fully open. Floribundas bloom continuously throughout their growing season.

Polyanthas

Similar to floribundas but technically older and less intensely bred, polyanthas are distinguished by a nice, compact, shrubby habit and a profusion of smaller-sized flowers. They bloom continuously throughout their growing season. Hardy to Zone 4 (a map of USDA Hardiness Zones is included in the regional section of this book).

Climbers/Ramblers

These are roses that naturally develop long, pliable canes, making them suitable for

Hybrid Tea

Grandiflora

Climber/Rambler, 'Social Climber'

Polyantha

training on a support (a tree, a trellis, a fence, an archway, etc.). Older rambling roses bloom just once every spring; modern ones bloom continuously. Climbing roses are not technically considered vines because they have no way to attach themselves well to a support —you, the gardener, must guide and help them along with judiciously placed ties.

Regional variations in English roses

Many of these roses are new enough that gardeners in North America are still in the process of discovering what climate conditions they can and cannot tolerate. So far, it appears that they are fairly cold hardy, more so than many hybrid teas, surviving winters in Zones 4 and 5. In warm climates, they seem to grow more vigorously.

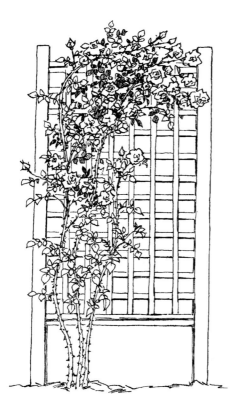

Climber/Rambler

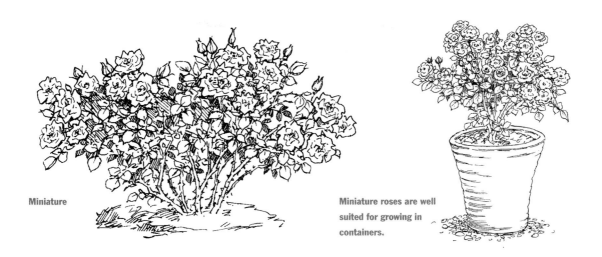

Miniature

Miniature roses are well suited for growing in containers.

Miniatures

These are little, compact rosebushes, with small leaves, small buds, and small flowers... all in scale with one another. They are full of color all season long, and often winter hardy because they are traditionally grown on their own roots. Miniature roses are also great for growing in pots.

English/Austin

Contemporary British nurseryman David Austin electrified the rose world by successfully combining beautiful, full-petaled, richly fragrant "old roses" with modern ones to get attractive, romantic plants that have improved disease-resistance and a much longer blooming period. For this reason, this group is frequently referred to as "Austin roses." But other breeders have waded in and occasionally a worthy new rose of this type is offered under the more generic term "English rose."

English/Austin

Miniature, 'Demitasse'   English/Austin, 'Graham Thomas'

'Simplicity'®

Shrub Roses

This is a "catch-all" term for a great many roses, which generally have the following characteristics: a big, broad shrubby habit; weather-resilience (cold hardy and able to tolerate hot, humid summers); disease resistance; and less refined but often lovely and fragrant flowers. Shrub roses are bred to be covered in blooms throughout the summer.

Below are some of the stars of the shrub rose world. These are all technically shrub roses, but frequently offered under their own names:

- *Rugosas/beach roses:* These are coarse-leaved, thorny shrub roses with single or double, super-fragrant flowers (spicy, like cloves) in shades of pink, white, red and occasionally maroon. Their hips are prominent and attractive—birds love them! Hardy to Zone 3 or 4.

- *Simplicity Hedge Rose® series:* Jackson & Perkins developed these enduringly popular, vigorous, easy-going shrubs; they are without peer when grown as hedges. Tough, handsome, dense bushes are awash in exuberant, informal blooms from spring to fall. The original version, 'Simplicity'®, introduced in 1978, is pink. There are also 'White Simplicity'® (1991), 'Yellow Simplicity'® (1998), and sweetly scented 'Purple Simplicity'® (1999).

- *Meidilands:* Weather-tough and disease-resistant, these European-bred roses also remain relatively under control once they reach their mature size of 2 to 4 feet wide and high, so less pruning is needed.

Shrub Rose, 'Greetings'

Rugosa Rose, 'Pink Grootendorst'

Meidiland Rose, 'Red Meidiland'

Explorer Rose, 'Henry Hudson'

- *Canadian roses/Explorer roses:* These very tough roses were selected and bred to survive the rigors of a chilly Northern winter. Many are named for famous Canadian explorers. To Zone 4, at least.

- *Griffith Buck roses:* The late Dr. Griffith Buck, a horticulture professor at the University of Iowa at Ames, succeeded in selecting and developing attractive shrub roses that are truly low-maintenance and able to tolerate that region's cold winters and blazing hot summers.

Buck Rose, 'Carefree Beauty'

Oldies but Goodies

Many roses have been lost to history because gardeners stopped sharing or growing them, or because they were superceded by improved editions. But many of the old-fashioned ones are still in commerce today and enjoying a resurgence in popularity, thanks to their tough, carefree nature, heady fragrance and/or romantic, petal-laden flower form.

Here are some of the "old-fashioned" types of roses still in commerce. If you have trouble finding them, seek out specialty mail-order nurseries on the Internet or in the classified ads found in gardening magazines. Each of these in some way, at some point, contributed genes to modern rose breeding— these are the distinguished ancestors in the rose family tree.

True antique or heritage roses are those bred prior to 1867, when 'La France' was introduced. A rose bred between 1867 and 1960 is referred to as a "vintage" or "heirloom" rose. All of these come under the general category of "old roses" or "old garden roses."

Antique Rose, 'Madame Plantier' (1835)

Rosa centifolia

flowers, they're usually pink or white and have a nice scent. Albas bloom only once a year, in spring, but the show lasts several weeks.

- *Bourbons:* These are the roses of Victorian England. Prized especially for their rich, romantic fragrance, bourbons feature red or pink flowers, often with a luminous sheen that is apparent in bright sunlight (this "sheen gene" from the bourbons reappears from time to time in modern hybrid teas). They bloom in spring and then repeat sporadically during the summer. As for the plants themselves, they tend to be manageable shrubs or restrained climbers, and are fairly cold hardy (to Zones 5 and 6, and further north with winter protection). Unfortunately, the glossy green foliage is often susceptible to black spot.

- *Albas:* You can tell these right away because of their unusual foliage— bluish-green and finely toothed. They're tough, too. They grow well in poor soil, tolerate partial shade, resist rose diseases very well, and they're cold hardy (to Zone 3). All this, plus their stems are thornless, or nearly so. As for the

- *Cabbage roses/Centifolias:* These beauties get the name "cabbage rose" from their densely petaled flowers, which come in shades of purple or pink. The bloom period, late each spring, tends to be brief but extravagant. The plants are usually large and shrubby. They've been

Alba,
'Mme Les Gras de St. Germain'

Bourbon,
'Honorine de Brabant'

China,
'Gloire de Rosomanes'

Damask,
'Rose de Rescht'

Gallica, 'Rosa Mundi'　　　　Hybrid Musk, 'Cornelia'　　　　Hybrid Perpetual, 'Reine de Violettes'

in cultivation a long time and were especially popular in Holland, which is why you often see them in the still-life paintings of Dutch Masters. Hardy to Zone 4.

- *China roses/China hybrids:* Chinas are smaller, shrubby roses with good disease resistance. They are valued for their ability to bloom over a longer period than most old roses. Flowers appear in clusters and are usually single, sometimes double. Their smaller size and attractive form make them suitable for large containers or placement in smaller gardens. Only hardy to Zone 7, for the most part.

- *Damasks:* Clusters of flowers cover these big, thorny plants, radiating intense, delicious fragrance. A very ancient group, damasks were first brought to Europe from the Middle East by the Crusaders. The plants bloom once, in spring. Fall brings big, colorful hips. Hardy to Zone 4.

- *Gallicas/French roses:* Extremely fragrant blossoms, usually in rich hues of red, purple, or pink (sometimes mottled or

striped) distinguish this ancient group of roses. The plants have an upright growth habit and are wonderfully tough: They can tolerate some shade, dry sites, poor soil, frigid temperatures, and even neglect. Hardy to Zone 4, at least.

- *Hybrid musks:* Flowers appear in large clusters and are prized for their strong, musky, "old rose" fragrance. Colors are delicate pink, apricot, or lemon yellow. Most are good repeat bloomers. The plants are handsome shrubs with dark green foliage, often adorned with orange hips by fall. Good up to Zone 6, perhaps 5 with winter protection.

- *Hybrid perpetuals:* Bushes are shrubby and feature arching, flexible canes. The densely petaled flowers are sweetly scented and come in red, purple, shades of pink, and even white. There is a big show every spring, followed by sporadic, light repeats for the rest of the season. Predecessor of the hybrid tea.

- *Moss roses:* Popular in Victorian England, these roses get their name from the fact that their stems and flower bases sport a mossy-looking fuzz of

Moss Rose, 'Perpetual White Moss'

little, prickly hairs (glands), which have a piney scent. The blooms repeat, and are typically "double" (loads of petals) and very fragrant; moss roses come in red, purple, pink, and white. Hardy to Zone 4.

- *Noisettes:* Two important characteristics of modern roses hail from noisettes. Many are climbers, with flexible canes that breeders of climbers covet. Color is the other contribution—noisettes come in cream-yellow, pink, and soft orange. Most are sweetly scented. Originally bred in the early 1800s by John Champney, a rice plantation owner in Charleston, South Carolina, by crossing 'Champney's Pink Cluster' (given to him by his neighbor Philippe Noisette) with *Rosa moschata*. They perform best in mild climates and are hardy only to Zone 7.

- *Portland roses:* Actually an old blend of China, damask, and gallica roses, these hybrids are more compact and manageable than those forebears. They repeat-bloom and flowers are usually in the pink-purple-red range. The flowers are frequently double and have a rich, heady fragrance. Hardy to Zone 4.

- *Scotch roses:* Very thorny, prickly stems! But the crinkly, ferny, forest-green foliage is tough and disease resistant. And the single flowers come in pink, white, or yellow, followed by jaunty, bright red hips in fall.

- *Tea roses:* Hybrids of complex origins, these forebears of modern hybrid teas have pointed buds and they repeat-bloom. They come in delicate pastel hues of pink, yellow, and cream, and some are fragrant. The plants, however, are not very cold hardy, surviving winters only to Zone 7 or 8.

Noisette Rose, 'Blush Noisette'

Portland Rose, 'Marchessa Boccella'

Scotch Rose, 'Golden Wings'

Tea Rose, 'Monsieur Tillier'

Species Rose, *Rosa moyesii*

Groundcover Rose, 'Flower Carpet Pink'

Tree Roses/Standards

You may remember these unusual roses from illustrations in *Alice in Wonderland*—compact, continuous-blooming shrubs atop a tall bare stem, like a fancy lollipop. They are gorgeous in the ground or displayed in pots, lining a walkway or entryway, or flanking a pool or formal garden area. They are not winter-hardy and must be protected.

Groundcover Roses

There are two kinds of "groundcovering" roses. Certain climbers or ramblers have been used to carpet a slope or strip or other broad area. As long as the rose has long, pliant canes, it can be anchored or pinned to the ground at intervals; horizontally trained stems tend to flower more, too, so this works fairly well. In recent years, however, rose breeders have succeeded in developing actual horizontally growing "groundcover" roses that are naturally low growing, dense in habit, and generous with flowers. These are a better choice because they've been developed for this purpose—there's no pinning down or pruning or fussing necessary, and they remain in bloom all summer. To Zone 5.

Species

Rose enthusiasts have saved or rescued some of the original, wild forebears of modern roses, lauding them for their vigor, natural toughness, and casual, exuberant beauty. Species roses tend to bloom only once a year, in spring—but often for an extended period.

Tree Rose, 'Prominent'

THE NEW WORLD OF ROSES

IN THIS CHAPTER:

- ■ **How the rose world has changed**
- ■ **Own-root and grafted**
- ■ **Roses in the landscape**
- ■ **Rose companions**

How New Roses Are Created

While no rose breeder wants to give away his or her secrets, it is possible for anyone to develop a new rose. All you need is patience and persistence—and a keen eye for roses with promise.

First, a little biology: Roses have both male (stamens) and female (pistils) parts on the same plant, and they can self-pollinate. Numerous seeds then develop within the fruit, called "hips." These can be collected and germinated. Sometimes they are not viable and don't grow. When they do sprout, they don't always resemble the parent plant.

Breeders intervene in this natural process when they cross two different roses in the hopes of making a good new one. Pollen is taken from the stamen of a flower on one plant and brushed onto the pistil of a flower on another plant. Later, when the hips swell and change in color from green to red or orange, they can be harvested. The breeder then extracts the seeds, plants them, and evaluates what develops.

Admittedly, this is a time-consuming process. It's preferable to have a greenhouse in which to pamper the seedlings while they're small, plus plenty of garden space to move them to when they're ready to go into the ground. Rose companies are able to do this on a large scale, but the entire process still requires time, expertise, record keeping, and patience. Jackson & Perkins and other large rose breeders typically introduce one new rose out of nearly 20,000 seedlings. (However, anyone might be fortunate enough to hit the jackpot with less effort. See the story of the shrub rose 'Knock Out'™ on page 172.)

Jackson & Perkins 2004 introduction 'Salsa'

Plant breeders create new roses by taking the golden dust of pollen from the anthers of one flower and applying it to the stigma of another flower, thus combining the genetic material of two separate plants. The resulting seeds are sowed and the rose seedlings evaluated over several years. It can take many attempts of this process before a worthy new rose is achieved.

What's New in Roses and Rose Gardening

It's an exciting time to grow roses these days. New colors, improved forms, and exciting scents, on tougher, more resilient plants—all these qualities continue to come to the fore. But perhaps the most significant development in roses and rose gardening is: ease. Modern gardeners are busy—they want to enjoy beautiful blossoms, but on low-maintenance plants.

What is an easy rose? It's one which is resistant to various pests and diseases, so it can be enjoyed without requiring the gardener to regularly defend it with chemical sprays. Its mature size fits the gardener's needs and space, whether it's on a trellis against the wall of a small garden, mid-border in a

mixed perennial bed, or in a container on a deck or patio

The truth is, roses these days are no more difficult than many perennials. Often, they're even lower-maintenance. And what other flower is able to deliver such spectacular color all season long, so dependably, year after glorious year?

Better Flowers

A Season of Color

Historically, many roses bloomed but once a season—in late spring or early summer. The show lasted a few weeks and then was over. Many of these are still in commerce, and so beautiful that lots of gardeners feel they're well worth growing. These are mainly the

The species rose *Rosa glauca*, while it only blooms once a year, has such beautiful dark pink flowers, handsome blue-green foliage, and attractive orange hips in the late summer and fall that it remains a popular landscape plant.

·ROSE TIP·

Something's always in bloom

Here's a trick used by the pros for hybrid teas, and it works beautifully in the home garden as well. Pinch off some of the tips of the side shoots on your rosebushes. This redirects energy into the remaining buds, which then develop into flowers. And you'll continue to get blooms later in the season.

Long-blooming roses such as 'Heaven on Earth' bring continuity to your garden design, providing color throughout the growing season, complementing perennials, annuals, and other shrubs as they come in and out of flower.

"old garden roses" and species types, such as 'Maiden's Blush' and *Rosa banksiae* 'Lutea,' the yellow Lady Banks' rose.

But there are numerous roses that continue to bloom throughout the summer, including hybrid teas and floribundas, as well as shrub roses and climbers. English roses, a combination of old roses and new, also bloom over a long period. The foremost breeder, David Austin, has succeeded in marrying the lush, beautiful, often intensely fragrant blooms of vintage roses with modern-day repeat-blooming roses. American-bred "modern antiques" also bring together qualities of heirloom and modern roses. The innovative, ever-expanding group of groundcover roses, relative newcomers to the rose world, are even starting to replace more traditional groundcovers in private and public landscapes, where their flower-studded, low-growing stems provide color over a long period.

Typically, to achieve blooming color throughout the growing season, a wide variety of plants need to be included in the garden, so that their bloom times are staggered. Many shrubs bloom in spring or early summer and then recede from attention. Many perennials are at their peak during early to midsummer, while others are autumn bloomers. Few plants can provide the full season of flowering that long-blooming roses do. They bring continuity, or a recurring theme, to your garden design over the course of the spring and summer months.

Groundcover roses such as 'Snow Shower' are an expanding category of roses, offering a low-maintenance, long-blooming alternative to traditional groundcovers.

A bright, spring blooming combination of hot-pink roses, yellow irises, and blue mealy-cup sage. Even after the irises have finished blooming, the roses will continue to be beautiful with the blue sage and the upright spikes of iris foliage.

Maximum Color Impact

When choosing a rose for its long bloom period, consider its color carefully, since it will be a continuing presence in the garden while other flower colors come and go. Rose flower color will have a significant influence on the "color impression" that the flower garden makes as a whole, up close as well as when viewed from across the yard. If they're going to have an important or starring role, it makes sense to plan for and around their colors.

Not only do season-long roses provide stability in the garden, they can also be the inspiration for a variety of color combinations from spring to fall, creating an ever-changing tapestry. You might prefer a "harmonious" hue, such as a pink or yellow rose, something that easily flatters other flower colors. For more dramatic impact, consider planting roses with "contrasting" colors, which highlight one another. For instance, two bright primary-color rosebushes in close proximity, such as a red and a yellow, have the effect of making both look more vivid. Similarly, a bright yellow rose near a tall, blue bloomer such as a campanula, butterfly bush, or caryopteris can make a genuine partnership or nicely balanced duo.

LONG-TERM TERMS

Rose catalogs, plant labels, and reference books may use the following special terms to describe blooming habits:

- **Ever-blooming:** Continuously in bloom; every new shoot produces a flower.
- **Flush:** An intense bloom period, with many flowers.
- **Remontant:** Having more than one period of bloom during the growing season.
- **Repeat-blooming:** A rose that blooms in cycles, running the course of one flowering period before starting up a new one, so it might bloom in the spring, then again in the summer or fall.

Repeat Bloomer, 'F.J. Grootendorst'

A white or yellow rose, such as butter-colored Lady Banks', would be a good choice for a garden with hot-colored plants, including red centranthus, orange helianthemum, and electric blue lithodora.

COLOR CHOICES

Your hot pink rose may look fabulous with your early-blooming purple irises, but will it be a good companion for the electric orange of your crocosmia later in the season? Maybe a white or yellow rose would be a better choice for the full-season picture. Consider your roses "anchor" plants in the garden and choose annuals, perennials, shrubs, and vines to complement and enhance them.

Flower Color and Design

Roses often bring to mind delicate pastel colors, which are perfect for many types of gardens and combine well with other plants, but roses also come in bright colors, which can be energizing and exciting. In recent years, bold, "hot" colors—red, magenta, orange, yellow—have come to the fore. Many of today's gardeners want sizzling drama in their gardens, to inspire traffic-stopping admiration. Stronger colors will deliver that impact. When adding roses to your garden, consider the colors of the plants already in place. Do you need a "connector" color to bring other plants together, or a bright accent? There are rose colors to suit every taste.

Also available are striking color blends, such as pink warmed with yellow, or orange-yellow and orange-yellow-red combinations. There are red roses with cream or white at the petal bases, giving the flower a bicolor effect. And some roses actually change over a period of days, often from darker buds to soft pastel flowers. *Rosa chinensis* 'Mutabilis', or China rose, progresses from yellow buds, to salmon pink flowers, to deep pink. 'Joseph's Coat' and 'Belinda' also have multi-colored floral displays. Capitalize on the variability, and place the rose with other roses or other flowers that echo or contrast with the show.

Longer-lasting color is another aspect to consider, and newer roses are wonderfully superior in this respect. While for some roses color tends to fade as the bloom ages, especially in hot sunshine, the color-saturated petals of recent introductions hold up longer. Your particular climate and soil can also affect the durability of flower color. Identify the ones that hold their color best in your area by observing roses in a neighbor's garden or in a public display, or even at a local garden center.

Rose buds generally form at the tips of new canes, so be careful not to snip them off by pruning early in the growing season.

What is "disbudding?"

This technique is used on hybrid teas and grandifloras to favor a single bud rather than allowing several buds to develop in the same place. If you peer closely at each stem, you may see tiny side buds growing just below the main bud. Rub or clip them off early in their development and the main bud will receive more energy from the plant, and be free to grow larger than it would have otherwise. So you will have fewer flowers, but the ones you have will be much larger.

Disbudding hybrid tea roses, such as 'Chicago Peace' (left), by removing side buds will create fewer but much larger blossoms. For floribundas, like 'Showbiz' (right), you can enhance the clustering habit by removing the center bud and allowing the numerous side buds to develop.

Disbudding may also be done on floribundas, but in this case you should remove the center bud and not the side ones, to show off the clustering habit.

This trick is especially popular with those who grow rose blossoms for show, but anyone who wants to grow their own big, beautiful bouquet flowers can do the same.

In Search of Fragrance

In general, the main goal of rose breeders is to develop a rosebush with beautiful flowers and a healthy, sturdy plant. Good strong fragrance can be a greater challenge, because rose genetics are complex. To achieve a good-quality rose flower that also has a good scent is a matter of trial and error and perseverance on the part of the breeder.

If you want a fragrant rose, there are a

Roses with numerous petals and old-rose genes are often highly scented, such as the English rose 'Gertrude Jekyll', which has a strong damask fragrance.

number of options. Many shrub roses are fragrant. Full-petaled roses are also frequently scented, due to both the sheer number of petals and their parentage, which often includes fragrant old-rose genes. And some single-form roses—like the rugosas—waft a rich, delicious scent. Hybrid teas, which are typically bred to emphasize superior flower color and form, often have a lighter scent, though there are plenty of fragrant hybrid teas.

One clue for breeders, and anyone shopping for a fragrant rose, is that in roses there are links between color and fragrance.

Though of course there are exceptions, your nose will notice, for example, that:

- Lavender roses are almost always very fragrant.
- Dark-colored roses, including every hue of red plus darker pink and bright orange blossoms, and blends thereof, are often at least slightly fragrant. It may not be a powerful scent, but it is classic and distinctive.

SELF-CLEANING ROSES

There's no doubt that spent blooms left on a plant can detract from its appearance. But many favorite garden plants "self-clean," meaning that the flowers naturally shed or shatter their petals when they're finished blooming. This characteristic spares the gardener from constantly grooming plants to keep them looking nice.

Some roses hang onto spent blooms, while others don't. The best "self-cleaners" seem to be shrub roses. If you're using them as a screen or hedge, this is a big advantage, as deadheading and bloom-by-bloom grooming is time-consuming on a large planting. Roses with single blossoms (that is, few petals) tend to self-clean better, for the obvious reason that there are fewer petals to drop. A classic example is the Simplicity® series of hedge roses from Jackson & Perkins.

To find other self-cleaning roses, check the American Rose Society's *Handbook for Selecting Roses;* this is one of the qualities rated for every rose they list. Visit the website of the ARS for more information on this valuable handbook.

'Sun Runner' is a "self-cleaning" rose, meaning it naturally sheds the petals of its spent blossoms, making for a tidier looking plant.

'Tropicana' has a fruity fragrance.

'Melody Parfumée' has an old-rose perfume.

'Fame!' has a scent like fresh-cut grass.

THE SCENT OF A ROSE

All scented roses do not smell the same, or the same to all noses. If you grow several different roses, or visit a garden with a rose collection, test the fragrance of each one in turn and you will notice variations. Savoring these distinctions is one of the great joys of growing roses. You may detect the following scents:

- **classic,** "old-fashioned tea rose," rose perfume
- **citrus** (lemon, orange, or grapefruit)
- **sweet violets**
- **sweet pea**
- **fresh-cut apples**
- **raspberry**
- **ripe currants**
- **honey**
- **fern**
- **parsley**
- **bay**
- **anise/sweet licorice**
- **ginger**
- **spice** (cloves or cinnamon)

- Striped roses or those with splashy-marked petals—often pink or red, like a peppermint stick—are often (though not always) sweetly fragrant, thanks to their old garden rose forebears, most notably gallicas such as 'Rosa Mundi' (*Rosa gallica* 'Versicolor').

- Yellow roses with the very old species rose *Rosa foetida* in their parentage are fragrant.

- Light colored and white roses traditionally have more subtle fragrances, unless they have old-rose genes in their background.

Enhancing Fragrance—What You Can Do

Here's how to help your roses achieve maximum fragrance in your garden:

- *Smart placement:* Your rose will perform best, and have the strongest scent, if it is happily growing in full sun, with plenty of room, in good soil with the proper pH. Good site selection is a key factor.

- *Ample water:* Rose fragrance resides within the cells of the petals and the higher the water content, the higher the amount of the scent ingredient. Keeping your plants well watered makes a significant difference in the strength of the scent.

To enjoy the most fragrance from roses in bouquets indoors:

- *Display in a low-light spot:* Too much light, from a window or even artificial light, shortens vase life and dissipates fragrance.

- *Put the bouquet in the refrigerator overnight:* This is a florists' trick that essentially holds the blooms in a suspended state, hoarding their scent and prolonging their vase life.

More Flowers Per Plant

In addition to having plants that bloom for a longer period of time, another goal for rose breeders—and rose gardeners—is having more flowers per rosebush. The key is having

Plant your roses in a sunny location to encourage the strongest fragrance.

ample foliage. With plenty of leaves, a rose plant has the fuel it needs to generate more buds, and more buds mean more flowers. This is especially true of the newest roses.

It's easy to help your rose plants be more flower-productive. Here's how:

- Plant your rose in full sun. Also, remove or cut back encroaching plants or tree branches. The more sun a rosebush gets, the more flowers it can make.

Color and scent are often closely connected, and lavender roses, such as 'Angel Face', are typically very fragrant.

How nature helps to enhance scent

Warm, sunny days bring out the most powerful, delicious fragrances—the volatile plant oils that contain fragrance are fully released under those conditions. And, interestingly, humidity also helps, because it slows or inhibits evaporation.

While pastel roses remain popular additions to gardens, bright, bold colored roses can add a dramatic focal point and create striking color combinations.

Some roses have flowers that are "color blends." 'Perfect Moment' is a vibrant red-yellow combination.

- "Deadhead," meaning remove faded blooms, right away. The goal of all flowering plants is to produce seed, and when that is accomplished they stop flowering. Removing spent flowers spares the rose the considerable effort of producing seeds (present in the rose hips), and "fools" it into continuing to bloom longer instead.

- Fertilize regularly. Roses really respond to plant food, generating more growth and, in turn, more flowers. (Follow package directions carefully.)

- Water faithfully. Lack of water or a period of drought, particularly while buds are swelling, is stressful. Your rosebush needs plentiful water at that critical point of development. Ample moisture after the buds unfurl also helps keep the flowers blooming longer.

- Never prune at the very beginning of the growing season. Buds generally form at the tips of new canes. If you snip off the ends, you'll lose the show. (The exception is deliberate "disbudding.")

MAXIMUM COLOR FROM YOUR ROSES

- Maintain the plants in top health, with proper watering and feeding.

- A little afternoon shade helps preserve flower color, particularly in areas where the summers are blazing hot.

- Choose companion plants that draw attention to the colors of the rose blossoms, rather than distract from them, including foliage plants. For example, gray-leaved artemisias or lamb's ears always seem to make bright colors look even brighter. Lime-green plants, such as sweet potato vine (*Ipomoea batatus*), also make great supporting actors, flattering any color of rose.

Better Plants

Growing beautiful roses means more than having lovely blossoms—it also means having attractive plants. Increasingly, roses are utilized in a variety of garden situations, and it has become more and more important for them to have pleasing shapes and handsome foliage.

Advances have been made toward improving the overall form of several types of rosebushes. For example, the leggy profile of older varieties of hybrid teas has been superceded by a handsome, vase-like form, clad with foliage high and low.

There has also been progress in creating smaller, more compact roses. From the point of view of many gardeners, especially those

The color-saturated 'Sundance' hybrid tea, a 2004 introduction from Jackson & Perkins, is an example of the expanding possibilities of brightly colored roses.

with small gardens in suburban or urban areas, smaller-sized plants are desirable. Recent years have brought smaller forms of many popular shrubs, including hydrangeas, lilacs, fothergillas, forsythias, crape myrtles, and weigelas. Smaller-sized, more manageable rosebushes are also part of this trend. Floribundas are typically 2 to 3 feet high and wide, and miniatures vary from 1 foot high and wide to 3 feet high and wide. There are even miniature climbing roses. Shrub roses are also being introduced every year that are more mannerly and compact, and thus require less pruning to remain in bounds.

A damaged or disease-prone rose can also detract from the floral display. The "total package" should include a tougher, disease-resistant, winter-hardier plant. New roses are extensively tested before ever being introduced—and hardiness and disease-resistance are obviously major considerations. By carefully choosing your roses, you can have lovely flowers and healthy, attractive plants as well.

Some roses change flower color as the blooms age, creating a lively display in the garden. 'Belinda' has flowers that begin dark pink, fade gradually to varying shades of light pink, and then turn white.

Here are some general tips for keeping your rose plants looking good:

- Choose wisely. If you know your area is prone to a certain pest or disease, seek out a rose that is resistant. If you have cold winters, pick a rose that is hardy.
- Keep them healthy by fertilizing appropriately and watering properly.
- Keep them well pruned and uncrowded to allow ample air circulation.
- Patrol the plants often and spring into action if you spot a problem.
- Spray preventatively.

Recent introductions of more compact roses are good choices for smaller gardens. 'Electric Blanket' grows to only 1½ feet high and 2 feet wide.

Several issues have traditionally marred the appearance of rose foliage, including black spot, powdery mildew, rust, and insects such as aphids and Japanese beetles. Black spot is a genetic propensity introduced at the turn of the twentieth century when roses were bred with the large, fragrant, yellow-flowered, but unfortunately black spot-prone, *Rosa foetida*. So a rose with this Austrian briar rose in its parentage can be susceptible. Powdery mildew and rust are problems for a number of plants, not just roses, and are more likely to be present on plants subjected to long, stressful periods of humid weather. Japanese beetles and aphids also occur on a wide variety of garden plants and, while they have a limited life cycle and will disappear partway through the growing season, the damage they cause can be discouraging for gardeners.

Observe your growing conditions carefully and then choose your roses wisely. The Explorer series of roses are particularly hardy and are suitable for cold climates. A wall or fence can give added protection from strong winds and create a microclimate of warmer temperatures.

The Roots of the Rose

Perhaps the biggest news in roses in recent years is the form in which the plants are sold. For over eighty years, rose growers have offered mainly grafted rose plants. But more and more, we are seeing "own-root" roses, in local garden centers as well as in specialty rose catalogs. What are they? What does this trend mean for you and your garden?

Grafted Roses

A grafted plant is really two plants. The stems (or "canes," as rose stems are called) and the root system. Grafting is not a difficult technique; anyone with a good sharp garden knife can marry one plant onto another, ideally while both are still young, then nurture the result until it becomes one strong plant.

Commercial growers "bud graft" roses, a special grafting technique that takes a little more expertise than a stem-to-stem graft. With

The floribunda 'Sunsprite' has been popular since its introduction in 1977 and is now available as an own-root rose.

a sharp, clean knife and a deft twist of the wrist, they remove a bud from the variety they want to propagate (from the point where a leaflet meets a stem or cane). This little bud is then inserted under a flap of bark, low down on a stem of the rootstock plant. Any growth above that point on the rootstock plant (leaves or stems) is snipped off at that time, leaving the introduced bud as the recipient of all the plant's growing energy. Thus a new rose begins to grow atop the rootstock.

Why do this in the first place? A grafted plant can be a great plant, a combination of a weather-tough, vigorously growing root system, called a rootstock, and a possibly more frail but desirable "scion" or top. A standard rootstock also leads to a uniform look in the roses you see for sale, in terms of size and shape. Certain rootstocks have also been used to confer disease resistance or adaptability to certain types of soil.

A successfully grafted rose plant is usually easy to spot. The place where the two plants were joined is visible as a scar or bulge. In rose parlance, this is called the "bud union." Look

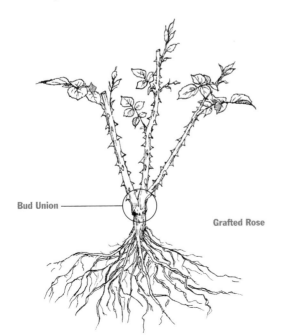

Bud Union

Grafted Rose

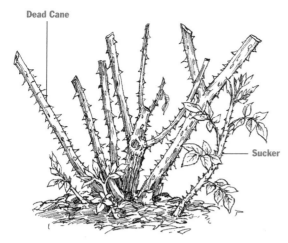

Dead Cane

Sucker

A winter-damaged rosebush.

for it at the base of the green stems, right where they meet the root system.

Many rootstocks have been used by rose growers, as many as fifteen different ones, for a variety of reasons. One in particular has dominated for many years. It is called 'Dr. Huey,' and has been prized for vigor, uniformity, and toughness. It made possible generations of good grafted roses. In colder regions *Rosa multiflora* was often used as the rootstock due to its exceptional hardiness.

The Disadvantages of Grafting

But all is not entirely "rosy" with grafted roses. Suckers (or errant canes), emerging from below the bud union, are unwelcome. They have the following telltale characteristics:

- Clearly different foliage from the rose you thought you had planted.

- Frequently lankier, thornier, leafier, and of a different hue than the rest of the stems on your rosebush.

- They grow to unwanted heights and in undesirable directions.

- And if these suckers produce flowers— usually a year or two after planting— inevitably they are "mongrel" blossoms,

smaller in size, with fewer petals and of a different color.

If you garden in a cold climate, it sometimes happens that the grafted top of a rosebush is killed by a harsh winter. The following spring and summer, the rose does not return in its expected glory. Instead, you get only those unwelcome suckers sprouting rampantly from the tougher rootstock, which did manage to survive the cold. At that point, unfortunately, you might as well declare the plant a loss and dig it out. Sometimes in colder regions, the 'Dr. Huey' rootstock might even be killed, which means you will lose the entire rosebush.

Bourbon roses such as 'Louise Odier' and other old-garden types have always been grown on their own roots. Growing roses by rooting cuttings rather than grafting is a propagation method now being applied to newer roses as well, creating hardier, more adaptable plants.

Own-root roses (left) are more supple and symmetrical and often have more branches, while grafted roses (right) have a more one-sided profile and are not as flexible.

Own-Root Roses: An Idea Whose Time Has Returned

Chronic grumbling among gardeners about unwanted suckers and winterkill on grafted roses has led rose growers to take a renewed look at growing roses on their own roots. This is not a new technique—all roses were once own-root and many shrub roses, including the resurgently popular old garden roses (including the richly fragrant bourbons and damasks) have always been grown from rooted cuttings. This old propagation method is now being applied to newer roses, with high standards for plant quality, adaptability, and toughness.

A cutting from a good rose variety—the classic red hybrid tea 'Ingrid Bergman', for instance—readily develops and grows well on its own root system. And many shrub roses are easy to raise this way. The more inherent vigor a rose variety has, the greater its chances are for growing on its own roots. And, of course, if the mother plant, which is the source of the cutting, is virus-free, or "clean," the offspring are guaranteed to be so as well.

Other virtues have revealed themselves as rose growers applied modern know-how, resources, and production methods to raising roses on their own roots. Interestingly, freed from the energy supplied in the past by an understock, own-root roses tend to develop more branches—and in a more evenly formed, symmetrical shape. (Grafted roses often have a one-sided profile.) Automatically, the bushes look fuller and more attractive. And, of course, more branches per plant means . . . more flowers per plant!

But the proof is in the roots, and there the advantages of own-root roses are evident. An own-root rose is healthy and ready to leave the growing fields for your garden at an earlier stage, so you are getting a younger plant. The roots are finer and more fibrous, poised to grow vigorously. Because the younger plant is a bit smaller than a traditional, grafted rose plant, it's easier to handle. Indeed, you can dig a smaller, shallower hole than roses have traditionally demanded (between one and two feet deep), and you can manipulate those pliable young roots into place with more ease. Transplant shock is less, too, because the younger plants are more adaptable.

Long-Term Benefits of Own-Root Roses:

- No more suckers to contend with!
- If a bitter winter kills the top of the plant, the resprouted plant will still be the same rose (in gardening parlance, your rose will "come back true to type").

YOUTHFUL VIGOR

Because they are basically rooted cuttings, own-root roses can grow faster than their grafted-on-understock counterparts. They require less time in the field before they are garden-ready. So you are getting a younger plant—with all the flexibility and vitality that implies. Younger roses are smaller, which not only makes them a bit easier to plant, it makes them easier to site. Tuck them into a new flower border or among younger plants and let them develop towards maturity together.

■ There's no variability in flower color over time because the plant is 100 percent unique (grafted roses sometimes produce variations in flower color).

■ And, finally, own-root roses appear to have greater longevity. A grafted rose subjected to annual springtime hard prunings can run out of steam after three or four or five years; whereas an own-root rose keeps on going, unfettered, relying on the stores of energy (stored starches) in its own root system.

And when you grow landscape or shrub roses, own-root offers yet another asset. These types of roses are popular for hedges, groupings, and foundation plantings and benefit from an annual shearing to shape them and keep them in bounds. They tend to respond to such pruning by sprouting at the base—which, because they are on their own roots is fine. Over time, a denser, fuller look is easily achieved.

Own-root shrub and hedge roses, such as 'Carefree Delight'®, make for easier maintenance, since they can be pruned and shaped by annual shearing and the subsequent new canes will be true to the cultivar.

A New Generation of Roses

Bear in mind that this trend toward own-root roses is still new. If a rose plant is not specifically labeled "own-root," it may not be (Jackson & Perkins calls their own-root roses "New Generation" roses). As they make the transition in their fields, some growers are offering gardeners a choice—that is, the same rose as own-root or grafted. If you have the inclination and garden space, you might try both and see the differences for yourself. If you already have—and like—a rose variety you know is grafted but is running out of steam or has tended to produce suckers, consider replacing it with its own-root counterpart. And for cold-climate gardeners who have lost favorite roses to harsh winters, own-root roses designated as cold hardy are definitely desirable.

'Key Largo' is a rose grown on its own roots, designated as "New Generation Roses®" by Jackson & Perkins.

ROSY GOALS

The roses of the future will be better than ever. Watch for these trends to continue:

- better disease-resistance
- longer bloom periods/cycles
- higher bloom production
- improved cold hardiness
- more roses grown as own-root
- improved fragrance, especially in traditionally mild-scented colors like white, yellow, and pastel blends
- better (thicker) petal "substance," for longer-lasting blooms in the garden as well as the vase
- richer, longer lasting colors

The 2004 introduction 'Fragrant Keepsake' is an own-root rose that combines intense, long lasting color and strong perfume.

Many roses combine well in a perennial border. In this garden the pink shrub rose continues to flower as other plants come in and out of bloom, is a backdrop for shorter plants, and creates a lovely color combination with the yellow columbine. The miniature white rose in the lower right serves as an edging plant and a "skirt" for taller perennials, performing the same function as the lamb's ear in the foreground, but with the added bonus of attractive flowers.

Certain roses balk at being grown on their own roots and will not be found as own-root, or at least not until some diligent horticulturist conquers their reluctance. (Examples include 'White Lightnin' and 'Angel Face'—attractive roses, but not abounding in the inherent vigor that would help them develop good strong roots of their own.) But don't be surprised to see many new introductions coming out in this form.

The New Tree Roses

A great way to bring extra or portable color to the garden is with tree roses, also called "standard" roses or "standards." Tree roses look fabulous in pots, placed strategically: flanking a walkway or entry, by the pool, or decorating a patio or terrace. They're usually between 2 and 6 feet tall, and the rose atop the bare stem can be almost anything you could wish: a favorite hybrid tea or floribunda, or a lovely "weeping" shrub variety (one with a cascading habit). There are even small tree roses, with bright, cheery miniature roses grafted atop 18-inch plants.

Traditionally, tree roses have been three-part plants: a rootstock (understock), then a sturdy, straight stem, then the rose itself. The trouble with this configuration is that the stem—the middle, or trunk, of the "tree"— has sometimes sprouted unwelcome growth. New tree roses are two-part, an own-root base with the chosen rose grafted on top. The goal is a more reliable and, because there are fewer parts, more physically stable plant.

Don't forget to protect your tree roses over the winter; see page 130 for details.

New Ideas in Rose Landscaping

Roses need not be grown as solitary plants or in beds designated solely for roses. The variety of forms and colors available, and the healthier foliage and handsome, more manageable plant profiles mean there are roses for every landscape situation.

Roses in New Places

Thanks to the variety of forms that roses are available in, there are a range of intriguing uses for them. Here are some ideas:

- *Perennial borders*: Many types of roses combine well with perennials. Their dependable color keeps the garden attractive as other blooms come and go. Miniature or floribunda roses can be tucked into traditional flowerbeds, where they will not overwhelm their neighbors because they are roughly the same size and height as many flowers.

- *Shrub borders*: Many shrub roses and hybrid teas are compatible in height and girth to other flowering shrubs. Remember that your roses are likely to remain in bloom longer than their companions—you'll now be enjoying color all season in an area that was once only green for most of the summer.

Roses are good additions to shrub borders, being comparable in size to many blooming and evergreen shrubs. The pale pink rose 'Felicia' and reddish pink 'Archduc Joseph' are here in full bloom, contrasting with the pittosporum between them, and providing color in the garden while their evergreen companion is out of bloom.

Groundcover and hedge roses have become popular for difficult to maintain sites such as slopes, curb strips, boundaries, and foundations. Their dense growth crowds out weeds and controls erosion. And their season-long blooms can provide beauty in previously overlooked locations, making them useful for their form as well as their function.

- *Patios, decks, terraces, poolsides*: These are ideal places for containerized plants. Minis are suitable, as are tree roses. If there is room, add shallow-rooted annuals or herbs to the pot for extra beauty, or even plant miniature roses around the base of your tree rose.

- *Foundations and boundaries*: The palette and quality of roses suitable for mass plantings, in rows or groupings, is astounding. Use all one color, all pastels, or create a rainbow sequence.

- *Banks, curb strips, slopes*: The increasing variety of groundcover roses will revolutionize home and municipal landscapes that have challenging sites. The thick growth excludes weeds, the low habit is less maintenance and reduces erosion, the thorns will discourage foot traffic and pets—and the parade of flowers all season long will bring welcome color.

- *Container gardening*: Many roses grow well in pots. This allows you to feature roses in more places, such as a deck or patio, or in an area of the garden where the soil is poor. You can even grow a mini rose or a Garden Ease® rose in a hanging basket. A few tips: pots dry out fast, so remember to water often; make sure there are drainage holes so excess water can drain away; frequent fertilizing will guarantee a great show; and give bigger roses bigger containers so their roots have plenty of room.

Roses As Partners

Roses combine well with other garden plants. Place them where they'll get plenty of sun, and allow "breathing room" around the roses, for air circulation and to allow access for watering, pruning, and fertilizing. Since roses have certain water and nutrient requirements, plant companions with them that need similar care.

Here are some principles that have led to successful combinations. You can substitute similar plants, and create your own "vignettes."

- *Spiky flowers*: The rounded forms of roses, particularly full-petaled types (like English roses and certain old-

Tree roses are a great way to add color to a walkway, patio, pool, or porch. They can be underplanted with miniature roses or annuals such as petunias, scaveola, lobelia, sweet potato vine, or ivy-leaved geranium.

MIXED BEDS

The needs of your roses are not so very different from many other garden shrubs and flowers. They thrive in reasonably good, well-drained soil and perform best in full sun. Like perennials and annuals, they benefit from occasional grooming, such as removing spent blossoms, pruning wayward stems, and snipping off foliage that doesn't look as neat as you'd like. Because many roses are larger in width and height than most annuals and perennials, you need to place them judiciously when they are planted in a mixed bed. Put a rosebush in the middle or towards the back if you think it could overwhelm smaller plants. If a flowerbed is not large, choose a smaller-growing rose. If a flowerbed is large, you may wish to tuck in several rosebushes here and there to provide definition, as well as a recurring color theme.

Roses can be located in the middle of the bed so as not to crowd smaller plants toward the front. In a large garden several roses can be placed throughout, to repeat their color and form, providing continuity in the landscape.

Rosa 'Clytemnestra' with *Clematis* 'Ernest Markham'

ROSES LOVE CLEMATIS

Roses and clematis are a mutually beneficial combination: The rose provides support for the vine, and the flowers of both provide color and interest whether the other plant is in or out of bloom. And growing the two together allows the possibility of two beautiful flowers intertwined.

The upright forms of spiky flowers like foxglove are a good contrast with the rounded forms of rose blossoms and their arching canes.

garden roses) are a good contrast to the vertical flowering stems of many perennials and herbs. Good choices include: salvia, foxglove, veronica, and lavender.

- *Ornamental grasses*: These also love full sun and can "fountain" around roses. Some have colored foliage—blood red, powder blue—that adds a dramatic color contrast. Good choices include blue fescue (*Festuca glauca*) and burgundy fountain grass (*Pennisetum setaceum* 'Rubrum').

- *Flowers of similar size*: A rose adjacent to a blossom of approximately the same diameter makes them equals. Many great color combinations are possible. Good choices include any larger-flowered clematis hybrid, ornamental onion (*Allium caeruleum, A. sphaerocephalum*), and daisies.

- *Skirts*: Roses can be bordered with annuals and perennials, both to add color and to hide the less-interesting bases of the roses. Good choices include sweet alyssum, pansies, lady's mantle, and mums.

- *Silvery leaves*: Plants with gray or silvery leaves are great rose companions, because their color enhances the colors of the roses. They also serve well as connector plants between flowers of widely different colors. Good choices include artemisia, lamb's ears, dusty miller, sage, santolina, and silver thyme.

The fleabane in the foreground not only serves as a skirt for the rose behind it, hiding the bare stems at the base of the rose, the pink of the flower buds also repeats the color of the rose blooms.

Roses and ornamental grasses combine well. Both enjoy full sun and the grass foliage, whether as a backdrop for the roses, as a filler between plants, or as a border in the front, is a striking textural contrast.

Gray-leaved plants like the herb in the lower left enhance the colors of your roses. The white-flowered sweet alyssum in the lower right has a similar effect.

■ *Strap-shaped leaves*: Roses look good with the grassy, flat leaves of a number of perennials long after the perennial blooms have gone. Good choices include any iris, from tall bearded ones to Siberian, and daylilies.

Herbs As Rose Companions

The foliage of many herbs looks sensational with roses. Lower-growing herbs with silvery leaves (such as lamb's ears, artemisia, or sage) go well with rose blossoms of many hues, from lavender to pink to crimson. Herbs of any foliage color can also create a pretty "skirt" at the base of a rosebush, which draws attention away from the rose's stems and leaves and highlights the flowers.

Glorious bouquets

If a rose looks great with another plant in the garden, by all means put them together in a bouquet. But bouquets also allow combinations that would not be possible in nature, such as white astilbes or fronds of Japanese painted fern (both of which are shade lovers) with a pink or magenta English rose; bright, spiky penstemons (from the dry part of the yard) with a cluster of floribunda blossoms; or big snowy white hydrangea flowers (from your shrub border) with big-blossomed hybrid teas in red or mauve.

Roses are attractive companions for grassy-leaved plants even when those plants are out of bloom, such as irises and daylilies.

Roses such as the antique damask rose 'Celsiana' are natural additions to an herb garden, here grown with onions, yarrow, thyme, and boxwood. Herbs and roses are a good combination in any garden, both for fragrance and form. Onions and garlic are also said to discourage insect pests.

Many herbs—from parsley to rosemary to towering fennel—have an informal growing habit that complements the elegance of the roses, conferring a "cottage garden" charm. They can fill in around a rosebush and anchor it to the garden, and serve as ideal supporting players, calling attention to the rose's glorious flowers.

And don't overlook herbal fragrance! A richly scented rose in the company of heady-scented lavender spires, for instance, is enchanting—in the garden as well as in bouquets.

·ROSE TIP·

Night lights

While some garden flowers close for the night and reopen in the morning, unfurled roses remain open day and night, usually for several days. White roses are spectacular on summer evenings, when they seem to emerge from the shadows and glow in the garden. Grow them among other white bloomers—white annual geraniums, white cosmos, daisies, white foxglove (*Digitalis purpurea* var. *albiflora*), white evening primrose (*Oenothera speciosa alba*), candytuft (*Iberis sempervirens*)—and you have your own lovely "moonlight garden." (Interesting to note—many white flowers are pollinated by moths and other insects that are active at night, when the white stands out in the landscape.)

'Blanc Double de Coubert'

A beautiful moonlight garden can be created using white-flowered roses, white foxglove, daisies, candytuft, moonvine, and white nicotiana.

SELECTING AND PLANTING ROSES

IN THIS CHAPTER:

- **Bareroot roses and potted roses**
- **What to look for**
- **Rose awards, rose tags, patents**
- **Site selection and preparation**
- **Pre-planting care**
- **How to plant step-by-step**
- **After-planting care**

Shopping for Roses

Selecting and bringing home your roses, after all your dreaming and planning, is exciting. Now is the time to choose a quality plant, one that you'll be enjoying for years to come.

'Intrigue'

Bareroot Roses

Good roses are widely available in bareroot form. There are many compelling reasons to invest in these.

- *Robust good health:* Bareroot roses are the form of choice for mail-order nurseries and some garden centers. They may look disconcertingly like a bundle of dry sticks. But don't be deceived by appearances—these are a wise purchase. The plants were harvested in the fall, when they were full of starch reserves; they will live off of these as they emerge from dormancy and begin life in your garden.

- *Dormant plants for earlier planting:* With bareroot plants, you can get an earlier start. They can be planted sooner in the spring than potted roses, and will make a slower and better-paced transition into life in your garden as the season ramps up. In other words, they tend to adjust well, without transplant trauma, easing into growth at a natural pace.

- *Ease:* The fact that the roots have never been cramped or confined also makes

If you are planning to install a hedge of roses, buying them bareroot can be a less expensive, easier approach.

'Iceberg'

planting a bareroot rose easy. They are literally "ready to go."

- *Affordability:* Bareroot roses are generally cheaper than already-growing, potted roses (except, of course, for the new small-pot Garden Ease® roses described on page 70). This is a consideration if you are putting in a hedge or boundary planting, or have an ambitious rose garden in mind.

Bareroot Rose Grades

As with other industries, the plant industry has certain set standards, with ratings indicated by numbers. The American Association of Nurserymen has established these numbers, and all reputable rose suppliers adhere to them. A plant is rated based on the number and thickness of its canes (stems).

Note that these standards only apply to two-year-old, field-grown roses, sold as bareroot plants. (Greenhouse-grown roses will not meet these standards, though they can reach rated sizes when grown for a year or two before sale. There are no sale or distribution standards for miniature roses.)

You will find grade information on the rose label or in the catalog.

- *#1 grade:* This is the highest designation and indicates a bigger, better plant, with more numerous and thicker canes.

- *#1¹/₂ grade:* This is a midway rating, indicating a rose that was harvested at a younger age. It has fewer and thinner canes than a #1. Yet it is still bigger and better than a #2. These often appear later in the season, when suppliers are trying to sell excess stock. They may also be offered when the supplier has run out of #1's, and the buyer is willing to take a lower grade to get the roses they want right now and for a lower price.

- *#2 grade:* This is the lowest rating, and designates smaller, less robust rose plants.

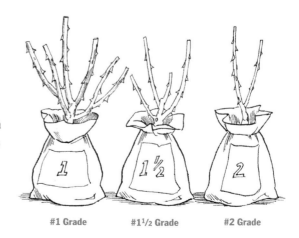

#1 Grade   #1¹/₂ Grade   #2 Grade

Not surprisingly, #1's are the most expensive. The two lower grades are frequently offered at discount prices and sometimes you can get a good deal on a decent plant, or save money if you are buying a lot of rosebushes for, say, a long, informal hedge. But generally, higher grade—and bigger—roses are far superior. They get off to a better start in your garden and perform better the first season and beyond.

Where and When to Buy Bareroot Roses

A little background will help you understand why bareroot roses are such a good choice. The rose-distribution system begins like this: Roses are raised in large production fields and harvested while young and full of energy reserves. They are dug up in the fall, their roots are cleaned of soil, and they are placed in cold storage, which keeps them safely dormant until springtime shipping arrives.

Note that freshness is important in plant quality, and roses are no exception. If a rosebush changes hands frequently on its way from the nursery to your yard, its quality is at risk and dependent on how it is handled. Chances are, the earlier in the spring you get a bareroot rose, the fresher it is.

Garden centers typically offer bareroot roses only in early spring. These were ordered in advance and are unpacked and kept cool (to prevent premature sprouting). Some garden centers soak the roots in water prior to sale.

Alternatively, some gardeners prefer to order their bareroot roses by mail, ordering in late winter for early-spring delivery. This is well worth doing. Advantages include:

Mail-order nurseries often offer a wide selection of unusual roses, such as this antique climbing noisette, called 'Jaune Desprez', which dates to 1830.

- *No middleman (or middlemen):* Less handling means freshness and better quality. It's the fastest possible journey from the field to your garden.

- *Top quality:* This is because specialists know best how to harvest, store, and ship.

- *You get a guarantee:* Catalog companies are ready, willing, and able to stand behind their product. Reassurance, advice, and a replacement or merchandise credit are a phone call away. This sort of service makes mail-order companies competitive with local garden centers.

Bareroot roses offer several advantages: They can be planted earlier, are less effort to plant, will make a smoother transition to the garden, and are usually cheaper than potted roses. Be sure to inspect your newly-arrived bareroot rose for plant quality and health.

■ *You have access to reliable information and expert advice:* Rose specialists know their products and are ready to answer your questions—check the catalog or packing slip for a customer-service phone number or website and don't hesitate to use these resources.

■ *A wider, more exciting selection:* Catalogs often debut exciting new varieties that are not produced in enough quantity to make it into national distribution networks. Mail-order companies are also able to offer a tantalizing array of interesting and rare roses that local garden centers typically don't stock.

How to Check for Plant Quality and Health

Although all reputable suppliers ship pest- and disease-free bareroot roses, it's just common sense to inspect a plant when you get it. Slide it out of its packaging and look for the following:

WHAT IS "VIRUS-FREE" AND WHY SHOULD A HOME GARDENER CARE?

"Rose virus" is not a rose disease that home gardeners commonly see or contend with because its effects, while ultimately insidious, may not be visible to the untrained eye. Fortunately, the industry as a whole has been working hard to eradicate it. These days unaffected, healthy plants sold by reputable growers are clearly labeled:

■ "virus-free"   ■ "certified"

■ "virus-indexed"   ■ "virus clean"

You should do your part, for your garden's health, longevity, and beauty, as well as for the greater good, by seeking out plants designated as free of virus.

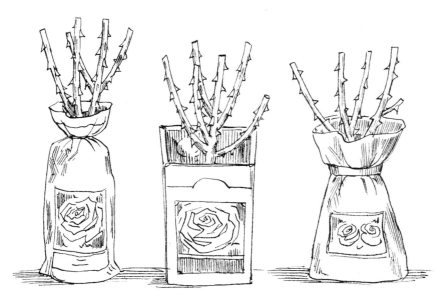

Roses can be purchased in several types of containers, including boxes and poly-bags.

- *Healthy stems:* The canes should be intact and undamaged, not snapped off in places or dried out at the tips. They should be thick, succulent, and green, but not yet really leafing out.

- *Healthy roots:* Living, viable roots are flexible and "crunchy." Damaged, dying, and dead roots are browned or black. (They may even have a telltale rotten smell.) If there are only a few they can be pinched or clipped off, but if many of the roots are in poor condition, the rose may not survive.

Potted Roses

Every spring, after the air and soil have warmed up, all danger of frost is past, and everybody has gardening fever, local garden centers traditionally offer potted roses for sale. The biggest advantage to these is that they are ready to go when you are. You can bring these actively growing roses home and plant them without delay. If growing conditions are

right—mild days and nights, with sufficient soil moisture—you'll be enjoying the closest thing to an instant garden. You also don't need to plant a potted rose immediately as you do a bareroot plant.

Remember, however, that buying a potted rose is somewhat like shopping for a tree or shrub—you may be impatient and want to acquire a bigger, more mature plant, large

Garden Ease® Rose,
'Wild Plum'

GARDEN EASE® POTTED ROSES

The problem of rootbound potted roses has been circumvented by this recent development, pioneered by Jackson & Perkins. Garden Ease® roses are small plants, not more than 8 inches high, and not large enough to have exceeded the limits of their pots. Rather than being offered in 1-gallon pots, these come in 4-inch nursery pots, similar to those often used for flowering perennials.

These scaled-down rose plants can remain in their containers until you are ready to plant them. Then they go easily from container to garden, and bloom profusely.

So small, inexpensive, and productive are these new little roses, that some gardeners and landscapers are even employing them for annual color. Some uses include:

- **Bedding displays:** Mixed or matched.
- **Groundcovers:** Because they are uniform and so colorful, they look beautiful massed.
- **Hanging baskets:** Some have a cascading habit that is perfect for hanging displays.
- **Quick color:** Anywhere in your garden, while you wait for other garden roses to get into full swing.

Look for Garden Ease® roses at local garden centers, or order them from the Jackson & Perkins catalog or website.

and lush with leaves and buds, but in the long run you'd be wise to invest in a smaller plant. True, a smaller plant is younger, but it is also less likely to have spent much time in the pot and therefore less likely to have become rootbound. If it has buds, and you get it into the ground quickly and properly, it won't be long until you are enjoying your first rose blossoms.

In short, your best bet is a smaller plant in a larger pot. It will make a smoother transition to garden life if it's just beginning to show new growth rather than completely leafed out or already blooming.

Where to Buy Potted Roses

When shopping for potted roses, your best bet is to visit a local garden center that has a big selection of rose plants. Big selections suggest that they know enough about roses to handle the shipment and care properly. Also, a big selection indicates a recent, fresh delivery. (If there are only a few roses left, chances are you are shopping late!)

Generally speaking, roses that travel directly from the grower to a garden center are in the best shape. Garden center staffers unload them into a holding area, where they immediately get a drink of water and protection from the hot sun.

If you spot a rosebush for sale in a non-traditional venue, such as the sidewalk in front of your local grocery store, or if a rosebush is on sale late in the planting season, buyer beware! In both cases, it is likely that the plant has traveled far and changed trucks and storage facilities several times and it is probably no longer in peak condition. It may not have gotten the care it needs, such as water or protection from hot sun, either. Bargain-priced potted roses may or may not look bedraggled at first glance, but chances are they have suffered during their journey—and therefore may struggle in your garden.

When to Buy Potted Roses

Springtime is prime potted-rose season. It is then that you will find them on display and in peak condition. Shop when the weather has turned warm and all danger of frost is past.

Sometimes garden centers unload excess rose plants later in the summer or fall at cheap prices. Not only could such plants be potbound (meaning the roots have filled the pot and become crowded), they may also have a tough time when they finally get planted in the ground. Hot, dry summer weather may

ROSE TIP

New growth is usually red

When rose leaves first appear—in almost every variety—they are briefly red or maroon in color. They soon turn green, some quite glossy, some more "matte green," once chlorophyll production gets underway. A potted rose with reddish leaves, then, is just getting started and may be a better buy than one that is further along.

New rose leaves are typically dark red when they first appear.

prove very stressful. The root systems may struggle to get established, the foliage may wilt, buds may fall unopened, and flowers may shatter their petals to the ground. If you decide to buy one of these, be prepared to invest extra care.

As for fall bargains, depending on your climate, these roses may not have enough time to get established before cold weather comes—and they can struggle and ultimately die.

So, it's best to spend more money on a young rose in the spring.

How to Check for Plant Quality and Health

Reputable suppliers are reliable as a source of roses that are pest- and disease-free. When shopping locally, it's still wise to check over a new plant for signs of insect damage or disease. If anything gives you cause for

Rose foliage with early signs of black spot. When shopping for roses, carefully inspect the plants for indications of insect pests and diseases.

To have a beautiful, healthy rose that will enhance your garden for years to come, buy one in peak condition in the spring and plant it well.

'Ballerina'

concern, don't buy. (If you've already purchased a rosebush that has a problem, return it if you can . . . or treat the rose appropriately. For more information on identifying and dealing with common rose problems, see the chapter on Rose Care.)

Top Growth Check

Certain pests like to congregate under leaves, at the junction of a stem and a cane, or on developing buds.

- *Chewed leaves:* Anything from a harmless caterpillar to voracious Japanese beetles could be responsible. If the creature is present in any significant numbers, there may be a problem. (If you only see one or two and still want the plant, pick off the bug and alert the garden-center staff. Don't bring trouble home with you!)

- *Chewed petals:* A small pest called "rose chafer" could cause this. Cucumber beetles, usually of greater concern in the vegetable garden, sometimes chew on rose blossoms. Often, chewing insects may be picked off by hand; however, if there are many, you may have to resort to a chemical treatment suggested by your supplier.

- *Webs:* These are made by spider mites, a very tiny pest related to spiders. Don't buy an infested plant!

- *Ants:* These little creatures don't harm roses *per se*, but can still be a bad sign, because they are drawn to the honeydew secreted by aphids, an often-serious rose pest.

Disease-infected plants may also show signs of damage. Sometimes you can just pick off and discard the afflicted leaves or flowers. But avoid a plant that is showing troublesome symptoms. Rusty, spotted, or blotchy leaves, or ones disfigured by gray powdery fuzz or mildew, are infected. Yellow leaves might be a sign of disease, or might be nothing more serious than the protest of a thirsty plant.

Root Check

A rose may look fine on the top, but what is going on below? Pick up or tilt a potted rosebush and look at the base of the pot. Are roots questing out of the holes in the bottom? This is a sure sign that the plant is potbound. And if you are able to slide out the rootball, even partway, you may observe a tangled, dense mat of roots that have been forced by their confinement to grow in and around one

WHY DO FLOWERS FALL OFF?

New, young potted plants, including roses, always give priority to new growth, including new roots, which help establish the rose in its new home in your garden, and new leaves and buds. A plant with blooming flowers that is under stress—traveling in a truck or car, not being properly cared for, in need of water—naturally jettisons its flower petals. In this way, the plant conserves its precious resources for new root and top growth.

·ROSE TIP·

Clip off flowers to relieve stress

When you get your potted rose home, if you think it is stressed, or has been under duress, clip off its flowers no matter what stage of development they are in. This will allow the plant to regroup. Once it's improving and has the basics of root growth and renewed leaf and stem growth underway, it will generate new buds and flowers.

Flowering takes a lot of energy, so clip off the flowers on newly purchased roses if you think the plants are stressed to give them a chance to recuperate.

another. This is not an ideal condition, but it can still be a viable rose for your garden. Just be sure to get it into the ground as soon as possible, since the roots of a potbound plant are difficult to keep watered in the container. Before placing it in the planting hole, tease apart and spread out the constricted roots.

When you are checking the roots before purchase, make sure it has healthy, "springy" roots; dead roots are dark and limp and may smell musty. The presence of a few dead roots is not a crisis, but a plant with predominantly unhealthy roots is not a good buy, despite what the top of the plant looks like.

When shopping for roses, researching which ones are award winners can help you make your selections. There are a number of awards, in the U.S. and in other countries. 'Maiden's Blush' is a winner of the Award of Garden Merit, given by the Royal Horticultural Society and Royal National Rose Society in England.

Rose Awards

There are so many enticing roses to choose from! As you shop, you will discover that some are award winners. Seeking these out is a good place to start and will help you wade through the multitude of choices with confidence. An award means there is a quality, or perhaps several qualities, superlative about the rose. Or it indicates that the rose outpaced many others in competition.

Please note that even if a rose was an award-winner long ago, it might still be a great rose. Twenty years may have gone by, but the qualities that caused it to take a top honor haven't changed—if it had fabulous fragrance then, it still does, if it exhibited excellent disease resistance then, it still does. The fact that an older rose is still in commerce indicates that it has stood the test of time and is still "a winner."

'Mister Lincoln', a past AARS winner, has been a popular rose since its introduction in 1965.

That said, you should also be sure to consider more current winners, for the simple reason that modern-day rose breeding has made such impressive improvements.

A newer red rose, 'Opening Night', introduced in 1998, is a more recent AARS winner.

'Memorial Day',
2004 AARS Winner

AARS Test Gardens

AARS stands for "All-America Rose Selections," and is an ongoing, annual competition that began in 1938. Each new rose variety submitted is grown in the AARS-accredited rose test gardens, for a period of two years. This is considered sufficient time to observe and rate its merits. Judges look at everything from growth habit and disease resistance to flower form and fragrance. Each characteristic is rated "poor," "fair," "good," "very good," or "excellent," and when the results are tallied, a score is assigned. Top scorers—and there may be a handful every year—are designated AARS winners.

The breeder or company who submitted the rose variety can then trumpet the award to you, the consumer. This is a very good system not only because it is rigorous, but also because the roses must prove themselves nationwide in a range of climates and growing conditions. Twenty-four rose gardens are spread across the United States, from Alabama to Colorado, from Maine to Hawaii. All are open to the public. To find one of these AARS-accredited gardens near you, check the website at www.rose.org.

The ARS Rating System

If you want to grow a rose that the experts have rated highly, consider the American Rose Society's system. Their goal is to evaluate all roses in commerce in the United States and Canada, assigning each one a number between 0 and 10, where 0 is not a good rose, and 10 is a stupendous rose. Most roses rate somewhere in the middle. Considered in the calculations are such things as plant quality, disease- and pest-resistance, blossom quality, and bloom period and longevity. Members nationwide send in their reports, which are compiled and averaged. Since the numerical rating is an average, it may not be applicable if you have special or extreme climatic or soil conditions. On the other hand, a higher rating indicates a resilient and adaptable rose, because it had to impress rose gardeners from all corners of the country.

Interestingly, the mathematical calculations are logarithmic, like the Richter Scale used for measuring earthquakes. So a rose that is rated 7.5 is actually 31.5 times

Based on a scale of 0 to 10, the shrub rose 'Robusta' has a high rating of 9 from the American Rose Society.

better than a rose rated 6.5.

You can browse the listings of roses in the ARS compilation, called *The Handbook for Selecting Roses.* It's revised and updated every year (there is a small fee to purchase it, which is less if you order in quantity, with a garden club or group of friends). The address is: P.O. Box 30,000, Shreveport, LA 71130, and their website is: www.ars.org.

'Grand Prize', a winner of The Hague Gold Medal, an international competition held in the Netherlands.

James Alexander Gamble Fragrance Medal

The American Rose Society decided in the early 1960s to honor especially fragrant roses that also meet high standards for plant and flower excellence (the rose has to be rated an 8.0 or better, out of a possible 10.0—see page 77 for more on this rating system). The award is not issued every year, only when a certain rose is deemed worthy. The contenders are judged over a five-year period in municipal and private gardens throughout the United States.

To date, less than a dozen roses have been thus honored—so the award is very prestigious and a great guide if you love fragrant roses. Past winners include the hybrid teas 'Fragrant Cloud' (1970) and 'Double Delight' (1986), and the beloved lavender floribunda 'Angel Face' (2002).

American Rose Society Award of Excellence for Miniature Roses

Not to be confused with the AARS, the ARS award is an honor bestowed by rose aficionados. The judges are American Rose Society members, who rate both old and new miniature roses according to a variety of traits, including appearance and health. Their much-anticipated *American Rose Annual* publishes the results, categorized by region. This award may point you to a mini, old or new, that performs particularly well in your area.

James Alexander Gamble Fragrance Medal Winner 'Double Delight'

ARS Award of Excellence for Miniature Roses Winner 'Tropical Twist'

2004 Jackson & Perkins Rose of the Year® Winner 'Sundance'

ROY®, or Rose of the Year®

Rose of the Year was started by Jackson & Perkins and is now a popular annual feature—look for a splashy announcement on the opening pages of their catalog. Culled from thousands of seedlings, a handful of promising new roses, unnamed and designated only by color, are put into limited production. Customers are then invited to order these at a discount price, then grow and judge them via the Rose Test Panel program (to participate, see a current catalog or visit the website at www.jacksonandperkins.com).

READING A ROSE TAG

Whether you shop for roses in a specialty catalog or look at the plant tag at the local garden center, you'll see conventional rose labeling. A typical label reads as follows: 'Scentimental'™ (WEKplapep), or 'Disneyland® Rose' (JACmouse). Sometimes there is also a patent number. The main name has been registered with the American Rose Society to protect it from being used on another rose.

As for the coding in parentheses, this information identifies and credits the hybridizer (WEK=Weeks Roses, JAC=Jackson & Perkins), and the lower-case letters that follow ("plapep" and "mouse") may flag the rose's parentage or be a unique code. The rose carried this coded name, and sometimes also a coded number, for the first part of its life—until it was ready to be marketed and given a descriptive name.

Tags are usually small, made out of weather-tough metal and attached to the rose plant at the base with a twist of wire. It's a good idea to leave them on—they'll be out of sight, but you'll be able to refresh your memory if you ever forget a rose's name. Since some roses can grow large enough to make it difficult to reach the tag at the base of the plant, it's a good idea to move the tag as the rosebush grows to allow easy access to it.

As seen on this rose tag, the patent code for 'Wildberry Breeze' is JACRULAV, meaning it is a rose patented by Jackson & Perkins (JAC), it's a rugosa rose (RU), and it has lavender flowers (LAV). PPAF means "patent pending/applied for."

The Jackson & Perkins rose '*Disneyland* ® Rose' is patented and the name has been registered with the American Rose Society.

judging, but they are good roses to begin with, and growing something "a jury of your peers" likes is appealing to many rose gardeners.

What Is a Patented Rose?

Occasionally, you will notice that a rose is "patented"—it either has a patent number listed next to its name or "PPAF" (which is shorthand for "patent pending/applied for"). Legislation allowing roses to be patented was passed in the 1930s. It is used now more than ever because modern-day rose breeding is proceeding at a dramatic pace, and those who have spent many years and a lot of effort, rightfully wish to protect their investment and achievement.

Results are tallied, participants are sent a signed certificate from the breeder thanking them, and the winning rose is given a name and offered to the general public. It's amateur

For the rose hybridizer, a patent protects his variety for seventeen years; someone else can propagate this rose during that time, but only if they pay the hybridizer a royalty fee

'Flirtatious', a rose patented in 2003 by Jackson & Perkins.

'Fabulous'

White and yellow roses hold their flowers longer, with better color, if they have a little protection from hot afternoon sun.

(usually a dollar or two per plant). For the home gardener, a patent indicates that in the judgment of its developer this rose shows great merit. Thus newer patented roses are often considered superior to older, non-patented ones.

If you are less careful or your garden simply doesn't offer ideal growing conditions, some roses are more forgiving than others. But a well-grown rose will be a source of great pride and joy for you for many years, so it makes sense to do it right.

Planting Your Roses

A well-planted rose becomes a beautiful, healthy rose. This is not a difficult or mysterious process. However, you should not cut corners. A good start will make all the difference in the plant's performance this year and in the years to come, beautifying your garden and firing your enthusiasm for rose growing.

A rose is really no more work to plant and care for than many other perennial flowers and shrubs—it may even be *less* work! Attention to a rose's requirements will save you work down the line and make sure that it makes the best possible debut.

Better, longer-lasting color

The only exception to the full-sun requirement is that, once in bloom, some flowers tend to last longer on the bush—and have richer color—if they get a little protection from the hottest afternoon sun, particularly white and yellow roses. In the Deep South and Gulf Coast, where summer afternoon sun can be severe, rosebushes welcome a little afternoon shelter from a nearby (but not too close!) tree, fence, house, or other building.

Site Choice

It's a good idea to choose an appropriate site and have a preparation plan before you have your new rosebush in hand. Keep the following guidelines in mind.

- *Full sun:* Roses are sun-lovers. With it they will produce plenty of leaves and burgeoning buds. The warmth of the sun coaxes the buds to open—and also draws out rose fragrance. Insufficient sunlight, on the other hand, can cause a rosebush to struggle, producing lankier stems, fewer leaves, and fewer buds. This weakens the plant and invites diseases and pests. Try to choose a spot that receives between six and eight hours of sun a day, though some roses will perform well with somewhat less.

- *Shelter from wind:* Use a windbreak, other plants, or a fence to protect roses that are growing in the open, on a hilltop, or along a ridgetop. Applying plenty of mulch will also keep roses from drying out too quickly. Better still, avoid such locations. Roses are happiest in the garden among other plants, a situation that is both protective and pretty.

- *Elbowroom:* Give your new roses space. The plant may be small now, but you need to allow for future growth. Crowded conditions also lead to poor

'Joseph's Coat'

Select an appropriate place to plant your roses. They need plenty of sunshine, and protection from wind if they are in an open location.

Not under a tree

Don't plant a rose under or close to a tree. The tree will shade the bush and inhibit its performance. Trees also have big, greedy root systems, and roses will have difficulty competing. Roses need all the water, nutrients, and sunshine you can provide them.

A well-planned garden that includes roses takes into account sunlight, shelter, and space.

air circulation, which can encourage disease. A good rule of thumb is to allow a typical rosebush (a hybrid tea, shrub, or floribunda) space that is as wide as it is tall. For example, 'Veterans' Honor', projected to grow 4 to 5 feet tall, should reach 4 to 5 feet wide (or, as some landscapers like to say, "a 4- to 5-foot footprint").

Planting Time

Like many other garden plants, roses are best planted in the spring, after danger of frost is past and the ground is workable. Of course, spring's arrival varies according to where you live. Consult your local Extension office for frost dates for your area.

As for mail-order nurseries, they have impressive national "weather-watch" computer shipping programs that allow them to send your roses at just the right time. They can even schedule to deliver your roses in the middle or at the end of the week, on the

Give your rose plenty of room to reach its natural size and to allow air circulation.

Roses can be planted in the summer but will need extra care, especially watering.

WHEN YOU CAN'T PLANT RIGHT AWAY

Too busy to plant promptly? Haven't had a chance to prepare the planting site yet? Rose shipment arrived a bit earlier than expected? Not to worry! Hold over a potted rose for several weeks in a cool, sheltered spot, watering every day or so. You can do the same with bareroot roses, for up to two weeks.

For bareroot roses, if you expect a longer delay, try "heeling in." To do this, simply dig a shallow "holding trench" in a semi-shady location (because full sun will bake the plants). Lay the plants in it nearly sideways—at about a 45-degree angle—so their roots can be completely covered with a protective blanket of soil. Cover up to a third of the stems (canes) as well, if you can. The object is to keep the plants shielded from sunlight and prevent dehydration, but not encourage them to sprout new growth.

correct assumption that most of us plant on the weekend. (If you are concerned about changes in local planting conditions, such as an unusual late snowstorm, or if you will unexpectedly be out of town when your shipment might arrive, call and make other arrangements.)

Bareroot roses can be planted earlier in the spring than potted roses, because they are dormant and will tolerate time in cooler soil and not-yet-warmed-up air.

Potted roses are actively growing and so are planted later, when spring is solidly underway. They can even be planted as late as midsummer, at least in most areas. But remember that the later you get them in the ground, the more pampering and watering they will need to get established and prosper under the stress of hot summertime weather.

Soil Preparation

The truth is, many gardens already have what roses need. Rose soil requirements are not difficult to provide. To boost performance, all you may have to do is add organic matter prior to planting. If your soil is poor, amending it will be the most important, cost-effective thing you can do in your garden. (This is what is meant by the old saying "It's better to dig a $10 hole for a 50¢ plant, rather than a 50¢ hole for a $10 plant.")

Rose lovers can apply the same planting trick that bulb gardeners use. Instead of going to the effort of preparing an entire bed, simply dig individual holes for each plant, and attend to the soil quality hole by hole. This works fine when you are only planting a few roses.

If you are breaking new ground for a larger rose bed, a lot of shoveling can be

Holes can be dug and amended for each individual rose, rather than preparing an entire bed.

backbreaking. Make the digging easier by giving the area a couple of good soakings in advance to soften the soil. You might want to use a small hand-held tiller to break up the soil and mix in amendments, or, if you have a big, ambitious planting plan, borrow a roto-tiller for an afternoon. The goal is to have good, loose soil about a foot deep, so the rose roots can grow freely.

Here's what a new rosebush really needs:

- *Good organic-matter content:* This means loamy soil rich in humus. Organic matter helps hold in soil moisture longer and will add nutrition—conditions your rosebush will love. This will mean less work for you since your rose will need less watering and fertilizing.

- *Good drainage:* Roses don't like "soggy feet," which deprives their roots of oxygen and leads to straggly growth. The best soil is one in which rain does not puddle up (clay soils), but also doesn't drain away too fast (sandy soils). Improve less-than-ideal spots by mixing in some organic material.

- *Proper pH:* Roses are not as particular about pH as some plants. They like their soil to be in the 5.6 to 7.2 range, or slightly acidic. If your soil's pH is higher or lower than that, the chemical reactions that make soil nutrients available to your rosebush may be interfered with or thwarted. Purchase a simple test kit at your local garden center. Or, if you are really concerned about your soil's quality, get a soil

Roses prefer loamy soil with good drainage and no serious obstructions such as large rocks or tree roots.

test from your local Cooperative Extension Service and follow the recommendations. Generally, overly acidic soils can be made more hospitable to roses by digging in dolomitic limestone, while soil sulfur will acidify overly alkaline ground.

■ *No obstructions:* Rose roots do not grow well if the soil is full of rocks and large tree roots, or is compacted. When you're preparing the site, get rid of all larger rocks. You may also encounter roots of other plants—if they come from long-gone plants, or ones that are not close by, it's fine to chop these out. The goal is loose, friable soil.

A RECIPE FOR SUCCESS

Roses grow beautifully in loamy soil, but what is "loam?"

Loam is ideal soil for almost all garden plants, including roses. If your garden doesn't have it naturally, it is not hard to create. Loam is organically rich soil that boasts a balance of large and small mineral particles. In texture and composition, it is midway between clay and sand. So it holds water well, allowing plant roots to get the moisture they need, but loam also drains well and is not soggy.

Organic matter builds up soil texture beautifully. If your soil is poor-draining clay, mix in organic matter; if your soil is quick-draining sand, mix in organic matter. Add it at planting time and then make a practice of adding more organic matter annually.

What qualifies as organic matter? Compost; dehydrated (composted) cow manure; shredded bark; shredded, rotted leaves ("leaf mold"); and peat moss (dampen it before use since it is difficult to dampen after it's mixed into the soil) are all good forms of organic matter. If you don't have these materials on hand, you can buy their packaged equivalents at a good garden center.

If your garden soil is uniformly poor, and you're not up to coaxing it along, you can have a truckload of garden loam delivered to your yard. Landscaping firms and larger garden centers can give you a quote. Have the soil unloaded in a location that allows easy access for you to transport it to the garden.

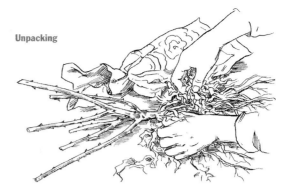

Pre-Planting Rose Care

Bareroot Roses

When you bring home a bareroot rose from a local nursery, or receive the box in the mail, give it tender loving care before putting it in the ground. This will delay planting for up to twenty-four hours, but it is well worth the time.

1. Unpacking

Slide the plant carefully out of its plastic or paper sleeve, and pick off any packing material such as wood shavings. Inspect the plant carefully.

Grooming

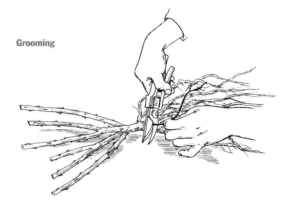

2. Grooming

Cut off any damaged, blackened, or rotten looking roots. Similarly, get rid of damaged stems. Use good sharp clippers for this work; scissors are not up to the job and tend to just mash the roots and stems.

Your rose will thrive in soil amended with organic matter, which builds soil texture, improves drainage, and adds nutrients.

Hardpan alert!

Many times, a gardener merrily digs down through topsoil to make way for new plants, only to run into a seemingly impenetrable layer of hard, compacted soil called "hardpan." This spells trouble for deeper-rooted plants like roses—they'll stop downward growth at the hardpan layer, and perhaps change direction and grow sideways. And water will not drain away properly. *You have four options:* Keep digging, in the hopes that the layer is not too thick and will eventually yield to your shovel. Install drainage pipes deep down to carry excess moisture away (or pay an experienced landscape contractor to do this). Pick another spot. Or, berm the soil to give added depth or use raised beds.

Shortening the canes

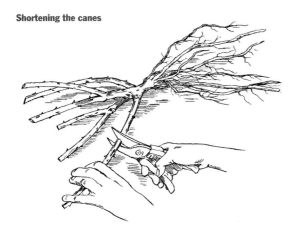

Shortening the roots

Re-hydrating

3. Shortening the canes

Bareroot roses vary in size and length, but you should shorten the canes upon arrival in any case. This reduces stress on the plant, so it can better make the transition into life in your garden. Each healthy, viable cane should be cut back to no more than 8 inches long. Cut to an outside eye to shape the plant, as this directs new growth outward.

4. Shortening the roots

The same practice applies to bareroot rose roots. Use sharp clippers to trim them just a little—no more than an inch.

5. Re-hydrating

This is the final, and most important, step in pre-planting. Prepare a bucket of lukewarm water, set it in a sheltered place (just inside the garage or on a covered porch), and put the roots in, right up to where they meet the canes, and let them drink in moisture for a few hours or overnight (up to twenty-four hours). *Optional:* After that, if you wish, you can remove the plant from the water and seal

Keep rose roots moist!

Particularly for bareroot roses, moist roots at planting time are important. Some gardeners add a bit of mud to the bucket of water, or even a handful of soil polymer powder (available from a garden center). Either substance will coat the soaking roots and prevent dehydration, helping to hold in crucial moisture.

After receiving bareroot roses, soak them for several hours in a bucket of water. Adding a little mud or soil polymer powder can help, as can a small amount of fertilizer.

it in a plastic bag for a few hours to let it further plump up. You may also add a small amount of fertilizer at this stage, such as Root Boost B1. Follow the dilution directions on the label.

Potted Roses

Pot-grown roses, too, appreciate a little pampering, just for a day or two, before you put them into the garden. It will definitely improve their performance.

1. Protect from sun and wind

Put the pots in a sheltered location out of hot sun and drying wind, such as on a porch, or against a north or east side of a house or garage. If you must keep them in a more exposed spot, just set a few lawn chairs over them for protection.

2. Water

Give them a good drink of water, until water runs out of their drainage holes.

3. Groom

Look them over and use clippers to take out damaged stems. Also, remove blooming flowers to direct energy to new roots, leaves, and stems. Leave on as much good foliage as you can, though, because it will manufacture the food that's needed for the rose to get established quickly once it's in the ground.

Put potted roses in a sheltered location until you are ready to plant them.

Remove damaged stems on new potted roses.

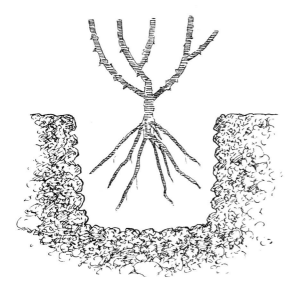
Dig your planting hole an appropriate size.

Step-By-Step How to Plant

Planting day can be stressful for a new rose. Plan to do it on a cooler—even a drizzly—day, or in the morning or evening, to avoid hot sun. Work quickly and efficiently.

1. Prepare the hole

Depth: A planting hole should be deep enough to accommodate the roots comfortably, without cramping, pushing, or bending. For a bareroot plant, this may be a foot deep, or as much as 2 feet deep. When planting potted roses, it's simple to check a hole's depth and width. Just set the plant in, pot and all. If the hole is not the right width or depth, make adjustments before removing the rose from its pot and planting it.

Width: Make the hole wider than the roots. This not only gives you room to work, it provides the roots with an area of loose soil to grow into.

Loosen: It's always a good idea to loosen the soil on the bottom and around the sides of the hole, to further make it a hospitable home for the incoming root system. Just roughen it a bit with the trowel. If the bottom and sides of the hole are smooth, it can act like a bucket and hold water, which will damage the rose roots.

Plant a grafted, bareroot rose with its bud union at or slightly below soil level. Spread roots over a mound of soil.

By watering as you plant you can eliminate air pockets.

2. Place the rose in its new home

Position it in the center of the hole. Hold the plant upright with one hand, and gently scoop soil back in around it. Tamp the soil down loosely to eliminate air pockets, but be gentle with the roots. (Later watering will further eliminate air pockets.)

For bareroot roses: Mound up a cone of back-filled garden soil in the center of the hole on which to rest the plant. This is much easier than trying to sift soil back in around the roots as you go.

Make a mound of soil in the bottom of the hole for bareroot roses, then spread the roots over the mound.

For potted roses: Using your fingers, gently tease the roots loose, on the sides as well as on the bottom, before setting the rose into the hole. This step encourages the roots to grow downward and outward in their new, bigger home. If the roots have formed a really tight mass, take a sharp, clean knife and score the outside of the rootball, top to bottom, in two or three spots. Don't cut too deeply—just a half-inch to an inch is sufficient. This inspires new roots to branch out where you cut, and from there they will grow into the surrounding soil.

Set the potted rose in the hole to check depth and width.

Tease roots apart and then place your potted rose in the hole.

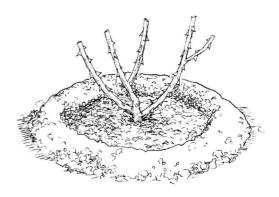

Make a basin of soil or mulch around your newly planted rosebush.

3. Make a basin

Once the rose is positioned upright and at the correct depth, and soil has been filled in around it, it's time to water. But first, create a holding basin around the plant—this makes the watering job much easier, not only now, but in subsequent watering. It also creates a buffer over those tender roots, which can be beneficial at this point in their life. Just make a low mounding circle around the plant beyond its outer limit, between 3 and 6 inches high, and about 18 inches across, for most plants.

4. Water well

With a hose or watering can, deliver a good, slow soaking to the newly planted rose. This eases the roots' transition into the hole and eliminates air pockets. If watering causes the rose to settle too deeply, just grasp the main stem and tug it gently back up to the proper spot, let go and see if that does the trick. If it doesn't settle higher, you may not have backfilled enough soil into the hole. Carefully remove the plant from the hole and try again.

5. Planting Climbers

Chances are, you have big plans for your climber. So you've positioned it by a fence, pillar, archway, trellis, at the base of a tree stump or big dead tree, or large garden structure.

DETERMINING PLANTING DEPTH

Grafted roses: In mild climates (Zones 8-10), the bud union—the swollen part where the roots meet the stems—can be positioned at or slightly above the soil surface. In cold climates (Zones 3-7), it's better to bury the bud union below the soil surface. This protects it from the chill of winter, and the plant may be inspired to generate some roots above the graft point, which not only further anchors it in place but creates new blooming canes of the variety you want.
Own-root/New Generation Roses®: Position the plant so the point where the stems emerge from the roots is just barely below the soil surface.
Potted roses: The bud union, if any, should be right above the soil surface in mild climates—and slightly below in cold climates.

On a grafted rose, the bud union is the swollen area just below the canes.

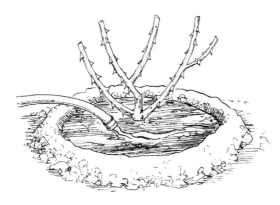

Water your new rose well.

Timing: If the intended support is not already in place at planting time, position it as soon as possible. Otherwise, you run the risk of damaging the rose's developing root system as you try to plunge the support into the ground.

Distance: Position the rose about a foot from its support; this is far enough away to allow the roots some room, but close enough for you to easily tie back the canes. If you place a rose too close to its support, the canes may cause you trouble later as they splay out and away from it. A little breathing room between plant and support is also good for air circulation—crowded stems and leaves can be vulnerable to plant diseases.

Climbers like 'Dream Weaver' should be planted a foot from their supports—close enough to attach but far enough away to allow good air circulation.

STEPS TO AVOID "TRANSPLANT TRAUMA"

A rosebush should have no trouble adjusting to life in your garden, but it helps if you minimize stress on the plant throughout the transition:

- Never place or store a new arrival in a hot, sunny spot.
- Always re-hydrate your roses before planting.
- Let the "good stuff" grow. Always trim out damaged or unhealthy-looking stems, roots, buds, and flowers. Clear the way for a fresh new growth spurt by eliminating any plant part that doesn't look promising.
- Plant at a "low-stress" time. Avoid planting in the middle of summer, on a hot day, or a few weeks before the first fall frost. A drizzly, late spring or early summer morning or evening is ideal.

A rose suffering from "transplant trauma" will signal its distress by not generating new leaves within a week or two of planting. Existing foliage may wilt. (Loss of blooming flowers is not a sign of transplant trauma but rather a natural survival mechanism.) Try watering—deeply and daily—and see if the plant perks up. Fertilizing with a chemical fertilizer at this time is not advisable; a rose needs to "get its legs under it" before it can respond to plant food. A slow-release, organic fertilizer would be safe to apply, however.

Plant climbers about 1 foot from their supports.

Canes on climbing roses tied horizontally produce more flowers.

- *Start tying early:* Unlike vines, roses do not have structures like tendrils or "holdfasts" to aid in climbing. Instead, they have long, supple canes that lend themselves to training. The gardener must intervene, especially in the early years, by tying the canes to the supports. If you wait until the rose has established itself, and the canes are older, it will be harder to train.

- *Work with new growth:* Like most roses, climbers produce their best growth and most flowers on new growth. This is good news, because it means you are going to be handling and tying the youngest, newest stems, which are always more pliant and easy to handle. Guide them to their support and tie them gently in place. (For more detailed advice on training climbing roses, including tying materials, see pages 126 to 127.)

Giving canes direction

Train young climber canes to grow upward on their support when they are just getting started. Later, when there is more growth, tie the canes more horizontally, since horizontal canes produce more flowers than those that are growing vertically.

Post-Planting Care

The days and weeks following initial planting are critical to your new rose's success. There are two simple things you must do to protect your investment and make sure the plant will thrive:

- *Water!* Newly planted roses are thirsty. If they were planted at the beginning of the season, warmer weather is coming and the plants will need more water to cope. Ample water also encourages root growth, so the plant can truly establish itself in your garden—and begin generating new stems and leaves, and of course a great show of beautiful flowers.

  The basin you created at planting time should be filled and refilled. The most efficient way to do this is to let water from a hose trickle in slowly and steadily over a period of at least an hour or two (if the water is running off and away from the plant, turn the hose flow down lower). This sort of "deep watering" not only hydrates the plant, but also seeps farther down into the soil, inspiring deeper root growth. Deeper roots, in the long run, help a plant cope with dry spells and drought, when the upper layers of soil dry out but lower layers are still moist.

  Water every day for the first week, especially if the weather is hot and dry. Thereafter, every three or so days is sufficient. Once the

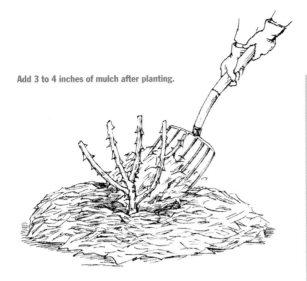

Add 3 to 4 inches of mulch after planting.

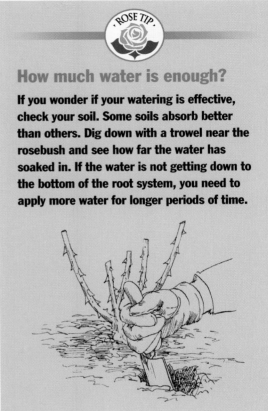

ROSE TIP

How much water is enough?

If you wonder if your watering is effective, check your soil. Some soils absorb better than others. Dig down with a trowel near the rosebush and see how far the water has soaked in. If the water is not getting down to the bottom of the root system, you need to apply more water for longer periods of time.

rose is thriving, you can change to weekly watering unless the weather is very hot or the plant looks stressed.

- *Mulch!* A layer of mulch at the base of a newly planted rose is a great asset. This helps hold in soil moisture by reducing evaporation, keeps the roots cooler, and moderates soil temperature fluctuations, reducing stress on the plant. It also inhibits weeds which are not only unsightly and a nuisance to the gardener, they may also hog the water and soil nutrients your new plant needs.

  Depending on the type of mulch you use, mulch can give your rose bed a more finished look, which is why bark chips are so popular.

  Three or 4 inches of mulch, loosely applied over the planting basin and just short of the stems, works best for most roses. The material will break down in time, and *you will have to replenish it.*

  For more details on types of mulches recommended for roses, see page 106.

Ample watering during and after planting helps your new roses become established in the garden.

ROSE CARE

IN THIS CHAPTER:

- ■ **Wise watering**
- ■ **Mulching is a must**
- ■ **Fertilizing simplified**
- ■ **Pruning basics**
- ■ **Seasonal care checklists**
- ■ **Troubleshooting pests and diseases**

Wise Watering

Beautiful roses are easy to grow. There really is no secret formula—just a few basic, easy caretaking principles. Rose maintenance is like anything else—if you do it right the first time, you are sure to avoid extra work or trouble down the line. Here, then, are the best ways to meet your roses' various needs.

It's easy to have beautiful roses. Choose appropriate roses for your area, plant them well, and follow basic guidelines for such maintenance practices as watering, pruning, and mulching.

Shallow watering does not reach the majority of rose roots, and will foster the growth of roots near the soil surface, which are less able to endure dry periods.

While some roses can get by on less than others, all roses need plentiful, consistent watering. During their first season, when the root system is getting established and probably also expanding outward underground, sufficient water is especially critical. In later years, your roses are likely to be more resilient and tolerate an occasional lapse in watering or a short dry spell.

The main thing to remember—and this principle holds true for many other flowers and shrubs—is that shallow watering encourages shallow roots, and deep watering encourages deep roots. You want your roses to develop deep-growing roots. Not only will this anchor the plants in place, but a deep-growing root system will also help the plant survive

drought. Garden soil tends to dry out quickly in the top few inches, especially on hot summer days, whereas deeply watered ground supplies moisture to deeply growing roots and thus sustains a plant better.

As you know from digging and planting, roses have long, downward-growing roots. So the moisture must be available where they are growing. The key is deep watering, to 12 to 18 inches down. And it is important to deliver that water as directly as possible to the right area.

Depending on the quality and porosity of your soil, it may or may not accept water well, which is another reason to prepare your soil well prior to planting. Generally speaking, roses do best when you give them a slow soaking from the hose. If the water is obviously running off onto the lawn, driveway, or other parts of the flowerbed and not soaking in where you want it, you have three options:

The best time to water

Water your roses early in the morning. As the day warms up, since the roses have had a good drink, they can enjoy the hot summer sun rather than become stressed by it. Afternoon watering is less efficient because some water is inevitably lost to evaporation. And evening watering is not the best idea, either, because dampness or humid air can persist around the plants all night long, possibly inviting disease.

- Lower the water flow to a trickle or use a slow "bubbler" attachment.

- Make or rebuild a mulch or soil "basin" around the base of each bush to hold the water; this way, it will penetrate eventually, and in the right area.

- Water for a short period of time, perhaps an hour, then turn it off. Wait an hour or so and water again, after the first watering has soaked in.

If rainfall is not adequate during the growing season, supplement by watering. Water deeply, and early in the morning.

Double-checking

If you want to make sure your watering is sufficient and effective, you can dig down near your rosebush afterwards and see how far moisture has soaked in. Remember, it should be around 12 to 18 inches down, for most roses. Or—easier still—use a "soil probe," an ingenious tool that is a hollow metal tube that removes a small core of soil for you to check for moisture. A rain gauge may also be worth investing in; it will keep track of the rainfall so you are alerted when moisture is low.

How Much Water and How Often?

The amount and frequency of watering needed in your location is a matter of trial and error. Traditionally, roses need up to 2 inches of water a week—but no region, not even the Pacific Northwest, can guarantee that kind of rainfall for the entire growing season. The plants will let you know when they are thirsty. If the foliage starts to droop or look dull (lose its lustrous shine), you've let too many days go by. But that kind of stop-start watering is stressful for a rose, especially a young one.

Try to establish a schedule. Water every two or three days, *before* a rose shows any signs of stress. Skip a watering, of course, if there has been a good, heavy rainfall. Running a bubbler or drip irrigation for thirty minutes at a time should do the trick for most soils.

Be careful not to overwater. This can suffocate the roots by depleting their oxygen supply.

Use a soil probe to find out if water is reaching deeply-growing rose roots.

Ways to Water

Watering Can

Advantages: You can visit each plant as an individual, taking a closer look at your rose as the water sprays down. Delivers water evenly and moderately.

Disadvantages: Not practical if you have lots of roses to water. You may have to make several trips to refill, per rose; a big planting can be a laborious watering job.

Hose

Advantages: Delivers water directly to the basin and your rose's root system.

Disadvantages: You have to move it from rose to rose. (If you "baby-sit" the hose, you could become impatient and underwater.)

Watering Can

Sprinkler

Advantages: Ease! Also, delivers water slowly and steadily.

Disadvantages: Wet foliage can get unsightly water spots, or develop disease problems. To minimize these possibilities, water in early morning or on a hot, bright day, so drops that fall on the leaves can quickly evaporate.

Bubbler

Advantages: Ease! Also, practical—delivers water at a slow gurgle.

Disadvantages: It's possible to overwater. To prevent this, add a timer to the system.

Soaker Hose

Advantages: The ideal way to water many roses or a large flowerbed. Delivers water slowly, directly to the root areas. Can be put on a timer.

Soaker Hose

Disadvantages: If you leave it in place, it's not a very attractive sight in the garden (unless you can find a way to hide it from view). But pulling it out of the garden—and laying it back down again each time you want to water—is a lot of work.

In-ground Systems

Advantages: Ease! Also, efficient—they provide water directly to the root area, at a measured rate, so there's little waste or runoff. Thus, these systems are an excellent choice for areas with regular droughts or water restrictions. Also a time-saver, if you have lots of roses needing water. It can even water your roses when you are away if you add a timer.

Disadvantages: Depending on the type you choose, and the extent of the system you want, it can be costly. Also, it's easier to install *before* you plant anything, so if your garden is established, installation might require more care to avoid damaging plants.

If you garden in a drought-prone region, plant your rose in a sheltered location to protect it from drying winds and to shade it from the hot afternoon sun.

Watering in Drought Areas

If you love roses but garden in a dry climate:

- Begin by choosing a variety known to be resilient to such conditions.

- Select a sheltered spot for your roses, so there will be less stress from drying winds and less exposure to full, blazing sunshine (a little afternoon shade will help). Good sites might be a walled, or courtyard, garden or a spot downwind from a fence or windbreak.

- Install a drip irrigation system in the planting bed *before* planting any roses. The emitters will drip, or lightly spray, water quite slowly, no faster than the root area can absorb it.

- Plant early in the growing season, so the roses can establish their roots before the weather gets really hot.

- Mulch!

- Water consistently. Roses really respond to a predictable watering program; this is even truer in drought-prone areas.

Growing Roses in Poorly Draining Soil

You can still grow roses, even if your soil or planting site drains poorly, as when the topsoil has been stripped off or your garden soil is high in clay. For some gardeners, the challenge is coping with heavy or soggy ground, or even occasional flooding. If you have these conditions, there are several options:

- *Improve the planting area before planting:* Dig and loosen the soil, and add lots of organic matter.

- *Install something underground that improves the drainage:* This can be a perforated pipe, a layer of stones or gravel, or even an adjacent sloped trench filled with loose stone and topped with coarse sand (a "French drain").

- *Make a raised bed:* This approach is popular with vegetable gardeners, but flower gardeners can enjoy the same benefits. A raised bed is a bottomless wooden frame set on top of the ground and filled with good soil. To accommodate deep rose roots (compared to vegetable plants), the raised bed will have to be at least a foot deep, but ideally deeper. This is admittedly a major project, but once in place, the results will be gratifying. (Alternatively, some roses can be grown fairly well in a half-barrel planter.)

If your soil has poor drainage, plant your roses in a raised bed. To allow ample room for rose roots, which are deep growers, make the bed a foot or more high.

Mulching Is a Must

Mulching is good for many plants, but it is especially beneficial for roses. It reduces stress in a variety of ways—and the less stress in a rose's life, especially in its first year in your garden, the better it will perform. Roses are even-tempered plants that prefer growing in a stable environment, which mulch promotes.

The Benefits of Mulch

- Mulch holds in soil moisture—so all the watering you are doing is retained.
- It moderates fluctuations in soil temperature, so even if your weather is unpredictable (especially in that turbulent period when spring segues into summer), your rose plants are spared the stress of temperature extremes. If the weather is really hot or windy, mulch will slow down the damaging effects of drying out.
- It smothers weeds and discourages weed-seed germination; weeds not only mar the appearance of your rose garden, the bigger and more aggressive ones will compete with your roses for soil moisture and nutrients. It's better to smother them before they ever get started.
- And last but not least, depending on the mulch material, as it breaks down it adds a bit of welcome nutrition to the soil around your roses.

Mulching benefits your roses by holding in soil moisture, moderating soil temperatures, discouraging weeds, and adding nutrients.

When to Apply Mulch

Apply mulch to your roses at planting time. (It is even more critical if you plant your roses a bit late, when the weather is getting hotter.) Thereafter, keep an eye on the growing area. Rainstorms, your own watering program, changing weather, and time will wear away mulch or encourage it to break down. Replenish it when you notice it is depleted—any time during the growing season.

   If you garden in an area of cold winters, be sure to mulch your roses in the fall. This is especially important if your snow cover is thin or unpredictable; cold, dry winters are very hard on most roses. A fall application of mulch can be made thicker than usual—like a protective blanket.

Growing season mulch should be 3 to 4 inches deep.

Applying a layer of mulch at planting time is one way of ensuring that the rose will adjust well to its new home.

When spring returns, chances are the mulch needs renewing. Make it an annual practice to always apply a fresh layer. Put it down early, before the weeds start to grow.

How to Apply Mulch to Roses
At planting time:
It's easy to put down mulch right after planting a rose. Just shovel it on (or scoop it on with a trowel) right into and over the basin you've constructed around the rose's base. Do not pile it up against the stems, however, not because the mulch may smother the plant (most mulches still admit some light and air) but because pests and diseases may be drawn to the damp conditions.

During the growing season:
Applying or replenishing mulch once the rose is growing vigorously can sometimes be a challenge. You may end up on your knees or stomach as you try to wriggle in close to the lush plant while avoiding thorns. Protective gloves can help. First, pull out any weeds that have managed to gain a foothold. Deliver the mulch to the base of the plant by the trowelful or shovelful, then spread it out carefully.

In the fall or for winter protection:
Do not cut back a rosebush's stems at this time, even though it means you may still have to contend with thick growth and grasping thorns as you try to get in close! On the other hand, you don't need to be as careful of the stems and leaves as in the spring, since the season of active growth is over.

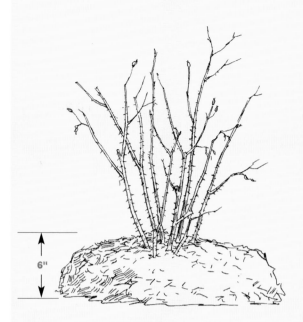

6"

Winter mulch should be at least 6 inches deep.

HOW MUCH MULCH?

You want to help your rosebushes thrive and protect them from cold, drought, and invading weeds—but you don't want, in your zeal, to bury them. Too much mulch can actually inhibit growth or invite small rodents or other pests to make a cozy home around your rosebushes. Too little mulch, on the other hand, and your rosebushes simply won't reap the benefits.

The general rule of thumb is 3 to 4 inches during the growing season, and at least 6 inches when it's a protective winter covering. Modify these amounts according to your own climate and unique growing conditions. If your roses look great, and they come through a cold winter to return in glory the following spring, you know you've done it right. If their performance is disappointing, don't rule out insufficient—or overzealous—mulching as a cause.

MANY MULCHES!

There is no "right" or best mulch for roses. Benefits will vary in different parts of the country. Some mulches are free, right in your own yard, others you may buy locally—so cost can be a factor. Experiment to see what kind your roses like best.

Wood or bark chips

Advantages: Looks neat and attractive, stays in place. Slow to decay. Free, if you chip your own (let it age a bit first—fresh wood chips rob the soil of nitrogen). Easily available at any garden center.

Disadvantages: If from pine trees, it's fairly acidic, which can make the soil pH too low for roses.

Grass clippings

Advantages: Cheap. Readily available. Easy to apply.

Disadvantages: Decays quickly and must be replenished often. If you have used weed killers (herbicides) or nitrogen-heavy fertilizers on your lawn, their residues might harm your roses. If your grass went to seed before you cut it, grass seed can germinate in your rose bed, which will require weeding later.

Straw

Advantages: Cheap. Easy to apply.

Disadvantages: So light it can blow away. Might harbor rodents, especially over the winter months.

Hay

Advantages: Cheap. Easy to apply.

Disadvantages: Contains weed seeds! Might harbor rodents, especially over the winter months.

Rotting leaves

Advantages: Smothers weeds very well. Helps hold in soil moisture well.

Disadvantages: Not especially attractive. If there are seeds (from maples, ashes, and acorns from oaks), they germinate and become a weed problem.

Compost

Advantages: Adds nutrients to the soil while it breaks down. Free and plentiful if you already have a compost bin or pile.

Disadvantages: Fresh compost can "burn" rose foliage due to high salts/minerals content.

Mushroom compost

Advantages: Organically rich—provides very good nutrition for the roses as it breaks down.

Disadvantages: Hard to find. Must be well composted, not fresh. May be high in salts.

Cocoa hulls

Advantages: Looks terrific!

Disadvantages: Can blow away in a stiff breeze. The chocolaty smell, usually appealing, can compete unfavorably with the rose's fragrance.

Peat moss

Advantages: Looks neat and tidy. Versatile—can also be used as an amendment in the planting process.

Disadvantages: Becomes crusty over time, and when the peat moss is dry it will repel water.

Sawdust

Advantages: Long-lasting. Looks neat.

Disadvantages: Needs extra nitrogen to break down properly (which you will have to add). If it's too deep, it makes a dense, impenetrable layer.

Gravel or stone

Advantages: Nice neat look. Easy to apply. No need to replenish over the course of a season. In cool climates, reflects welcome warmth and light into the rose plant.

Disadvantages: No benefits to the soil. Doesn't look natural.

Plastic (garden plastic, black plastic)

Advantages: Keeps weeds out! Holds moisture and warmth in.

Disadvantages: Can be hard to apply (before or after planting—tricky at either time). Inhibits access of water and fertilizer (exception: permeable "landscape fabric"). Unattractive.

'Lady of the Dawn'

A rose that receives ample fertilizer has healthy foliage and plenty of flowers, and is more resistant to pests.

Fertilizing Simplified

There are really only two things you should know about fertilizing roses: Roses benefit greatly from fertilizing, and soil pH is important. The most critical reason to feed your roses is that they actually need it. Some garden flowers don't, while other flowers perform better but don't really require feeding. Roses actually do respond to fertilizer, even in the most wonderful, well-drained, compost-enhanced garden loam.

For fertilizing to work, however, the soil must have an appropriate pH. If it is too high or two low, fertilizer simply isn't as effective. Luckily, roses prefer a moderate, and commonly found, pH level of between 5.6 and 7.2. So, most of us don't encounter pH problems. But if you suspect your soil is poor, and notice that your roses aren't thriving, even after an application of fertilizer, try a soil test. You may only need to add certain amendments to the soil to grow great roses.

What Fertilizer Does for Roses

Fertilizer is plant food. A well-nourished plant grows with more gusto—it's bigger, it has more leaves and more stems (canes), it generates more buds and therefore more flowers. And a well-nourished plant is healthier, because it receives the nutrition it needs to resist diseases and pests.

Nitrogen Is the Priority

All balanced fertilizers contain nitrogen, and you'll notice that fertilizers sold expressly for roses emphasize nitrogen. This may surprise you, if you only think of nitrogen as the element that keeps your grass greened up.

Nitrogen keeps your roses green, too. It goes to the leaves, which are the "engine room" of your rosebush, so to speak. They generate the energy that leads to bud formation, and thus, more flowers. So make sure you use a fertilizer with plenty of nitrogen.

'Bella'roma'

Roses thrive on regular applications of fertilizer.

'Ferdinand Pitchard'
Rose leaves generate the energy that leads to flower bud formation.
Healthy foliage results in more flowers per plant.

Of course, you should use a fertilizer that also provides the other two main nutrients plants need to thrive, phosphorus (P) and potassium (K).

When to Start, and When to Stop

Basically, you need to supply your roses with food throughout the growing season. Start in springtime, when your roses have already leafed out and the flower buds are beginning to swell.

Stop fertilizer applications early in the fall, before the cold weather arrives. Feeding

What the numbers and letters mean

All common plant fertilizers show three numerical values on their labels, in order, for the following elements.

- **N (nitrogen):** For enhancing the growth of leaves and stems.
- **P (phosphorus):** For good flowering and strong root growth.
- **K (potassium):** For overall good growth, vigor, and resistance to disease.

A "complete" fertilizer (meaning it includes all three elements, N, P, and K) with a label listing of 20-20-20 is an equal dose of all three; the "incomplete" fertilizer bonemeal, at 2.5-24-0, is a specialized amendment high in phosphorous. The best rose fertilizers are complete and balanced (with the three numbers being close in value), such as Once at 10-18-10, or Rose Food at 5-9-6.

For the best rose flowers and foliage, use a fertilizer that is complete and balanced, having similar amounts of the three elements nitrogen, phosphorous, and potassium.

For optimum performance throughout the growing season, fertilize your roses from spring to late summer.

That said, here's a good place to start: Feed your roses every four to six weeks throughout the growing season. That's not too demanding, as you'll discover—depending on where you live, it could amount to no more than four or five feedings per growing season. And the results are certainly worth the effort!

What's Up with Epsom Salts?

You may have heard, or seen, more experienced rose growers applying Epsom salts to their plants and been curious. This is not a traditional fertilizer, and it is an optional addition. It is a rose "treat" if you will, inspiring the plants to generate more flowering canes. Some say it also makes flower colors more intense, more even, and more fade-resistant.

Technically, Epsom salts is magnesium sulfate. Some garden soils are low in magnesium and when this chemical is added, the boost is obvious. (If your soil is not magnesium deficient, you may see little effect from adding Epsom salts.) But it can be worth a try.

generates fresh green growth and more flower buds, which would be vulnerable to cold weather, and there's no point in stimulating growth only to have it nipped by frost. Fertilizing late in the fall also inhibits a rose's ability to slow down and begin to go dormant for the winter. A good rule of thumb is to count back about six weeks before your first predicted/expected fall frost and let that be your last feeding application of the season.

How Often?

Of course, requirements and results vary in different parts of the country, with different roses, and even from one year to the next. But feeding your roses on a regular schedule throughout the growing season is always wise. You can watch the results—and adjust your timing accordingly, once you see how your plants respond.

· ROSE TIP ·

Water your rosebushes before you fertilize

That way, they're full of moisture ("well-plumped") and under no stress. Then, when you add the plant food, it will enter the soil more evenly and more gradually. If possible, also water immediately after you feed—this moves the nutrients into the root zone faster. Better still: Water with a hose-end fertilizer attachment.

If your soil is low in magnesium an application of Epsom salts can be beneficial.

Or, get a soil test first to find out if this "treat" is needed.

The standard application is a half-cup, or less, sprinkled around the base of the plant. Water it in well. Applying it once—no more than twice—during a growing season should be sufficient.

Are "Micronutrients" Important for Roses?

If your roses do not appear to be suffering and you don't see the need to order a soil test, you needn't bother with micronutrients. But they may be of interest to you if you garden in difficult soil (very alkaline, for instance); if your roses are simply not responding to traditional, nitrogen-heavy fertilizer; or if you see the characteristic symptom of yellowing leaves lined with green veins.

The micronutrients roses typically require that are either already present in the soil, or need to be added, are:

- Iron
- Manganese
- Zinc

The easiest way to deliver these nutrients to your rose is actually not directly to the soil, where they may dissipate quickly. Instead, get a bottle of "chelated micronutrients," add the amount of water recommended on the label,

DON'T BURN YOUR ROSES!

Too much fertilizer, or fertilizer applied too often, can lead to "burning." Your rose's foliage gets brown edges, or the leaves may even turn yellow or brown, dry up, and fall off. That's the damage you can see. What you can't see is that, under the ground, the tender feeder roots that received the heavy a blast of fertilizer may have been harmed.

To prevent or moderate the effects of too much fertilizer, you can:

- Apply less fertilizer per feeding.
- Feed less often.
- Water your plants well before AND after feeding, so the nutrients are diluted and delivered in a moderate fashion.
- Use an organic fertilizer (such as fish emulsion, cottonseed meal, or alfalfa meal); these are quite slow acting.

and spray the brew onto your rosebushes' leaves—on a mild or cool day, or in the morning or evening. This way, the nutrients are absorbed more quickly and delivered where they are needed. If your diagnosis was correct, the rose will perk up noticeably within a day or so.

Delivering Fertilizer

There are a variety of ways to feed your roses. Try them all and choose the one you prefer, or use different ones at different times.

- *Dry:* A grainy or powdery fertilizer is best sprinkled around the base of a rose plant. To make distribution even, some gardeners put the plant food in a cup, kneel down close to the spot, and shake it carefully all around the target area.

- *Water-soluble:* Either add it to the watering can, use a fertilizer attachment on your hose, or put the right amount in a sprayer.

Read the label!

Never assume you know how much fertilizer to use, or how much it should be diluted. Always follow the label instructions to the letter, for your plant's health as well as your own safety. (The only exception: If you wish, you can feed your roses more often, at half-strength. Just be sure to get your measurements right.)

TYPES OF FERTILIZERS

Granular

Advantages: Easy to apply, no mixing—just sprinkle on the ground and water in.

Disadvantages: Needs to be replenished every four to six weeks.

Powdered

Advantages: Gets to roots quickly.

Disadvantages: Must be diluted in water first.

Liquid

Advantages: Concentrated—a little goes a long way. Gets to roots quickly.

Disadvantages: Concentrated—you need to dilute it according to label directions.

Slow-release (Timed-release)

Advantages: Very convenient—apply once, maybe twice, in a season.

Disadvantages: May not be enough, so may need to be supplemented. May cost more than the alternatives.

Organic (examples: composted manure, fish emulsion, alfalfa meal, blood meal, cottonseed meal)

Advantages: Adds valuable/desirable organic matter to your garden soil. Acts slowly (less chance of "burning"). More in harmony with various soil microorganisms.

Disadvantages: Acts slowly, so the results are less dramatic. Not a precise science since nutrient content varies.

Roses can absorb rose food faster by foliar feeding.

Foliar Feeding

Traditionally, rose food goes into the plant through the root system—after you apply it to the soil. But rose leaves can also absorb nutrition. Indeed, this method gets the food into the plant faster.

Choose a water-soluble fertilizer and check the label to make sure it's okay to spray it on the leaves. Then dilute it according to the label directions and spray it on (see the information on various types of sprayers later in this chapter). Ideally, you want to do this on a relatively dry day and in the morning, to give the leaves the best chance of absorbing the maximum nutrition.

FIVE REASONS TO PRUNE ROSES

- **Prune for health:** When you cut out older, dead, diseased, and damaged wood, light and air are admitted once again and a rosebush is revitalized. A well-pruned rose tends to live longer, too.

- **Prune to improve quality:** A properly pruned rosebush has more and better flowers. The entire plant looks nicer, making it a real garden asset.

- **Prune to control size:** Once a rose reaches its mature size, judicious cutting keeps it in bounds, filling but not crowding its allotted space in your garden.

- **Prune for beauty:** Pruning is something of an art. With the right cuts in the right places, you can shape a bush attractively, encouraging it to grow where you want it to and displaying its flowers where they can be most enjoyed.

- **Prune to get to know your roses:** Something happens when you care for a plant in this way over the years. You learn about its habits and quirks. You know its history. You discover how to encourage its best performance. This kind of intimacy with a plant is an important reason why gardening is such an absorbing activity and such a joy.

Pruning Basics

Pruning your roses is always beneficial. They'll perform better and look better if you do—indeed, appropriate pruning brings out the best in them.

Fortunately, pruning roses is not mysterious. Remember, a rose is basically a flowering shrub. You may have other flowering shrubs in your yard, and you may prune those from time to time. So don't be intimidated.

When to Prune

Early spring is the best time to prune roses. Hard frosts are over, the buds are just beginning to swell, and the plants are ramping up for the new season—the plants have the energy and vigor to survive your cuts and generate fresh growth and soil and weather conditions are warmer.

Pruning can improve both the health and appearance of your roses. A rose with a nice shape displays its flowers better.

The best time to prune your roses is in early spring when the buds are just starting to swell.

Step One: Always Prune Out "Non-negotiable" Growth

Whether you are growing an elegant new hybrid tea or a somewhat unruly old-fashioned shrub rose, there are some general rules that apply to all roses. If you do no other pruning, there is some wood you simply must clip out, without exception:

Don't wait too late!

If the sap is already flowing in your roses—spring is well underway, in other words—the plants can suffer a loss of fluid from the cuts. This loss won't kill them, but it does slow down their recovery.

In the mild South and parts of the Gulf Coast, it's permissible to prune roses in the fall or winter. Just avoid pruning in freezing weather, which is sure to damage the now-vulnerable plants. If you aren't confident with this timing, just follow the rest of the country and wait until early spring.

Cut Out Dead Wood

You can tell when a stem is dead or dying (from damage or disease)—it's a different color, not green, not reddish, not lustrous brown. Instead, it's dull brown or gray. No new growth is sprouting from it. Cut it off as close to the base of the plant or to the point where the wood is still alive as possible, since there's no hope of renewed growth.

You'll notice that dead wood is dry and brittle, with dead or desiccated, darkened pith inside—and not always easy to clip off neatly. Be patient and careful; avoid wrestling with it and tugging on it, or you may unintentionally damage good wood in the process.

Cut Out Damaged Wood

Sometimes winter conditions (ice and snow) will snap, bend, or crack stems, and sometimes stems are broken by a car, bicycle, or errant soccer ball. These stems are not going to recover. You do not have to cut them all the way back to the base, however. If, lower down, undamaged parts show signs of life, just cut

Cut out damaged wood.

back below the damage and at the point of viable pith and hope for the best.

Remove Misplaced Stems

This includes ones that are rubbing together (choose one, spare the other), and stems that are growing in the wrong direction (toward the center of the bush, or into an adjacent fence or wall), or trailing on the ground. Again, cut these off as far back as you can.

Cut out dead wood.

Make sure it's dead wood!

While some pruning is best done at certain times of the year, dead wood can be cut out any time—whenever you notice it, whenever you want, even in fall or winter. Just be sure it's truly dead (if you're *not* totally sure, then wait until the growing season is in full swing and its status will be obvious).

Dead wood is dull brown or gray, brittle, and has no new growth. Cut back to live wood, which can be recognized in the early spring by the new buds forming along the stems.

Remove Suckers

These are errant canes that emerge from below the graft union, or bulge, at the base of the rosebush. They are sprouting from the rootstock and don't match or belong to the top part of the plant. In fact, they detract from the plant's overall attractiveness.

WE'VE GOT A LIVE ONE!

The condition of the pith, or innermost part of the stem, is the best clue to whether a stem is still alive and viable. Healthy wood has white pith. Dead wood pith is dried out and dark in color.

Suckers are easy to spot because they look so different. They're usually a different color, or smoother, or exhibit a lankier, wilder habit. (If you leave suckers on the plant long enough to generate leaves and flowers, you'll quickly see that they are alien to the rest of the plant's top growth. The leaves will look distinctly different, often smaller or a different shade of green, and the flowers are not at all what you expect and indeed are usually quite inferior to the rest of the plant.)

Remove stems that are rubbing together, growing in the wrong direction, or trailing on the ground.

Cut back damaged wood to just below the injury and at the point of active growth. Remember to prune at an angle.

Own-root roses, such as the New Generation Rose® 'Artistry,' are not grafted onto rootstocks, so suckers are not an issue.

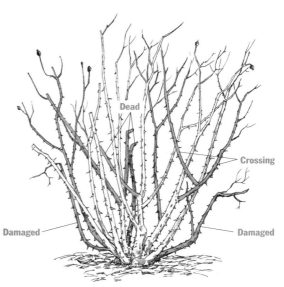

To thin out the canes of a rose that has become overgrown, first clip out branches that are damaged, dead, or crossing.

Not all roses generate suckers. Only grafted roses do. So you usually see them on hybrid teas and floribundas, which traditionally have been grafted onto hardy rootstock. Suckers are not an issue with own-root or New Generation® roses, including many shrub roses.

Step Two: Thinning

A rosebush that has never been pruned or has been neglected can be very congested. To restore order, begin by clipping out thinner, twiggy growth. That will clean up the plant dramatically. After that, your options require more thought. When in doubt, leave a branch in place. You can always cut it later, but you can't put it back after you've cut it and had second thoughts about its removal.

Remove suckers, which are sprouting from the rootstock, below the bud union.

Remove canes that will make the rosebush crowded. The goal is an open form that allows light and air to reach the interior of the plant.

Buds on rose canes face in different directions. Generally you should prune back to buds growing away from the center of the rosebush.

Thin Out Crowded Stems

Stems that are jostling for limited space need to be thinned out. Some must go and some can stay. The goal is to have the remaining stems separated from each other a bit—to give them growing room, light, and air.

Thin Out Crossed Stems

Stems that rest on each other have to go, too. Otherwise, the plant will only become more and more tangled up and dense. Canes growing sideways, especially, should be removed, so that the ones left growing upright will then grow more freely.

Cut Back Trailing Stems

These are the "pioneer" stems, or the ones that are heading upward and outward. Shortening them is advisable because it keeps a bush looking neater and also—by the same principle as pinching back your houseplants—inspires fresh new growth lower down. So you get a more compact, less lanky plant.

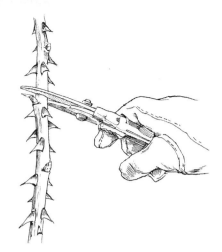

To encourage a rose branch to be spreading, prune to an outward facing bud.

Step Three: Strategic Pruning

Now that you've taken all the non-negotiable stems out of the way, and done some thinning, you have the chance to encourage your rosebush to develop an attractive profile and to grow in the directions you want. All it takes are some savvy cuts.

Aim for an "Urn" or "Vase" Shape

This is standard rose-pruning advice and works for most (but not all) roses. The goal is to have evenly spaced stems (flowering canes) on all sides of the bush, with the center of the plant somewhat open.

How much should you cut back good stems?

The general rule of thumb is: Cut back flowering stems by a third. A bit more, perhaps half, may be warranted on older, bigger bushes. Don't worry if this seems drastic. Roses are lusty growers and by midsummer, all your qualms will be banished as you admire your handsome, healthy rosebushes.

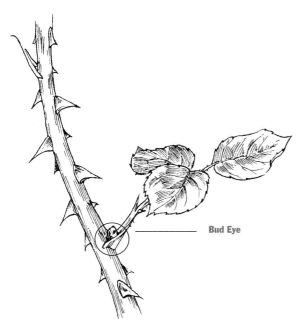

Not to be confused with the thorns, a bud eye is reddish and occurs just above a branch or leaf.

Fine-tuning

You will see that new growth alternates along a stem, or cane. Some buds are facing outward, some inward, some to the side. When these begin to swell and send out new growth, that's the direction they will be headed.

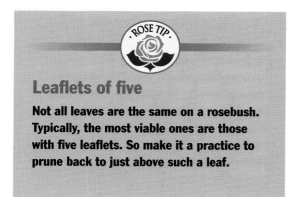

Leaflets of five

Not all leaves are the same on a rosebush. Typically, the most viable ones are those with five leaflets. So make it a practice to prune back to just above such a leaf.

Easy does it!

Generally speaking, vigorously growing roses can take more pruning, and recover and regenerate well. You might also think that heavy pruning would inspire weaker, slower-growing roses to make a fresh spurt of growth, but that actually doesn't work. Remember, "rose leaves are the engine room," and if you take off too much foliage in the course of pruning, a plant may lose vigor.

To fill in the center of the bush: If your pruning efforts have resulted in a rather thin, empty-looking plant and you now want to see some denser growth, here's what to do. Cut stems back to an "inside eye," that is, cut the stem just above a bud or eye that is pointing into the center of the bush.

To direct outward growth: Where you want a branch to be spreading, simply cut it back to an outside, or outward facing, bud.

The Kindest Cut

It's best not to prune at random or make blunt cuts since you may compromise the plant's health, not to mention its good looks.

Find a Bud Eye

Usually, thorns abound on a rose stem. These are not to be confused with bud eyes, which are tucked just above the branches and are quite small at the beginning of the season. And bud eyes are brown or reddish.

Cut Near a Bud Eye

Make the cut about $1/4$ inch from the bud eye—not too close, and not too far away. If you cut right on top of a bud eye or even accidentally slice into one, it may not grow or grow well. The too-close cut may cause the bud to dry out, it may not receive enough sap, or it may fail due to physical damage. (The bud eye could also be killed by a late frost, if you are pruning in early spring.) If you cut too far above a bud eye, when it begins to grow the result will look clunky and unattractive. The dead stub will rot and look bad, plus you risk giving rot a foothold and having it travel down the stem.

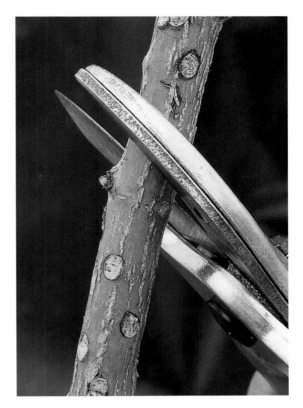

Cut rose stems at an angle.

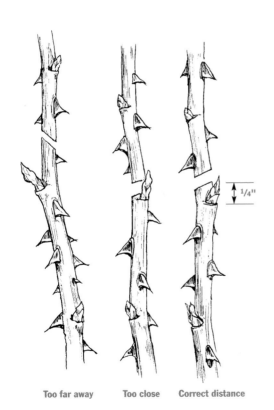

Too far away   Too close   Correct distance

Locate a cut at an appropriate distance from a bud eye, which is a quarter of an inch above it.

Cut on a Slant

This sort of cut is advised for many plants, not just roses. The theory is, water will run off a slanted cut, whereas a blunt cut is slower to dry out after a rain and rot or disease can enter the stem. A slanted cut also leaves a smaller stub, which is better for the plant's health and appearance.

Deadheading Demystified

Less-experienced gardeners and non-gardeners are often perplexed by the term "deadhead." It really only means cutting off dead or dying flowers. There are compelling reasons to deadhead your roses as often as you can:

- *It looks better:* Limp, dried out, old flowers are ugly and make the whole bush look bad, even when—or some feel, especially when—fresh new color-ful ones are appearing.

'Marmalade Skies'™

Long-blooming roses can be aided by deadheading.

- *It conserves energy:* The natural life cycle of a flowering plant is that the flower begins to fade as the seeds, or seedpods, develop. In the case of roses, it's the rose hips that are forming. Removing the flower before this happens, averts the exhausting, energy-depleting process of seed formation.

- *It encourages re-flowering:* When the hips, or seeds, are thwarted and removed, the plant returns its energies to flower production. So diligent deadheading leads to more flowers—and a longer blooming period for the bush overall.

- *There will be a better show next year:* The energy not spent on forming hips is also redirected into forming plentiful buds on the stems—the buds that will generate new stems, and new flowers, next season.

Deadheading your roses means removing spent flowers. This improves the appearance of the rosebush and encourages re-flowering.

'Pristine'™

Cutting flowers for arrangements has the same effect as deadheading—your rosebush will produce more blooms.

ROSE TIP

Picking bouquets is a win-win tactic!

Of course, you don't have to wait for flowers to flag before removing them from your rosebush. When you cut homegrown bouquets the benefits are the same. While you are proudly filling vases in the house or bestowing bouquets on your friends, the plant is promptly putting its energy into producing another round of blossoms.

Some rose varieties make beautiful hips in the late summer and fall, adding another season of interest.

In hybrid tea roses, disbudding by removing side buds will cause the main flower to be larger.

A BIG, BIG ROSE

Rose aficionados, who like to show off the fabulous roses in their garden or even enter them in competitions, use a pruning trick. Exhibition sized blooms can be generated by *disbudding*. Find a stem with a large flower bud, then remove all the other buds on side stems branching off that main stem. This way, all the energy resources are directed into that one bud. The resulting bloom is sensational—bigger than usual, sometimes even with richer color! Try this once or twice and see how your plant performs and how you like the result.

You can simply snap off spent rose blossoms at their bases. If the stems are a bit tough or you prefer clean cuts, clip them out with sharp pruners. You *will* need the clippers to remove entire flower clusters.

When deadheading, avoid leaving a stub. It's better to cut back to a leaf with a bud between it and the stem.

Be Tidy!

After a pruning session, clean up. Not only are thorny twigs scattered around the yard a nuisance, they make the garden look messy. And plant debris left lying around can create a breeding ground for pests and diseases. Cart the clippings off to the town dump's compost pile, or discard them some place far from the rosebush, where they can decay

'New Dawn'
Don't cut climbing roses too drastically or you will lose the framework of older stems.

Keep those hips?

There are times when a gardener wants to let nature take its course and leave the rose hips to develop. Some roses, notably some old-fashioned shrub roses, have gorgeous hips. (These are usually vigorous plants and the "energy drain" of hips production doesn't set them back.) Dangling on the bush through fall and winter, they bring welcome color to the garden. Also, rose hips are extremely high in vitamin C and some gardeners harvest them to make jelly or tea. Finally, bird-loving gardeners may leave hips in the hopes of attracting hungry migrating birds.

without being in the way. (They're a bit too woody, not to mention thorny, for inclusion in most home composters.)

Pruning Certain Types of Roses

In addition to the instructions above, which work well for most roses, here are some customized tips for pruning certain kinds of roses.

Climbers

These should not be cut drastically, or you will lose the framework formed over time by the older stems. Very old canes should be taken out at the base in early spring—this will stimulate young replacement canes. Flowering branches growing from the big, main canes can be shortened immediately after blooming. Prune off the top few inches of non-branching canes to inspire branching, and flowering, below the cuts.

'Betty Boop'™

Prune floribundas into a mound shape so you will have flowers covering the plant.

Don't overdo

Many hybrid teas have been bred to have long cutting stems that fit well in a vase. But too much cutting of these, in full bloom, leads to the need for summer pruning—and your plants can look unkempt. So harvest flowers judiciously!

Floribundas

These bushes must be pruned annually or they will become very twiggy, especially towards the interior. But prune conservatively, because old stems bear the first flowers of the season and you don't want to lose that show. Young stems will generate their flowers later in the season—you can shorten these stems by about a third early each spring. Aim for a mound shape, so you'll get flowers all over the plant.

Grandifloras

These are more like floribundas in habit and bloom than like hybrid teas. So follow the directions for floribundas. The main difference is that they can support a few more flowering stems (canes).

Groundcover Roses

These are bred to sprawl and pruning will only slow their establishment. Prune only to remove dead wood and any rogue stems that are too lanky or are trying to grow vertically. (To wade out into the bed to prune in early spring, wear heavy boots and thick trousers.)

Hybrid Teas

These should be pruned every year to keep them blooming well. Early spring is the best time. In addition to the general pruning described above, you should cut back all but five or so of the best stems, or canes. While you're at it, cut back older main stems to strong new shoots. When you finish, the canes that remain should be well spaced apart and the center of the plant rather open.

'Magic Blanket'

Prune groundcover roses only to remove dead wood and wayward stems.

'Baby Darling'

Lightly prune miniature roses to keep them in bounds.

Rosa banksiae 'Lutea', Lady Banks' Rose

For vintage and species roses that only bloom once a year, never prune early in the spring or you will remove the flower buds.

Miniature Roses

Because they are small to begin with, you don't want to prune too zealously. Cut out old stems after a few years, and shape the bushes lightly each spring, shortening strong growth to keep the plant in bounds.

Old Garden Roses

This term applies to a varied group but, for the most part, your pruning policy should be "less is more," that is, confine your cuts to cosmetic trimming and shaping. For those vintage varieties and species roses that bloom once a year, usually in June, you must never prune them in early spring or you will be removing the upcoming show. You can do some grooming right after they finish blooming, however, if you wish. And dead, wayward, and older canes should always be taken out—this you can do in late winter or early spring as the plants begin to emerge from dormancy. "Ramblers" tend to produce lots of stems and you can thin the plants back to four to eight canes.

Shrub Roses

This group includes everything from informal "landscape roses" to the modern English roses. While it's hard to generalize, most of these will respond very well to an annual clean up. Vigorous shoots originating near the ground can be cut back by a third. Branches coming off these can be shortened to about a foot long. And keep pruning away the twiggy

'Midas Touch'™

Prune hybrid tea roses every year in early spring to ensure plentiful blooms.

Over time some shrub roses, such as *Rosa rugosa*, can become a dense thicket of stems. This can be controlled with an annual thinning.

growth, or you will have an unmanageable thicket in a few years.

Tree Roses

Aim for a balanced, rounded shape, with the flowers displayed at eye level. Watch for suckers along the stem and clip them off immediately.

Pruning Tools

You may already have some of these in your arsenal. Just remember to keep everything nice and sharp; dull cutters mash rose stems, causing unwanted damage.

The tools most often used to cut and prune roses are:

- *Clippers/Pruners:* These are indispensable, useful for everything from pruning out twigs to cutting bouquets. They should also be able to handle most canes.

  Scissors-type: These feature a sharp blade moving past an edged blade.

  Anvil-style: A sharp blade hits squarely against a flat surface for a "snap cut."

- *Loppers:* Use these when taking out thick canes, especially at ground level, so that you can get the leverage you need to make a good, clean cut.

·ROSE TIP·

Shearing hedge roses

Use hedge clippers to take off a third to a half of the growth. As you work, if possible, strive for an attractive "dome" shape for each individual plant.

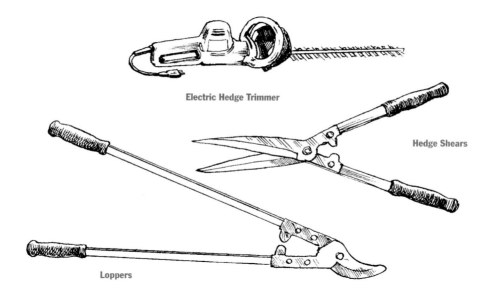

Electric Hedge Trimmer

Hedge Shears

Loppers

■ *Hedge Trimmers/Clippers:* Roses with more twiggy growth can be cut along the tops and sides with these. So they're good for shaping, especially early in the season when growth is new and pliable.

Manual: These are fine for "spot" pruning or if you want to shape only a few bushes.

Electric: These allow you to shear an entire hedge more easily and neatly.

And don't forget a good pair of *gloves,* to protect you from those thorns! Some rose growers keep two pairs on hand—the regular ones and a pair that goes all the way up the arm for wrestling with climbers and really thorny bushes.

Training Roses

Well-shaped roses can be achieved not only through pruning but also with a few simple training techniques. Climbing roses don't naturally climb on their own and need to be secured to a structure. Use ties that will hold the canes securely but are flexible enough not to damage or constrict the stems as they grow

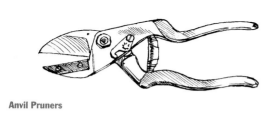

Anvil Pruners

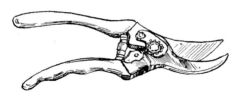

Scissors-type or Bypass Pruners

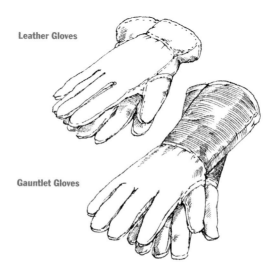

Leather Gloves

Gauntlet Gloves

Canes of this hybrid perpetual rose 'John Hopper' have been pegged and tied horizontally to stakes to increase flower production.

and increase in diameter. Canes growing horizontally produce more buds, so for the most abundant floral display, train climber canes to horizontal supports. Allow canes to harden a bit before tying them; they should still be flexible but not so tender that they will break as they are bent over.

A pillar rose can be created on a sturdy post using a climbing rose, typically a type with somewhat shorter canes that will reach its maximum height at the top of the post. If a larger climber is used, the canes that overtop the post can be secured to a nearby arbor or fence, pruned back, or splayed our like the ribs of an umbrella and allowed to cascade down. Wrap the canes around the post as they grow, or braid canes, and secure them to the structure. Here, too, use flexible ties so as not to damage the stems.

An old method of training some types of roses, including hybrid perpetuals and bourbons, is called "pegging" or "pegging down." Again, to take advantage of increased bloom production on horizontal stems, pegging canes means bending them over to the ground and attaching the ends to a stake or peg to secure them in an arched position.

Short of pegging canes completely to the ground, these roses can also be tied horizontally to plant stakes.

Since a climbing rose cannot attach itself to a wall, provide something to tie the canes to, such as wires or a trellis.

Seasonal Care Checklists

Spring

- Remove winter mulch. It's best to do this gradually, scraping away a little bit each day over a week or two.
- Plant bareroot roses.
- Prune roses. This is the time to do the annual substantial cutting and shaping.
- Apply the first fertilizer dose.
- If you wish, take softwood cuttings and pot them.

Establishing a regular maintenance program will foster healthy, beautiful roses.

Summer

- Plant potted roses.
- Deadhead diligently (remove spent flowers); keep the plants well groomed.
- Water at least once a week with a good soaking; more often if the weather is dry.
- Maintain or replenish mulch around the base of the plants to help retain soil moisture and inhibit weed growth.
- Fertilize every six weeks or so.

- Spray with pesticides or disease treatments where necessary.
- Release beneficial insect predators where necessary.
- Manage the growth of climbing roses by tying lengthening canes to their supports at frequent intervals.
- Pick bouquets!

Fall

- Stop fertilizing, about six weeks before your first expected frost, so the plant can gradually go dormant.
- Clean up all debris on the ground.
- Do NOT prune.
- Before the ground freezes but after a frost, give the rose one last good deep soaking drink, so it goes into winter well-hydrated.
- If you wish, spray with an antidessicant to seal in moisture and minimize damage from freeze-thaw cycles to come.

ROSE TIP

Wash it away

Rather than using a trowel, shovel, or your hands to remove a protective winter mulch, try washing it away with the hose— gradually.

If you live in a region of cold winter temperatures, give your roses winter protection by adding extra mulch.

Mound soil, compost, or mulch over the bases of your rosebushes to protect the crowns in areas where winters are frigid.

Winter

- Let a rose plant "harden off" (become accustomed to cold weather) by exposing it to about two weeks of below-freezing temperatures.
- Then, put a protective mulch or covering in place. If it's a grafted plant, make sure to bury the graft union.
- Spray dormant oils and fungicides where necessary.

Preparing for Winter

Most roses will tolerate moderately cold winters. But when your average wintertime temperatures regularly drop below 15 degrees Fahrenheit for example, you'd be wise to give your rose plants some extra protection.

Mounding

Simply push up soil, compost, or mulch, or a combination of the three, right over the base of the plant. Don't raid the surrounding area for this material or you'll risk exposing vulnerable plant roots. Bring the material from elsewhere (compost heap, bagged mulch, pile of extra soil, etc.). Depending on the severity of your climate, this layer can be a few inches deep to a foot thick.

ALWAYS, ANYTIME CHORES

- Clip off any suckers that are generated low on the plant, below the graft union.
- Pull weeds that encroach on the rose plants.
- Remove fallen leaves and destroy diseased clippings, to prevent pests or diseases from gaining a foothold.
- Cut out dead or diseased wood whenever you see it.
- When spraying anything, never spray on a windy day. Always follow label instructions to the letter. Wear gloves and other protective clothing.

Wrap tree roses for winter protection.

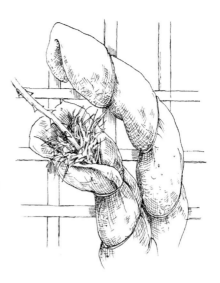

To protect your climbing roses during the winter, wrap the canes on their supports.

Wrapping

In severe climates, gardeners can protect their roses by placing a wire cage or cylinder, snow fencing, or burlap or tarpaper casing, around the outside of the plant, and stuff it with straw or leaves.

Cones

You can buy a protective plastic or Styrofoam cap and set it over a rose; ideally, it should be stuffed with organic matter, too, but getting enough under the cover can be tricky.

Special Cases

Tree roses: Wrap the plants, pots and all, in insulating material and stuff the interior with straw or leaves. If they are growing in the ground, dig them up and store them in a cool, but not freezing, place so they remain dormant. (An unheated basement or garage is ideal.)

Climbers: If possible, wrap the canes on their supports. Or untie them, lay the stems on the ground, and apply a blanket of soil or mulch. You might have to at least partially dig up the roots to allow the stems to truly lay flat; if this becomes necessary, be sure to cover over the unearthed roots so they are shielded from winter weather.

Troubleshooting Pests and Diseases

Novices hesitate at the thought of constantly spraying rosebushes with chemicals, even to the point of forgoing growing roses altogether. Meanwhile rose aficionados may have sophisticated, season-long "spraying programs." For most of us, however, the reality of rose growing lies somewhere in between. A pragmatic approach will allow you to enjoy your roses without undue fussing.

It's true that roses are not always trouble-free, but many garden plants are vulnerable to various pests and diseases, and they are

'Hansa'

The first step toward having healthy roses is to choose your varieties carefully.

still popular. And still worth growing. The sheer pleasure that a beautifully grown rose brings can banish your misgivings or complaints. The key here is not to enter into the relationship blindly.

Prevention: Ways to Stay Out of Trouble

There are many things you can do, right from the start, to minimize or even eliminate pest and disease trouble with your roses. The less stress a rose has to endure, the more resilient it will be, and the less vulnerable it will be.

- *Choose a tough rose:* Do your homework; a rose that shines in one region may struggle in another. Seek advice from a good local nursery or from gardeners in your area who have gorgeous roses thriving in their yards.

- *Minimize stress:* Plant your rose in full sun, in good soil. Give it elbowroom so it has space to grow and good air circulation. Water faithfully (don't let the plant suffer drought and then get drenched—instead, keep the water applications steady and consistent).

To avoid rose-growing pitfalls, plant your rose in full sun with plenty of room, keep weeds under control, and include a variety of other plants in the garden.

- *Be neat:* Pull out encroaching weeds. Never let leaf litter accumulate at a rosebush's feet. When you clip out dead, damaged, or diseased stems, don't leave the debris lying around—get rid of it. (Don't even compost it. Throw it out!) The reason? If you don't, disease can spread. Also, such debris can shelter pests and allow them a breeding ground.

- *Encourage beneficial insects:* Take advantage of nature's own system of checks and balances by allowing insects that prey on rose pests to live in your garden (ladybugs and lacewings, primarily).

- *Try companion planting:* Some gardeners feel that certain plants keep rose pests and diseases at bay. Garlic, in particular, is touted as a deterrent for aphids and even Japanese beetles. The concept of diversity is certainly valid: If there is a variety of plants in a certain area, the pests will have a harder time finding what they want.

Plant resistant roses

If you know you live in an area where a certain problem is prevalent—for example, your summers are quite hot and humid and you've seen roses afflicted with black spot—seek out a variety that is specifically touted as resistant to that problem.

Japanese Beetles

Rose Borer Damage

COMMON ROSE PESTS

Symptom: *Young leaves are curled up or distorted; sooty mold on leaves.*
Possible diagnosis: Aphids—tiny, pear-shaped, sucking insects.
Remarks: These insects love new growth! They excrete honeydew, a sticky, sweet substance that can turn black as sooty mold grows on it. Ants may dine on the honeydew but not otherwise harm the plant.
Recommended less-toxic treatments: Knock the aphids off with a blast from the hose. Treat with neem or pyrethrum. Spray with insecticidal soap.
Recommended chemical controls: Spray with malathion.

Symptom: *Nibbled leaves and flowers.*
Possible diagnosis: Japanese beetles—half-inch long, metallic copper-and-green bugs.
Remarks: They travel in groups—if you see one, there are more.
Recommended less-toxic treatments: Pick off and kill individual beetles—evening is best, and you can drop them in a bucket of soapy water (don't squash them since that releases pheromones that attract other Japanese beetles). Go after their larvae by treating your lawn (where they live before they change to beetles and attack your roses) with milky spore or parasitic nematodes. Use rotenone. Use pyrethrum.
Recommended chemical controls: Use carbaryl (Sevin).

Symptom: *Wilting, dying canes.*
Possible diagnosis: Borers—tiny, worm-like larvae.
Remarks: Entry holes are usually visible, often lower down on the canes. These insects like young canes or recently cut ones.
Recommended less-toxic treatments: Immediately cut out and destroy affected canes.
Recommended chemical controls: None.

Symptom: *Stunted growth.*
Possible diagnosis: Nematodes in the soil—microscopic worms.
Remarks: Check the roots for telltale galls.
Recommended less-toxic treatments: Pull out and destroy infected plants and do not replant in that area for a few seasons. Apply chitin (ground crab shells) or a chitin-containing product to the soil.
Recommended chemical controls: None.

Symptom: *Tiny, shell-like bumps "glued" to the stems.*
Possible diagnosis: Scale insects—tiny bugs that create a protective scaly or crusty shell over themselves.
Remarks: These insects suck plant juices from the stems, sometimes also the leaves.
Recommended less-toxic treatments: Spray with horticultural oil when the pest is in its crawling stage. Try releasing parasitic wasps in the rose garden.
Recommended chemical controls: Spray with malathion or carbaryl (Sevin).

Symptom: *Leaves are mottled yellow, especially during hot, dry spells; over time, you can see a silver stippling or sheen.*
Possible diagnosis: Spider mites—tiny spider relatives, specks the size of pepper grains, in green, red, or yellow.
Remarks: The pests themselves are almost too tiny to see, but you can observe their webs on an infected plant, particularly on the undersides of the leaves. They thrive during hot, dry summers on dusty plants.
Recommended less-toxic treatments: Hit the bush with blasts of hose water, aiming especially for leaf undersides. Spray with insecticidal soap, sulfur, or horticultural oil. Try releasing predatory mites in the rose garden.
Recommended chemical controls: Spray with a miticide such as Avid or Ortho Isotox Formula IV.

Symptom: *Misshapen leaves, deformed buds, flowers discolored and with brown spots.*
Possible diagnosis: Thrips—tiny yellow or brown insects.
Remarks: Most common in early summer. Most common on light-colored roses.
Recommended less-toxic treatments: Spray with insecticidal soap. Spray with neem, rotenone, or pyrethrum.
Recommended chemical controls: None.

Symptom: *No flowers. Buds shrivel and turn black.*
Possible diagnosis: Rose midges—tiny insects.
Remarks: These insects are barely visible.
Recommended less-toxic treatments: Spray with insecticidal soap.
Recommended chemical controls: Combat the soil-borne larvae with an organo-phosphate insecticide such as Permethrin.

Botrytis blight, a type of fungus, attacks rose flowers.

ROSE TIP

"Broad-spectrum" insecticides

These products typically kill more than just the target pest. Also, once applied, they tend to break down and become less effective—which means you may have to spray again. Better to spray with a product that targets exactly the pest you are battling.

COMMON ROSE DISEASES

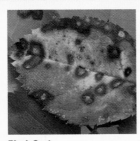

Black Spot

Symptom: *Small black spots on the leaves, with fringed edges.*
Possible diagnosis:
Black spot.
Remarks: Common in hot, humid weather.
Recommended less-toxic treatments: Promptly remove and destroy affected leaves. Prune the bush to improve air circulation. Deliver water to the soil; do not let it splash on the leaves. Water in the morning so the plant can dry out over the course of the day. Spray with summer oil. Spray with a dormant spray that includes lime sulfur

(only in late fall or early spring). Spray with neem.
Recommended chemical controls: Spray with chlorothanonil (Daconil).

Symptom: *White powdery residue on the leaves, sometimes also on flower petals; leaves and flowers become crinkled and distorted.*
Possible diagnosis:
Powdery mildew—a fungus.
Remarks: Thrives in dry conditions.
Recommended less-toxic treatments: Spray with summer oil or baking soda solution. Spray the foliage with an antidessicant (antitranspirant) product, which makes a thin, waxy layer over the leaves that shields them from this disease.
Recommended chemical controls: Spray with a fungicide. Sulfur-based ones are the most effective.

Symptom: *Yellow-edged purple blotches on leaf surfaces; grayish fuzz on the undersides.*
Possible diagnosis:
Downy mildew—a fungus.
Remarks: Often seen in cool, damp weather.
Recommended less-toxic treatments: Prune the bush to improve air circulation. Deliver water to the soil; do not let it splash on the leaves. Water in the morning. Spray with a dormant oil.
Recommended chemical controls: Spray with a sulfur- or copper-based fungicide.

Symptom: *Undersides of leaves develop rusty spots; yellow spots appear on the tops.*
Possible diagnosis:
Rust—a fungus.
Remarks: Often seen in dry areas. Thrives when there are warm days coupled with cool nights.

Recommended less-toxic treatments: Remove and destroy affected leaves. Deliver water to the soil; do not let it splash on the leaves. Spray with a dormant oil.
Recommended chemical controls: Spray with a lime-sulfur fungicide or rusticide.

Symptom: *Deformed new growth, yellow mottling on leaves.*
Possible diagnosis:
Rose mosaic virus.
Remarks: Can't spread by plant-to-plant contact (but will be spread via pruners used on diseased roses).
Recommended less-toxic treatments: Remove and destroy affected leaves. Severely affected plants should be destroyed and you should contact the nursery where you bought the rose and get a replacement.
Recommended chemical controls: None.

A rose planted in the right location will thrive.

ROSE TIP

Act fast!

If you suspect, or spot, a problem with a rose plant, don't procrastinate, or a small problem can become a crisis. Not only might you lose that plant, but the problem could spread to other roses in your garden (or your neighbor's). Severely afflicted plants should be dug up and destroyed. But try not to let it come to that. Be observant of your roses and proactive.

Know Thine Enemy

When you think you spot a problem with a rose plant, don't jump to conclusions. Observe closely. Take an afflicted leaflet, stem, bud, or blossom, or a live insect if you can capture one, to someone who can help you identify it—an accomplished rose gardener in your area, a knowledgeable garden-center staffer, your local Extension service, or a reputable landscaper.

TROUBLE SPOTS

You are asking for rose troubles when you:

- **Plant a rose in too much shade:** The recommended requirement of "full sun" means *lots* of sun—six to eight hours a day. Insufficient sunlight weakens a plant and invites disease. In addition, moisture from rain or irrigation will be slow to dry in the shade.

- **Crowd your roses:** Roses struggle when they are jammed too close together, with other roses, other shrubs, or other garden plants. They have to compete for the precious resources of soil nutrients and water, and they may suffer from poor air circulation.

- **Neglect garden sanitation:** Leaving afflicted or damaged leaves, buds, or blossoms on a bush only accelerates problems. Worse still is to let this debris accumulate under rose plants, where diseases can survive and pests can breed. So groom your plants and rake out debris from their bases—as often as needed.

Once you know what you're dealing with, you can take action. If some sort of treatment or spray is recommended, you can buy the right product. Then, *read the label* and follow the directions on dosage and application to the letter. Just as with any chemical, more is *not* better! Timing is also important—you don't want to spray for a certain pest at the wrong time in its life cycle, or the treatment will be totally ineffective. This information is also on the label.

To Spray or Not to Spray

You may be a reluctant sprayer. Perhaps, as a matter of personal policy, you want to protect yourself and your family and pets from chemicals. Perhaps you want to shield your garden and any beneficial insects that are present, and don't think roses should get special coddling.

Whatever the reason—and these objections may all be valid—realize that spraying can be a last resort. If you've chosen your rose varieties wisely, planted them correctly, and worked to keep your roses healthy, you may never have to apply any chemical controls. If you monitor the condition of your roses and catch a problem early, you may never have to do any spraying.

But if you find yourself confronted with a pest or disease that is ruining a beloved rose, or if one rose in your garden develops a problem and you don't want it to spread, you may decide to spray in a bid to save it.

Here are some guidelines as you ponder the option of spraying:

- Ask yourself: Is it too far gone? A pest-ridden rose or one whose foliage is full

of signs of disease may not even be salvageable. Consider whether you should just dig it up and discard it (especially if other, nearby roses could also be attacked).

- Make absolutely certain you have the correct diagnosis.
- Weigh other options (less-toxic approaches are listed on pages 132 to 133).
- Purchase the right product for treatment.

What to Spray

In the world of gardening, there are organic "botanical" controls and chemical ones. It's generally best to start with the less-intense choices because they are short-lived (though you might have to repeat applications because they are not as potent as their chemical counterparts). Please note that many rose treatments are concentrated and will need to be diluted with water before use. Always read the label, mix carefully, and wear protective clothing, including gloves, if recommended.

Here are the treatments most often suggested for controlling common rose problems:

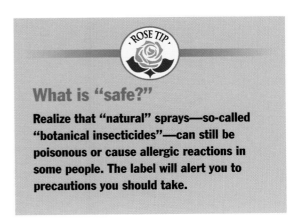

What is "safe?"

Realize that "natural" sprays—so-called "botanical insecticides"—can still be poisonous or cause allergic reactions in some people. The label will alert you to precautions you should take.

Neem Oil

This is derived from a tropical Asian tree and, although it works slowly, it has been proven effective against aphids, thrips, and even Japanese beetles. Unfortunately it also kills ladybugs, so spray when they are not present on the rosebush.

TIP: Interestingly—luckily—neem oil is also an effective treatment against some rose diseases as well: powdery mildew, rust, and black spot.

Pyrethroid Chemicals

These insecticides are variants of pyrethrum, derived from a relative of the common chrysanthemum. They kill landscape pests (except mites) quickly and are not harmful to people or animals; indeed, they are considered safer for humans and animals than organo-phosphates. However, they can kill bees, so spray when bees are not as active, in the evening hours. Among the variations are: pyrethrin, permethrin, cylfulthrin, deltamethrin, and bifenthrin (brand names include Bayer

WHAT IS ROSE VIRUS?

Rose virus is a chronic problem that has plagued commercial rose growers, the people who have production fields full of roses they plan to send to market. Apparently the virus can enter a plant, traveling through its sap, via either the rootstock or the "top plant" (also called the "budded plant" or "scion"). Thus it infects the plant grafted onto it—in other words, the entire plant ends up being afflicted. The disease shortens a rose plant's life span; the plant may do well for a season or two, but eventually it declines and may not survive a cold winter. Other signs of infection include a reduced number of buds and therefore flowers (as much as 20% less), and yellow streaking on the leaves, which may not be obvious to the untrained eye, or may be so pronounced as to be visible from a distance.

The problem appears when a perfectly healthy budwood is grafted onto infected rootstock, or vice-versa.

Concerned growers are combating rose virus in two ways. They are making every effort to graft budwood onto healthy root-stock. And some are going around the problem completely by raising certified virus-free own-root roses, which are healthy from top to bottom.

Two final notes: Rose virus does not appear to be a problem with roses originating in Europe; it has been mainly a problem in North American growing fields. And although it has been observed on various roses, rose virus has been distressingly recurrent on old-garden rose varieties.

'Buff Beauty'

By carefully monitoring your roses you can attend to problems early and avoid using chemical sprays. If a favorite rose does need to be sprayed, however, use caution in choosing a chemical control and always follow label directions.

products, Bonide products, Green Light Conquest, Ortho products, and Spectracide products—read the labels carefully).

Horticultural Oils

These smother insects and their eggs; they're fairly nontoxic and short-lived. Dormant oils are used when roses are dormant (wintertime, early spring) and are frequently combined with fungicides to help kill overwintering disease spores. Summer oils are used during the summer when roses are actively growing.

Insecticidal Soaps

You can buy these, or make your own (simply put one part dish soap and ten parts water into a spray bottle). They work quickly and break down quickly and are harmless to humans and pets. They kill aphids, spider mites, and sometimes have an effect on Japanese beetles. These soaps have to be sprayed directly on the pests to be effective.

Baking Soda

This is an effective homemade remedy for powdery mildew and sometimes diminishes black spot as well. Mix one tablespoon of household baking soda and one tablespoon of summer oil or vegetable oil into one gallon of water. Spray weekly.

Wear recommended protective clothing, gloves, and goggles, when spraying roses with chemicals. You might also choose to wear a respirator.

Fungicides

These chemicals kill fungi or prevent them from attacking healthy tissues. They include: chlorothalonil, mancozeb, thiophanate-methyl, and mycobutanil. If you find you need to use these products often, it's sometimes wise to rotate the products so the fungus doesn't build up a resistance, or to discover which ones work best on your particular roses in your particular area.

Spraying Protocol

Once you've decided to spray and you have the right product in hand, here's how to proceed:

- Spray at the right time in the pest's life cycle, or in the disease's life cycle.

- Spray on a day that is dry (so it doesn't wash off) and windless (to avoid wasteful "drift"). Do not spray when the temperature climbs above 85 degrees F.

- Spray in the morning so the plant has all day to absorb the treatment.

- Protect yourself. Wear gloves. Wear a long-sleeved shirt and long pants and sturdy boots. Wear a hat and goggles. Launder the clothing immediately afterwards.

- Protect adjacent plants. Prop up newspaper tents over them or use old sheets, and throw out these coverings after you finish.

- Water the plant first. A drought-stressed plant responds poorly to spray treatments.

- Be thorough. Take your time and spray the entire plant, including the undersides of leaves.

Safe Storage

Keep the container as well as the sprayer in a cool, dry place well out of reach of children and pets (even under lock and key). Many organic and chemical spray products come in concentrated form and must be diluted before they can be used. Label any such bucket, jar, or sprayer bottle with the name of the product so it isn't accidentally put to some other use.

Preventative Spraying

Some rose gardeners like to make pre-emptive strikes. They anticipate certain pests or diseases, or they have knowingly chosen to grow a beautiful rose that is likely to develop a problem. This is especially true of rose gardeners in areas where various fungi thrive. So they spray every week to ten days throughout the

Use simpler sprayers

If a sprayer has complicated assembly instructions, you might want to pass it by. Clean-up could be bothersome and you might not have the patience for it after spending time bent over your roses in the garden.

summer to keep their roses healthy and looking great.

Such a program may be warranted if you are a perfectionist or are growing your roses for show or for a midsummer garden wedding. But if it's not necessary, spare yourself the effort and expense.

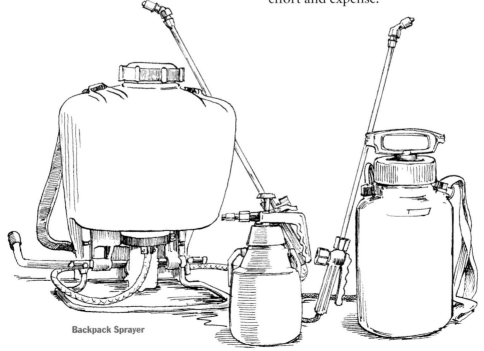

Backpack Sprayer

Hand-held Sprayer

Shoulder-strap Sprayer

Ladybug adults and larvae can consume hundreds of aphids.

Spraying Equipment

Rose growers who choose to spray have many options, and the good news is that sprayers have come a long way in recent years in terms of convenience, efficiency, and safety. These days, the tanks where the treatment material and water are mixed are made of special lightweight plastics. So they're corrosion-free but still able to withstand high pressures. And the tanks are made of a substance that blocks ultraviolet light, so they last much longer; even the valve seals are tougher, so corrosion and leakage are no longer a concern.

Here are some of the available products that might be appropriate for rose care:

Hand-held Sprayers

These are the smallest, most manageable, and probably the most practical for the majority of rose-spraying projects. They're usually 1 quart (or 1 liter) and thus are easy to carry around. Pressure is provided by a simple hand pump.

Shoulder-Strap Sprayers

The reason these come with a strap is that they are heavier, with generally a capacity of 2 or 3 gallons, allowing you to get more done in one trip to the garden. Check that the strap has comfortable padding.

Backpack Sprayers

These hold up to 4 gallons. The hand-operated pump makes it possible to handle higher pressures. The placement of the pump and the amount of padding should be assessed—try it on and make sure the sprayer is comfortable for you. This is only worth investing in if you have a large garden.

Beneficial Insects Are Your Roses' Friends

Certain insects are good to have around when you are growing roses. They prey on rose pests, saving you the effort of other control measures. If they don't occur naturally in your garden, you have the option of buying them—often in egg form—at a local garden center, or ordering them through the mail. You can release these beneficial insects into your yard to see if they help, especially if you can time their release to coincide with the appearance of certain pests.

If that's an option you want to consider, scan gardening magazine ads for mail-order suppliers and follow the supplier's advice explicitly. (For example, it's often suggested that you release beneficial insects at sundown— that way, at least you know they'll stick around for one night! Other beneficial insects need to be released in warm weather or they won't be mobile.)

Ladybugs

Both the adult and larval stages of ladybugs eat aphids (learn to recognize ladybug larvae, which look nothing like ladybugs). They also like to dine on thrips.

Trichogramma Wasps

These are not the stinging wasps that build nests by your attic window, but rather are tiny little wasps that never attack people. They feed on butterfly and moth eggs, which reduces the

The complete picture

The healthiest garden is one with a balanced system—plants, animals, insects, and microorganisms. Keep in mind that not all "bugs," or even all fungi, are bad (black spot is detrimental but mycorrhizal fungi in the soil benefit plants). Be conscious of all the garden's inhabitants when you are amending your soil, adding fertilizer, or using a chemical control. To attract beneficial insects to combat the damaging ones, and enjoyable insects like butterflies, provide a variety of plants for shelter and food (butterfly caterpillars favor certain plants). Diversity can keep problems to a minimum.

Some plants provide natural insect control. The tansy in the lower left, with its bright green, ferny leaves, was used in the eighteenth century as an insect repellant, and its presence in the garden can inhibit such insect pests as green peach aphids, squash bugs, and potato beetles. It makes a good rose companion since it also repels Japanese beetles. Other plants that help keep pests off your roses are feverfew, garlic, pennyroyal, and rue.

nibbling caterpillar population, though it also affects the adult butterfly and moth populations as well.

Predatory Mites

These like to eat spider mites. They may also go after thrips.

Green Lacewings

The larvae, not the adults, are the big eaters. They dine mostly on aphids but also thrips, mites, and eggs of various other insects.

Parasitic Nematodes

If Japanese beetles are a problem for your rose garden, these tiny worms are a weapon to use early in the season, when the beetles are in the grub phase of their life cycle and living in your lawn or garden soil.

ROSE DIRECTORY

O f the many, many beautiful roses you can choose to grow, the following ones are considered among the very best for the home garden. Some have won awards, others are old favorites that are tried-and-true, and still others are state-of-the-art newcomers that have debuted to high praise. To qualify for this list, a rose must have demonstrated these valuable qualities:

- **Resilience**—The vagaries of any given season's weather, not to mention your yard's particular soil and microclimate conditions, can put garden plants under some stress. A rose that can tolerate a variety of challenges, and still look good and produce gorgeous blooms, is a worthwhile rose indeed.

- **Availability**—These are not rare roses. Find them at your local garden center, or buy them through a mail-order or an internet catalog.

- **Proven performer**—Other rose-lovers have grown these roses and found them to be tough, adaptable, and dependable. Experts have rated them highly and/or they have won awards.

'Bella'roma'

MATURE PLANT HEIGHT: 4½ ft.
BLOOM SIZE: 4 in. to 4½ in.
BLOOM TIME: all season
FRAGRANCE: strong rose perfume
YEAR INTRODUCED: 2003
AWARDS WON: Jackson & Perkins Rose of the Year®, 2003

At last, a worthy substitute for the ever-popular 'Peace' rose. This relative newcomer has the same sumptuous color blend of golden yellow petals blushed with pink, but the coloration is richer and slower to fade. 'Bella'roma' also wafts a glorious, strong perfume. Disease-resistant foliage is yet another significant improvement over 'Peace'. A strong, attractive plant, it blooms profusely all summer and is sure to impress all who see—and smell—it.

SUBSTITUTIONS/SIMILAR ROSES:
'Double Delight'™
'Fragrant Keepsake'
'Fragrant Perfume'
'Peace'
'Success Story'™

'Dainty Bess'

MATURE PLANT HEIGHT: 4 ft. to 4½ ft.
BLOOM SIZE: 3½ in. to 4 in.
BLOOM TIME: all season
FRAGRANCE: moderate, sweet scent
YEAR INTRODUCED: 1925
AWARDS WON: Royal National Rose Society Gold Medal, 1925

One of the oldest hybrid teas still around, 'Dainty Bess' appeared in 1925 and has proven herself ever since. The sweetly scented flowers, while large, are quite unusual for a hybrid tea because they are single. This allows the shell-pink petals to show off the center spray of raspberry-red stamens. These beauties are carried in airy clusters and, despite their delicate appearance, hold up very well.

The bush itself is upright and sturdy, clothed in plentiful thorns and handsome, disease-resistant foliage. It's also fairly cold hardy. All of these qualities recommend 'Dainty Bess' for an informal, cottage-garden setting in need of a charming but tough pastel rose.

SUBSTITUTIONS/SIMILAR ROSES:
Also available as a climber.
'Betty Prior' (floribunda, dark pink)
'Frau Dagmar Hastrup' (rugosa shrub)
'Golden Wings' (shrub)
'Kathleen' (hybrid musk)
'Mrs. Oakley Fisher'

'Double Delight'™
MATURE PLANT HEIGHT: 3½ ft. to 4 ft.
BLOOM SIZE: 5½ in.
BLOOM TIME: all season
FRAGRANCE: spicy, strong
YEAR INTRODUCED: 1977
AWARDS WON: AARS, 1977; Gamble Fragrance Award, 1986

This splendid rose has enjoyed great popularity from the moment it appeared on the scene, thanks to its unusually colored and richly scented flowers. Classically formed, urn-shaped ruby-red buds swirl open to a cream-washed pink; when fully open, the flowers become buttery yellow and strawberry red. There is one bloom to each long (12 to 18 inches) cutting stem, making 'Double Delight' an irresistible bouquet rose.

In the garden, it forms a medium-sized, irregularly bushy plant and wafts that intense fragrance for up to 10 feet in all directions. Unfortunately, it's susceptible to mildew in cool, damp climates, but a great performer elsewhere.

SUBSTITUTIONS/SIMILAR ROSES:
Also available as a tree rose.
'Bella'roma'
'Fragrant Keepsake'
'Fragrant Perfume'
'Peace'
'Success Story'™

'First Prize'
MATURE PLANT HEIGHT: 3 ft. to 5 ft.
BLOOM SIZE: 5 in. to 5½ in.
BLOOM TIME: all season
FRAGRANCE: moderate, old-rose perfume
YEAR INTRODUCED: 1970
AWARDS WON: AARS, 1970; American Rose Society Gertrude
   M. Hubbard Gold Medal, 1971

The darling of rose exhibitors, those aficionados who grow rose blossoms for show, 'First Prize' deserves their adulation. Its big, classic blossoms are perfectly formed and balanced, and the swirled, shimmering hues of pure pink always enchant. The spectacular flowers hold up longer than most pink roses in the garden as well as in the vase. Long, strong, straight cutting stems are also an asset. This was the last hybrid tea bred by the late great Jackson & Perkins hybridizer Gene Boerner, and many consider it to be his very best.

The plant itself, while attractive, is vulnerable to disease and not very cold hardy. But if large, peerless bouquet flowers are your wish and your climate is not harsh, this is the pink rose for you.

SUBSTITUTIONS/SIMILAR ROSES:
'Barbra Streisand'
'Gerda Hnatyshyn'
'Pearl Essence'™

'Fragrant Cloud'

MATURE PLANT HEIGHT: 4 ft. to 5 ft.
BLOOM SIZE: 5 in.
BLOOM TIME: all season
FRAGRANCE: powerful tea rose
YEAR INTRODUCED: 1967
AWARDS WON: Royal National Rose Society Gold Medal, 1963; Portland Gold Medal, 1967; Gamble Fragrance Award, 1964

Big, gorgeous, coral-red blooms unlike any other rose! They are produced nonstop all summer long, and their color is even deeper in cooler weather. The plant is medium-sized, vigorous, and fits well in a border with other hot-colored flowers.

The heady, award-winning fragrance has been giddily described as a rich blend of cloves and orange blossoms—not an exaggeration! This is a superb rose to grow for bouquets.

SUBSTITUTIONS/SIMILAR ROSES:
'Artistry'™
'Spice Twice'™
'Tropicana'
'Wildfire'

'Gemini'™

MATURE PLANT HEIGHT: 5½ ft.
BLOOM SIZE: 4½ in.
BLOOM TIME: all season
FRAGRANCE: mild berry
YEAR INTRODUCED: 2000
AWARDS WON: AARS, 2000

An elegant flower and a tough, vigorous plant. The blooms, carried high on long cutting stems, are bicolored—cream, bordered in rich coral pink. They're at their best in areas with moderate to hot summer temperatures. Sunshine intensifies the fabulous coloration.

'Gemini' grows larger than some hybrid teas, and thus is ideal for the back of a flower border or as a "focal point" plant.

SUBSTITUTIONS/SIMILAR ROSES:
Also available as a tree rose.
'Barbara Bush'
'Brigadoon'
'Diana, Princess of Wales'™
'Love & Peace'™

'Honor'™

MATURE PLANT HEIGHT: 5 ft. to 5½ ft.
BLOOM SIZE: 4 in. to 5 in.
BLOOM TIME: all season
FRAGRANCE: slight
YEAR INTRODUCED: 1980
AWARDS WON: AARS, 1980

There are other white hybrid teas, but this gorgeous award-winner stands out. The flowers are an exceptionally pure, sugared white; toward the center, they gain a soft peach hue. The buds on this prolific bloomer are big and stately, and unfurl to large, double blossoms that flatten out to a saucer shape without losing their grace. And the cutting stems are nice and long. Best of all, while white roses aren't usually scented, 'Honor' radiates a sweet, delicate scent that suits the plant's cool, soothing personality.

The dark glossy-green foliage is nicely in scale with the big, beautiful flowers and the plant's habit is upright and vigorous. With these many sterling qualities, it's no wonder 'Honor' continues to be popular. If you have a white house or fence, this rose is a must.

SUBSTITUTIONS/SIMILAR ROSES:
'John F. Kennedy'
'Sheer Bliss'
'Whisper'

'Just Joey'

MATURE PLANT HEIGHT: 3 ft. to 3½ ft.
BLOOM SIZE: 4 in. to 5 in.
BLOOM TIME: all season
FRAGRANCE: intense fruity scent
YEAR INTRODUCED: 1972
**AWARDS WON: Royal National Rose Society's James Mason
Gold Medal, 1986**

Long considered to be among the loveliest of all apricot-hued roses, 'Just Joey' has certainly stood the test of time. The spicily scented blossoms are especially ruffled. Dark green, mahogany-tinted, disease-resistant foliage makes an elegant contrast. Also, the plant is not especially large or spreading, so you can fit it into most mixed flower borders or a smaller garden setting.

Just be aware that 'Just Joey' is not as prolific in really hot summers, nor does it tolerate cold winters well (it's fine up to about Zone 6; north of that, winter protection is necessary). That said, it remains one of the finest soft-colored roses.

SUBSTITUTIONS/SIMILAR ROSES:
'Medallion'
'Nancy Reagan Rose'
'Sunset Celebration'
'Warm Wishes'

'Marijke Koopman'

MATURE PLANT HEIGHT: 4½ ft. to 5½ ft.

BLOOM SIZE: 4 in. to 5 in.

BLOOM TIME: all season

FRAGRANCE: moderate rose perfume

YEAR INTRODUCED: 1979

AWARDS WON: Gold Medal at The Hague, 1978

An especially profuse bloomer, 'Marijke Koopman' carries her lovely blooms singly and in small clusters, an impressive show that continues all season long. Each one is a picture, with classic high-centered form, in sweet, candied pink, with plenty of petals and an enticing, romantic fragrance. The plant itself is top-quality, too—it's handsome, very bushy, and clothed in dark green leaves that show excellent resistance to weather-spotting.

SUBSTITUTIONS/SIMILAR ROSES:

'Perfume Delight'

'Signature'®

'Tiffany'

'Midas Touch'™

MATURE PLANT HEIGHT: 4 ft. to 4½ ft.

BLOOM SIZE: 5 in.

BLOOM TIME: all season

FRAGRANCE: moderate, fruity

YEAR INTRODUCED: 1994

AWARDS WON: AARS, 1994

Aptly named, this sensational yellow rose impresses everyone who sees it and performs well in almost any climate. Especially valuable is its enviable ability to hold onto its radiant, deep-yellow coloration, no matter how hot the sun or how variable the weather (the very best show, however, occurs in areas with cooler summers). Plus, they're wonderfully fragrant, with a scent reminiscent of sun-ripened nectarines. And they make dazzling bouquets.

This is a vigorous, easy-going plant that blooms heavily all summer long. It's a bit on the tall side, so it's best sited at the back of a flower border.

SUBSTITUTIONS/SIMILAR ROSES:

Also available as a tree rose.

'Apéritif'

'Henry Fonda'

'Oregold'

'Olympiad'
MATURE PLANT HEIGHT: 4 ft. to 5 ft.
BLOOM SIZE: 4½ in. to 5 in.
BLOOM TIME: all season
FRAGRANCE: slight, sweet
YEAR INTRODUCED: 1984
AWARDS WON: AARS, 1984

'Opening Night'™
MATURE PLANT HEIGHT: 4 ft.
BLOOM SIZE: 4½ in.
BLOOM TIME: all season
FRAGRANCE: mild, fruity
YEAR INTRODUCED: 1998
AWARDS WON: AARS, 1998

Brilliant ruby red petals make the classically formed flowers of this excellent rose stand out dramatically in any garden. Up close, you'll admire their velvety texture and sweet, gentle aroma. The bright color holds up magnificently (it is very slow to fade) and, as a bouquet flower, 'Olympiad' is especially long lasting.

The strong, weather-tough bush is upright and vase-shaped, like other hybrid teas, but more compact than some, so it's a nice choice for solo plantings where you want a show-off rose. It's also good in a mixed border with other strong colors.

SUBSTITUTIONS/SIMILAR ROSES:
'Cesar E. Chavez Rose' ('Olympiad' is parent)
'Chrysler Imperial'
'Dame de Coeur'
'Opening Night'™ ('Olympiad' is parent)
'Royal William'

Derived from the superb 'Olympiad', 'Opening Night' is another outstanding red rose. It holds its rich color amazingly well, even in hot climates. The dark green foliage sets a perfect stage for the blooms. Long, strong cutting stems make the large, elegant blossoms irresistible for dazzling bouquets.

The bush is medium to tall, with a slightly spreading growth habit. Bred by Keith Zary of Jackson & Perkins, it is perhaps his finest red rose to date.

SUBSTITUTIONS/SIMILAR ROSES:
'Cesar E. Chavez Rose'
'Dame de Coeur'
'Ingrid Bergman'
'Olympiad'
'Royal William'

'Pristine'™

MATURE PLANT HEIGHT: 4 ft. to 4½ ft.
BLOOM SIZE: 4½ in. to 6 in.
BLOOM TIME: all season
FRAGRANCE: mild, sweet
YEAR INTRODUCED: 1978

'St. Patrick'

MATURE PLANT HEIGHT: 4 ft.
BLOOM SIZE: 4 in. to 5 in.
BLOOM TIME: all season
FRAGRANCE: light, sweet perfume
YEAR INTRODUCED: 1996
AWARDS WON: AARS, 1996

One of the prettiest older roses that are still widely available, thanks to its general excellence and wide adaptability. Each perfectly formed blossom has an almost pearl-like purity. Pink, urn-shaped buds open to full-petaled flowers that are ivory in the center, gradually blushing to soft, sweet, lavender-pink on the outer petals. These tend to remain poised in the half-open stage for a few days, which prolongs the show when you cut it for bouquets. As for fragrance, it seems to vary according to growing conditions and climate, but when present is light and sweet.

The foliage of 'Pristine' is especially good. It's dark, glossy green, large enough to be nicely in scale with the flowers, and quite disease-resistant. Truly an elegant plant, 'Pristine' deserves a starring role and is well suited to a formal-style garden.

SUBSTITUTIONS/SIMILAR ROSES:
'Garden Party' (pale yellow tinged pink)
'La France'
'Rosemary Harkness'
'Sheer Bliss' (white with pink blush)

Perhaps the best yellow rose for steamy summers! This is a rose of amazing stamina—when sweltering days cause other roses to flag, 'St. Patrick' just keeps on producing big, bright blooms. A hint of green in the petals gives the flowers a citrusy pizzazz. They tend to unfurl slowly, prolonging the show and making for dramatic gift bouquets.

The plant itself has a rounded, upright habit and subdued foliage with a gray-green tinge. Because it's of medium height, it's a good choice for a border or mixed flower bed.

SUBSTITUTIONS/SIMILAR ROSES:
Also available as a tree rose.
'Buttercream'
'Selfridges'
'Sunbright'

'Tiffany'

MATURE PLANT HEIGHT: 4 ft. to 4½ ft.
BLOOM SIZE: 4 in. to 5 in.
BLOOM TIME: all season
FRAGRANCE: rich rose perfume
YEAR INTRODUCED: 1954
AWARDS WON: AARS, 1955; David Fuerstenberg Prize, 1957;
   Gamble Fragrance Medal, 1962

A classic! This romantic pink has been winning hearts for over a generation. Each big blossom is laden with gorgeous, richly blended hues of pink, centered with a subtle yellow inner glow, and radiates a heady fragrance. These appear singly and in clusters, making quite a show out in the garden. They keep coming on all summer long, so you should feel free to pick bouquets for your home and for your friends, who are sure to be enchanted.

Bushy and quite vigorous, this plant is a good choice for a mixed garden, where it will fill its allotted spot with plenty of wonderful color and sweet scent.

SUBSTITUTIONS/SIMILAR ROSES:
There is a climbing form.
'Barbara Bush' ('Tiffany' is parent)
'Belinda's Dream' ('Tiffany' is parent)
'Gerda Hnatyshyn'
'Perfume Delight'
'Sweet Surrender' ('Tiffany' is parent)

'Touch of Class'™

MATURE PLANT HEIGHT: 4 ft. to 5 ft.
BLOOM SIZE: 5 in. to 5½ in.
BLOOM TIME: all season
FRAGRANCE: mild tea fragrance
YEAR INTRODUCED: 1984
AWARDS WON: AARS, 1986; Portland Gold Medal, 1988

Utterly glorious color! Starting out as a warm, coral pink, the flowers mellow to rich salmon, underlain with a barely perceptible but elegant cream reverse to the petals. This thrilling show emerges from shapely, long buds that spiral open to high-centered blossoms with slightly ruffled petals. The petals are also heavy-textured, which means they last longer on the plant and in bouquets. Understandably, 'Touch of Class' has been extremely popular with those who grow roses for show.

Rather tall for a hybrid tea plant, 'Touch of Class' is best placed to the back of a garden or along a fence, where it can show off its fabulous flowers without blocking other plants. The foliage is handsome and dark green in color but can get mildew in some climates.

SUBSTITUTIONS/SIMILAR ROSES:
'Brigadoon'
'Gemini'™
'Key Largo'

'Veterans' Honor'®

MATURE PLANT HEIGHT: 5 ft.
BLOOM SIZE: 5 in. to 5½ in.
BLOOM TIME: all season
FRAGRANCE: light, fruity
YEAR INTRODUCED: 2000
AWARDS WON: Jackson & Perkins Rose of the Year®, 2000

'Whisper'

MATURE PLANT HEIGHT: 5½ ft.
BLOOM SIZE: 5 in.
BLOOM TIME: all season
FRAGRANCE: light musk
YEAR INTRODUCED: 2003
AWARDS WON: AARS, 2003

A truly great newer red rose. High-centered blooms of rich ruby red waft a tantalizing, light raspberry scent. As they mature, the color moderates to dark pink. Thick, high-quality petals and especially long cutting stems (up to 22 inches long!) make 'Veterans' Honor' a spectacular, long-lasting bouquet flower. Out in the garden, the handsome and prolific bush always commands attention.

SUBSTITUTIONS/SIMILAR ROSES:
Available as a tree rose.
'Cesar E. Chavez Rose'
'Mister Lincoln'
'Olympiad'
'Opening Night'

Quite possibly the most beautiful and romantic of all white hybrid teas, 'Whisper' is actually a rich, splendid ivory. Flawless satiny petals and symmetrical flower form, plus a hint of musk-rose perfume, add to the seductive appeal. These beauties are splendidly contrasted with ample dark-green leaves.

A strong, adaptable plant, 'Whisper' resists disease and keeps those glorious flowers coming all summer long.

This gorgeous rose swept the AARS judges in 2003, the first white hybrid tea to do so since 1980!

SUBSTITUTIONS/SIMILAR ROSES:
'Elina'
'Honor'™
'John F. Kennedy'
'Pascali'

'Candelabra'™

MATURE PLANT HEIGHT: 4 ft.
BLOOM SIZE: 4 in.
BLOOM TIME: all season
FRAGRANCE: light, sweet
YEAR INTRODUCED: 1999
AWARDS WON: AARS, 1999

'Cherry Parfait'

MATURE PLANT HEIGHT: 5 ft.
BLOOM SIZE: 4 in.
BLOOM TIME: all season
FRAGRANCE: mild and sweet
YEAR INTRODUCED: 2002
AWARDS WON: AARS, 2003

Radiant, top-quality, mango-orange blossoms burst forth in singles and clusters from this exceptionally robust, healthy plant. (They're bigger and hold their color better in somewhat cooler summers.) A proven performer nationwide, as evidenced by its 1999 AARS award. Sure to be a classic.

Such a superior orange flower deserves thoughtful placement in your garden. Because the plant forms a tall bush, it's well suited to the rear of a flower border or inclusion in a shrub border. Against the dark backdrop of shrubbery, its bright color glows.

SUBSTITUTIONS/SIMILAR ROSES:
Also available as own-root (New Generation®).
'Gingersnap' (floribunda)
'Prominent'

Sprays of white blossoms edged in cherry red cover this big, rounded plant of excellent, disease-resistant foliage. Everyone admires the flowers—they're so full and beautiful, and they hold up very well in the heat.

Like other grandifloras, you get bountiful clusters as well as some single blooms, all on nice long cutting stems. Don't hesitate to cut bouquets—'Cherry Parfait' is quick to renew the show. This is exactly the sort of rose you want to display in the front yard, because it is so reliable, so durable, and so spectacular.

SUBSTITUTIONS/SIMILAR ROSES:
Also available as own-root (New Generation®).
'Pink Parfait'
'Betty Boop'™ (floribunda, soft yellow edged in red)
'Double Delight'™ (hybrid tea)

'Crimson Bouquet'™

MATURE PLANT HEIGHT: 4½ ft.
BLOOM SIZE: 4 in.
BLOOM TIME: all season
FRAGRANCE: mild and sweet
YEAR INTRODUCED: 2000
AWARDS WON: AARS, 2000

The ultimate red grandiflora, without a doubt! Numerous vibrant red blooms with luscious, velvety petals adorn a strong, vigorously growing bush, in great clusters. So prolific, you can harvest bouquets freely all summer and still more flowers will continue coming on to keep the show going in your garden.

Dark-green foliage resists disease and shows off the vivid flowers perfectly. Not as tall or upright as some grandifloras, so you can include it easily in a mixed planting. No wonder the AARS judges bestowed this excellent rose with their top award!

SUBSTITUTIONS/SIMILAR ROSES:
Also available as a tree rose.
'Cesar E. Chavez Rose' (hybrid tea)
'Love' (red with white reverse)
'Showbiz' (floribunda)
'Veterans' Honor'® (hybrid tea)

'Fame!'™

MATURE PLANT HEIGHT: 4 ft.
BLOOM SIZE: 4½ in.
BLOOM TIME: all season
FRAGRANCE: mild and sweet
YEAR INTRODUCED: 1998
AWARDS WON: AARS, 1998

There's something so optimistic and upbeat about this rose. The color is a vibrant, luscious, hot pink. Scalloped edges to the petals make the open blooms full and exuberant. And the plant produces these big beauties continuously throughout the summer months. They hold up well in the garden and are especially long lasting in bouquets.

All this, on a vigorous, easy-care bush with a spreading, upright habit. No doubt about it, 'Fame!' is a show—be sure to plant it in a prominent spot where it can be admired daily, such as an entryway garden or foundation area.

SUBSTITUTIONS/SIMILAR ROSES:
Also available as own-root (New Generation®).
'Melody Parfumée'™ (plum colored)
'Queen Elizabeth' (lighter pink)

'Glowing Peace'™

MATURE PLANT HEIGHT: 4 ft.
BLOOM SIZE: 3 in.
BLOOM TIME: all season
FRAGRANCE: mild, tea rose scent
YEAR INTRODUCED: 2001
AWARDS WON: AARS, 2001

Reminiscent of the popular old hybrid tea 'Peace', award-winning 'Glowing Peace' is superior in every way. It flowers much more freely, and in generous clusters that beg to be cut for bountiful bouquets. The coloration is far better, with a rich golden amber radiance to the petals and luscious melon orange along the edges as accent. Deep-green, glossy foliage that resists disease is also a plus. In all, a terrific relative newcomer that is sure to become a classic.

SUBSTITUTIONS/SIMILAR ROSES:
Also available as own-root (New Generation®).
'Day Breaker'™ (floribunda, yellow-apricot-pink blend)
'Love & Peace'™ (hybrid tea, amber-pink blend)
'Sultry'™ (hybrid tea, apricot and amber)

'Gold Medal'

MATURE PLANT HEIGHT: 4 ft.
BLOOM SIZE: 3½ in. to 4½ in.
BLOOM TIME: all season
FRAGRANCE: moderate, fruit-and-spice
YEAR INTRODUCED: 1982

Enticing fragrance! Reminiscent of sun-warmed nectarines with a slight nutmeg spiciness, these beauties are saturated with golden yellow color, outlined in orange-red. Abundant blossoms cloak a tough, handsome bush in clusters and singles, making for an impressive show! Thorns are sparse on the long stems, which makes them easy for cutting bouquets.

Grow 'Gold Medal' where you want plenty of bright, cheerful color and enticing fragrance. It will deliver, all summer long.

SUBSTITUTIONS/SIMILAR ROSES:
Available as own-root (New Generation®).
'Rio Samba'™ (hybrid tea, yellow with orange edging)
'Sheila's Perfume' (floribunda)
'Sundance' (hybrid tea, gold with orange-pink edging)

'Melody Parfumée'™

MATURE PLANT HEIGHT: 5 ft.
BLOOM SIZE: 4½ in.
BLOOM TIME: all season
FRAGRANCE: powerful, rich perfume
YEAR INTRODUCED: 1999

Deep plum-purple, pointed buds gradually unfurl to reveal a lavender blossom of intense, delicious fragrance. They last a long time in the garden or in a vase, eventually softening to a silvery-lilac hue.

Bred in France, this rose's scent is so intoxicating that it has been selected to provide rose essence for perfume making. You'll be equally captivated by its charms.

A medium-sized bush with dark-green, disease-resistant leaves, 'Melody Parfumée' makes a good show in any cutting garden or mixed border.

SUBSTITUTIONS/SIMILAR ROSES:
Also available as a tree rose.
'Heirloom' (hybrid tea, lilac purple)
'Love Potion'™ (floribunda, dark lavender)
'Moon Shadow'® (hybrid tea, silvery lavender)
'Purple Passion'™ (dark purple)

'Queen Elizabeth'

MATURE PLANT HEIGHT: 5 ft. to 7 ft.
BLOOM SIZE: 3½ in. to 4 in.
BLOOM TIME: midseason, repeats
FRAGRANCE: mild tea rose fragrance
YEAR INTRODUCED: 1954
AWARDS WON: AARS, 1955; ARS Gertrude M. Hubbard Gold Medal, 1957; ARS National Gold Medal Certificate, 1960; Golden Rose of The Hague, 1968

'Queen Elizabeth' was the first, back in the mid-1950s, and is still considered by many to be the best grandiflora rose. The plant is incredibly robust, shooting up tall and proud and covering itself in fabulous flowers. They're a sweet, clear pink, large size, and waft a gentle, haunting scent.

The long stems are impressive, whether bearing clusters of flowers or the occasional single bloom. On the plant, they are held aloft and give the plant an impressive appearance. Cut for bouquets, they make a big, dazzling show.

Owing to her tall profile and large flowers, 'Queen Elizabeth' needs to be appropriately placed. She looks regal flanking a doorway or garden entrance, or grown against the side of house or other building in need of spectacular, reliable color.

SUBSTITUTIONS/SIMILAR ROSES:
Also available as a tree rose.
Also available as own-root (New Generation®).
'First Prize' (hybrid tea)
'Perfume Delight' (hybrid tea)
'Sexy Rexy' (floribunda)

'Angel Face'

MATURE PLANT HEIGHT: 2½ ft. to 3 ft.

BLOOM SIZE: 3½ in. to 4 in.

BLOOM TIME: midseason, repeats

FRAGRANCE: intense, citrusy

YEAR INTRODUCED: 1969

AWARDS WON: Gamble Fragrance Medal, 2002; AARS, 1969 (first lavender rose ever to win this award); ARS John Cook Medal, 1979

Considered by many rose-lovers to be the finest lavender-hued rose. The delightful, ruffle-edged flowers are saturated with rich color and delicious, strong perfume. They're carried in large sprays, with some of the flowers in bud and others fully open—an arresting sight in the garden and ideal for impressive "one-snip" bouquets.

Low-growing 'Angel Face' is ideal for mixed borders, where it settles in, spreads out a bit, and dependably produces those enchanting flowers all summer long. The coppery, dark-green foliage is also attractive in such a setting. A great rose that has stood the test of time!

SUBSTITUTIONS/SIMILAR ROSES:

Available as a tree rose.

'Climbing Angel Face'

'Love Potion'™

'Simply Marvelous!'™

'Betty Boop'™

MATURE PLANT HEIGHT: 3 ft.

BLOOM SIZE: 4 in.

BLOOM TIME: all season

FRAGRANCE: moderate, fruity

YEAR INTRODUCED: 1999

AWARDS WON: AARS, 1999

As spunky as its namesake, this attractive little bush covers itself in stylish blooms and repeats all summer long. The nearly single flowers are truly unique—creamy white with broad lipstick-red petal edges, with a flashy boss of bright yellow stamens in the center. They're especially durable, on the bush or in a vase, and the plant produces them continuously (no deadheading or shaping required).

The plant itself is not large and maintains a nice, dense, rounded shape that tucks into flower beds well. 'Betty Boop' also makes a fun, dependable mass planting, such as along a fence, pool area, or foundation planting in a front yard.

SUBSTITUTIONS/SIMILAR ROSES:

Available as own-root (New Generation®).

'Eyepaint'

'Playboy' (orange and red)

'Showbiz' (red)

'Betty Prior'
MATURE PLANT HEIGHT: 5 ft. to 7 ft.
BLOOM SIZE: 3 in. to 3½ in.
BLOOM TIME: midseason, excellent repeat
FRAGRANCE: moderate
YEAR INTRODUCED: 1935

'*Disneyland* ® Rose'
MATURE PLANT HEIGHT: 3 ft.
BLOOM SIZE: 3 in. to 4 in.
BLOOM TIME: all season
FRAGRANCE: light, spicy
YEAR INTRODUCED: 2003

An oldie-but-goodie, 'Betty Prior' has been around since 1935 and has been widely planted. You sometimes see it in the yards of older homes or churchyards. Its survival may be due to the fact that it is more cold hardy than some, surviving Zone 5 winters with aplomb. However, it also performs very well in the South, with an impressively long bloom period.

Its lush clusters of bright pink, single-form flowers might remind you of a wild rose, but it is better behaved. Others have compared the blossoms to those of a pink flowering dogwood, but they are decidedly rose-like when you admire them up close, and exude a delicate sweet-rose perfume.

'Betty Prior' is, however, much taller than modern floribundas, so be sure to allow it sufficient elbowroom. It's lovely along a fence or as a hedge, where it will prove its dependability and delight you with its durable beauty.

SUBSTITUTIONS/SIMILAR ROSES:
'Carefree Delight'® (shrub)
'Nearly Wild' (shrub)
'Wildberry Breeze' (rugosa)

Unique among floribundas, this exuberant newer rose delivers a parade of multi-colored blooms in big, lush clusters, each one a spirited blend of apricot, orange, and sweet pink. A flower this vibrant will get lots of attention, whether you tuck one or two into a mixed flower border—it only grows to 3 feet tall, so should fit in easily— or plant a bed or row of them en masse. (Its developer, Jackson & Perkins, has supplied plants to the Magic Kingdom in the *Disneyland*® Park in Anaheim, California, so you can admire them on your next visit.)

The plant itself is strong, vigorous and laden with dark-green leaves that resist disease. This is a fun and dependable rose, ideal where you want plenty of spectacular color with little effort.

SUBSTITUTIONS/SIMILAR ROSES:
Available as own-root (New Generation®).
Also offered as Garden Ease®.
'Day Breaker'™
'Gingersnap'
'Hot Cocoa'™ (chocolate-orange)

'Eureka'™

MATURE PLANT HEIGHT: 3½ ft.
BLOOM SIZE: 4 in.
BLOOM TIME: all season
FRAGRANCE: mild, sweet
YEAR INTRODUCED: 2003
AWARDS WON: AARS, 2003

'Hot Cocoa'™

MATURE PLANT HEIGHT: 3 ft. to 4 ft.
BLOOM SIZE: 4 in.
BLOOM TIME: all season
FRAGRANCE: moderate, sweet spice
YEAR INTRODUCED: 2003
AWARDS WON: AARS, 2003

When the AARS judges gave 'Eureka' their top award in 2003, they raved about its exceptional reblooming ability—it just doesn't quit! This rose also gets high marks for its unique (among floribundas) blossoms, which are plush and full enough to invite favorable comparisons to English roses. They're a splendid, consistent, warm gold, underlain with delicious hints of soft apricot and offering a sweet, light scent. Glossy green, disease-resistant leaves are a perfect contrast.

This is a vigorous, healthy, easy plant that grows almost as wide as it is tall. So it's an outstanding choice for small groupings or accent plantings.

SUBSTITUTIONS/SIMILAR ROSES:
'Fellowship'
'Honey Bouquet'™
'Honey Perfume'
'Sun Flare'

Very unique color! 'Hot Cocoa' flowers are chocolate, almost deep purple, enriched with cinnamon-orange. The form is flawless and the petals are thick and velvety, which helps them last longer in your garden or in a vase. Though still a fairly new variety, its glorious, durable color and strong, healthy growth have received raves—and it took top AARS honors in 2003, the year it debuted.

Grow 'Hot Cocoa' in a prominent spot where it can get a lot of attention. If you mix it with other flowers, be daring: Try it with bright orange roses or other hot-colored flowers. Or display them along a white building or fence to boldly show off their flowers.

SUBSTITUTIONS/SIMILAR ROSES:
'Leonidas'™ (named for a brand of Belgian chocolate)

'Iceberg'

MATURE PLANT HEIGHT: 3 ft. to 4 ft.
BLOOM SIZE: 3 in.
BLOOM TIME: midseason, repeats
FRAGRANCE: moderate, honey-sweet
YEAR INTRODUCED: 1958
AWARDS WON: Royal National Rose Society Gold Medal, 1958

'Intrigue'

MATURE PLANT HEIGHT: 3 ft.
BLOOM SIZE: 3 in.
BLOOM TIME: all season
FRAGRANCE: intense, rich perfume
YEAR INTRODUCED: 1984
AWARDS WON: AARS, 1984

Considered one of the best roses of all time, 'Iceberg' deserves all the praise. A low-maintenance, easy-going, trouble-free shrub, it is most popular as a hedge rose or in mass plantings. But the flowers are excellent—they're large, pure white, and sweetly scented—lovely in the garden and equally nice for bouquets! Individual sprays can have up to a dozen flowers. These appear a bit later than some other roses, but carry on nonstop for the rest of the summer.

One great virtue of 'Iceberg' is that it is so easily managed. If you keep the bushes pruned low, they stay in bounds and provide you with loads of blooms on long cutting stems. If you let them grow taller, you'll still get a great show but the flowers will be carried on shorter stems. Either way, it's hard to find a better landscape rose.

SUBSTITUTIONS/SIMILAR ROSES:
Also available as a tree rose. There is a superb climbing version.
'Fabulous!'™
'Guinevere' (shrub)
'Margaret Merrill' (better for black spot-prone areas)
'White Pet' (polyantha, 1 to 3 feet)
'Yvonne Rabier' (polyantha, 1 to 3 feet)

On hot summer days, a heady, delicious, almost lemony scent radiates from this bush. And the flowers are magnificent, a deep, rich plum, rare in floribundas, and indeed in all roses. The petals are especially ruffled, giving the blooms an old-fashioned look. 'Intrigue' is gorgeous in combination with white or yellow flowers—roses, or other flowers—in the garden or in a vase.

Expect flowers all summer long, in waves, so you will have plenty of opportunities to pick bouquets. The cluster-blooming habit means you can do so without stripping the bush of color. This is an attractive, compact plant, well suited for inclusion in a romantic, cottage garden setting. Needs winter protection in colder areas.

SUBSTITUTIONS/SIMILAR ROSES:
'Love Potion'™
'Melody Parfumée'™ (grandiflora)
'Simply Marvelous!'™

'Marmalade Skies'™

MATURE PLANT HEIGHT: 3 ft.
BLOOM SIZE: 2½ in. to 3 in.
BLOOM TIME: all season
FRAGRANCE: slight, fruity
YEAR INTRODUCED: 2001
AWARDS WON: AARS, 2001

Fiery, tropical red-orange flowers envelop a nice, tidy bush, making 'Marmalade Skies' one of the finest newer floribundas. It has everything going for it: stunning color; the valuable ability to bloom continuously and heavily; a light, sweet scent; and a neat growth habit that makes it easy to place in any garden. Once established, this rose delivers consistently fabulous annual shows.

Big clusters of these beauties adorn a medium-sized, rounded bush. It's great for a low border or hedge, and is compact enough to prosper in a large container.

SUBSTITUTIONS/SIMILAR ROSES:
'Disneyland® Rose'
'Fellowship'
'Hot Cocoa'™ (chocolate orange)
'Morden Fireglow' (shrub)

'Our Lady of Guadalupe'™

MATURE PLANT HEIGHT: 2½ ft. to 3 ft.
BLOOM SIZE: 3 in.
BLOOM TIME: all season
FRAGRANCE: light, sweet rose perfume
YEAR INTRODUCED: 2001

Named for the patroness of the Americas, this glorious pink floribunda is destined for wide popularity. The plants have a full, rounded growth habit and exhibit exceptional disease-resistance. And the flowers, which are produced in profusion all summer long, are especially lovely—a dark, rich pink that matures to silvery pink over a period of several days. They're wonderfully durable, in the garden or in a bouquet.

Grow 'Our Lady of Guadalupe' in a bed of pastel-hued flowers and you can count on her summer-long, beautiful show. Or plant a grouping in a spot where the remarkable blooms can be admired up close.

SUBSTITUTIONS/SIMILAR ROSES:
Also available as a tree rose.
'Gruss an Aachen' (3 to 4 feet)
'Memorial Day' (hybrid tea, lavender pink)
'Pearl Essence'™ (hybrid tea, light pink blend)
'Pensioner's Voice'
'Sexy Rexy'

'Playboy'

MATURE PLANT HEIGHT: 2½ ft. to 3 ft.
BLOOM SIZE: 3½ in.
BLOOM TIME: all season
FRAGRANCE: light, sweet
YEAR INTRODUCED: 1976
AWARDS WON: Portland Gold Medal, 1989

Cherry red petals are underlain with glowing yellow and centered with golden stamens. The color lasts for days on end, in your garden or in a vase. The petal count is low and the perky blooms are carried in great sprays. They come with a fresh, sweet scent, reminiscent of ripe, crisp apples.

These vivacious flowers cover a dense, healthy bush of glossy foliage, so even if you have a small garden, you can fit 'Playboy' in. It's also a great choice for a hot-colored border or cutting garden, and may even be grown in a container.

SUBSTITUTIONS/SIMILAR ROSES:
'Miss Behavin'™ (dark pink with yellow reverse)
'Perfect Moment' (red-yellow blend)

'Purple Tiger'

MATURE PLANT HEIGHT: 2 ft. to 4 ft.
BLOOM SIZE: 3 in. to 4 in.
BLOOM TIME: all season
FRAGRANCE: moderate, old rose
YEAR INTRODUCED: 1992

A modern, especially long-blooming rose that gets its fabulous color and scent from its old-rose parentage. Wildly splashed and striped purple-and-white petals make for a strikingly beautiful blossom, and the fragrance is delicious—it's been compared to the fruity-sweet scent of ripe currants. Like all floribundas, it blooms in clusters, which adds to the impact. All this, plus it's nearly thornless.

A medium-sized plant, 'Purple Tiger' has good vigor and flowers freely. It makes quite a show in the garden or in bouquets—try it alongside any white rose or white perennial—spectacular! Because the flowers are so unusual, you may prefer to show off 'Purple Tiger' in a large pot or tub on a patio or terrace.

SUBSTITUTIONS/SIMILAR ROSES:
'Ferdinand Pichard' (hybrid perpetual, red and white striped)
'Honorine de Brabant' (bourbon, red and white striped)
'Scentimental'™ (burgundy and white striped)
'Tigress' (grandiflora, 'Purple Tiger' is parent)
'Tropical Sunset'™ (hybrid tea, yellow and orange striped)

'Scentimental'™

MATURE PLANT HEIGHT: 3 ft. to 4 ft.
BLOOM SIZE: 4 in.
BLOOM TIME: all season
FRAGRANCE: strong and spicy
YEAR INTRODUCED: 1997
AWARDS WON: AARS, 1997

Splashy, peppermint-candy blossoms—no two alike!—decorate this award-winning rose bush. The wonderful scent is a great match, richly spicy and utterly tantalizing. Because 'Scentimental' is a floribunda, you get these unique and flashy flowers in large clusters. Just one or two stems make for an unforgettable bouquet.

There are old-fashioned roses with similar coloration, but their bloom period is brief as opposed to all summer, and their color may not be quite as vivid. Distinctive, quilted, dark-green foliage that resists disease well adds to this exceptional rose's appeal. It's also heat and humidity tolerant.

SUBSTITUTIONS/SIMILAR ROSES:
'Ferdinand Pichard' (hybrid perpetual, red and white striped)
'Fourth of July' (climber)
'Honorine de Brabant' (bourbon, red and white striped)
'Purple Tiger' (purple and white striped)
'Tigress' (grandiflora)
'Tropical Sunset'™ (hybrid tea, yellow and orange striped)

'Sunsprite'

MATURE PLANT HEIGHT: 2½ ft. to 3 ft.
BLOOM SIZE: 3 in.
BLOOM TIME: midseason, repeats
FRAGRANCE: strong, sweet licorice
YEAR INTRODUCED: 1977
AWARDS WON: Gamble Fragrance Award, 1979; Baden-Baden Gold Medal, 1972

Bright, crisp, sweetly scented, true yellow flowers, in generous clusters, adorn a handsome, bushy plant with good disease-resistance. Continuously in bloom. No wonder many experts consider it among the top yellow roses of all time!

Medium-sized 'Sunsprite' has such excellent and dependable color, it is often used as a hedge plant. But single plants make a cheerful addition to a mixed flowerbed. And because it is so productive, you can harvest bouquets for the house and still continue to enjoy a good show in the garden.

SUBSTITUTIONS/SIMILAR ROSES:
Available in a climbing form and as a tree rose.
'Easy Going'
'Eureka'™
'Sun Flare'

'Abraham Darby'®

MATURE PLANT HEIGHT: 5 ft. to 6 ft.
BLOOM SIZE: 4½ in. to 5 in.
BLOOM TIME: midseason, repeats
FRAGRANCE: intense
YEAR INTRODUCED: 1985

Beautiful! A light, delicate apricot-orange warmed with yellow towards the center, and dense with petals, the cupped blossoms of 'Abraham Darby' always stand out. Plus, the fragrance is rich and romantic.

This is a tough, durable plant and grows rather tall—in fact, its long, arching stems are easy to train on a small trellis or along and over a fence. Just watch out for the thorns, which are up to an inch long.

Glossy, deep green leaves add to this English rose's appeal. (The foliage is especially resistant to mildew, but may require protection from black spot.) All these excellent qualities account for the plant's enduring popularity.

SUBSTITUTIONS/SIMILAR ROSES:
'Adam' (tea)
'Crown Princess Margareta' (shrub, darker apricot hue)
'Evelyn'
'Geoff Hamilton'
'Pat Austin'

'Fair Bianca'®

MATURE PLANT HEIGHT: 2½ to 3 ft.
BLOOM SIZE: 3 to 3½ in.
BLOOM TIME: midseason, repeats
FRAGRANCE: intense
YEAR INTRODUCED: 1982

Because of its small, compact size, 'Fair Bianca' is perfect for a smaller garden, or for tucking into an old-fashioned flower border. Indeed, it is one of the smallest David Austin English roses.

And yet the flowers are everything you could wish for—they're plush with satiny white petals, endowed with a heady, spicy perfume, and displayed in a cupped shape with "quartered" form that gives them formal yet old-fashioned appeal.

'Fair Bianca' is a ravishing addition to any garden (the bright white stands out especially well in summer twilight, a plus for those who don't get to savor their garden until they get home from work). And the flower clusters make for delightful bouquets.

SUBSTITUTIONS/SIMILAR ROSES:
'Glamis Castle'
'Mme Hardy' (damask)
'Stanwell Perpetual' (old garden)

'Golden Celebration'
MATURE PLANT HEIGHT: 5 ft.
BLOOM SIZE: 5 in.
BLOOM TIME: midseason, repeats
FRAGRANCE: sweet honey
YEAR INTRODUCED: 1992

'Graham Thomas'®
MATURE PLANT HEIGHT: 5 ft. to 7 ft.,
    10 ft. to 12 ft. as a climber
BLOOM SIZE: 3½ in. to 4 in.
BLOOM TIME: late in season, repeats
FRAGRANCE: intense tea rose
YEAR INTRODUCED: 1983

You will be dazzled! These are big, glorious, ruffle-edged blossoms—up to 5 inches across and laden with rich golden color that seems to capture and hold summer sunshine like no other yellow. And the fragrance is equally irresistible, like sweet, warm honey! A fabulous bouquet rose.

Contrasting with the luminous flowers is the distinctive, lightly curved, forest-green foliage. It cloaks the plant and adds to its handsome, attention-grabbing presence in the garden.

SUBSTITUTIONS/SIMILAR ROSES:
Also available as own-root (New Generation®).
'Buff Beauty' (noisette, climber)
'Graham Thomas'®
'Pat Austin'
'Teasing Georgia'

This was the first yellow English rose, and has held up well. When it debuted at London's prestigious Chelsea Flower Show, it caused a sensation with its luminous golden yellow color, so rarely seen in old or new roses. The flowers are extremely full petaled and generously scented with old-rose perfume; they make an irresistible cut flower. Its performance in this country has perhaps exceeded even its European reputation—particularly since it flourishes in hot American summers!

The plant is a vigorous one, and can get quite large if you let it—up to 7 feet tall and nearly as wide. It may need supporting or reining in. Some gardeners let it go, and then train its bulk into a climbing form. If you want your 'Graham Thomas' to stay in bounds in a perennial border or in a spot by a wall or fence, simply prune it hard early every spring.

SUBSTITUTIONS/SIMILAR ROSES:
'Buff Beauty' (noisette, climber)
'Golden Celebration'
'Teasing Georgia'

'Heritage'™

MATURE PLANT HEIGHT: 5 ft. to 6 ft.
BLOOM SIZE: 4½ in. to 5 in.
BLOOM TIME: midseason, repeats
FRAGRANCE: intense, citrusy
YEAR INTRODUCED: 1985

'Mary Rose'

MATURE PLANT HEIGHT: 4 ft. to 6 ft.
BLOOM SIZE: 4 in. to 4½ in.
BLOOM TIME: all season
FRAGRANCE: moderate, anise fragrance
YEAR INTRODUCED: 1983

Classic loveliness. 'Heritage' boasts the finest qualities of this class of roses: gorgeous, old-fashioned flower form and heady fragrance, combined with good repeat bloom so you can enjoy its charms all summer. The foliage is handsome, and the stems are nearly thornless. Indeed, breeder David Austin has declared this one to be his most beautiful.

Borne singly and in lush clusters, the plush blossoms are utterly romantic soft shell-pink. And the scent is tantalizing and delicious, reminiscent of a just-baked lemon cake. Just imagine the fabulous bouquets you will harvest!

Considered to be among the most prolific of all English roses, 'Mary Rose' is one of the earliest to start blooming and continues with her fetching pink flowers for nearly the entire summer. The color is a darker hue, reminiscent of dark pink peonies—the full petal count further invites this comparison. The aroma is sweet though not overpowering, with a gentle hint of spice.

This is a bigger bush than some and grows quite vigorously; a row of plants makes an excellent hedge. It resists disease well and earns your praise with a consistently pretty show, year after glorious year.

SUBSTITUTIONS/SIMILAR ROSES:
'Fantin-Latour' (old garden)
'Jacques Cartier' (old garden)
'Mary Rose' (darker pink)
'Morden Ruby' (shrub)
'Geoff Hamilton' (soft pink)

SUBSTITUTIONS/SIMILAR ROSES:
'Gertrude Jekyll'
'Hénri Martin' (old garden)
'Lavender Lassie' (shrub)
'Morden Blush' (shrub)
'Roseraie de l'Hay' (rugosa)
'Sharifa Asma'
'Winchester Cathedral' (white sport of 'Mary Rose')

'Ballerina'
MATURE PLANT HEIGHT: 3 ft. to 4 ft.
BLOOM SIZE: 2 in.
BLOOM TIME: midseason, repeats
FRAGRANCE: mild, musky
YEAR INTRODUCED: 1937

'Bonica'™
MATURE PLANT HEIGHT: 2 ft. to 4 ft.
BLOOM SIZE: 1 in. to 2½ in.
BLOOM TIME: all season
FRAGRANCE: none
YEAR INTRODUCED: 1987
AWARDS WON: AARS, 1987

Generous clusters of dainty, single flowers cascade down the practically thorn-free stems of this old favorite. Though small, there are so many blossoms that 'Ballerina' always makes a big impression. They look bicolored, but on close inspection are dark pink on the petal edges, lighter pink for most of the petals, and white towards the center, which displays a frilly boss of golden stamens. A soft, musky-sweet scent adds to their appeal.

The stems arch gracefully yet the plant is not unruly—it grows densely and stays compact, growing about as wide as it is tall. As such, it can be used out in the open as a garden focal point. But it suits equally well as a natural-looking hedge or draped over a fence.

SUBSTITUTIONS/SIMILAR ROSES:
'Belinda'
'Frau Dagmar Hastrup' (rugosa)
'Marie Pavié' (semi-double)
'Marjorie Fair' (red)
'The Fairy'

Once upon a time, this excellent rose made history—in 1987, it was the first shrub rose ever to win top AARS honors. The judges were very impressed with the beauty of its flowers and the durability of the plant.

Borne in generous sprays, the flowers are prettier and fuller than those of some other hedge or landscaping roses. They're small, full petaled, and a sweet shell-pink color. The leaves, too, are small and generally disease-free.

'Bonica' plants are indeed very tough. They tolerate cold winters and blazing-hot summers, continuing to perform admirably year after year. Though well suited to screen, hedge, and foundation plantings, individual plants are a lovely, no-nonsense, low-maintenance addition to a flower border.

SUBSTITUTIONS/SIMILAR ROSES:
'Baby Blanket'
'English Sachet'™ (English style)
'Royal Bonica'™
'Vancouver Belle'

'Brilliant Pink Iceberg'

MATURE PLANT HEIGHT: 3 ft. to 4 ft.
BLOOM SIZE: 3 in. to 4 in.
BLOOM TIME: all season
FRAGRANCE: moderate, sweet honey
YEAR INTRODUCED: 2002

'Carefree Beauty'™

MATURE PLANT HEIGHT: 5 ft. to 6 ft.
BLOOM SIZE: 4 in. to 4½ in.
BLOOM TIME: midseason, repeats well
FRAGRANCE: moderate perfume
YEAR INTRODUCED: 1977

For those who enjoy what 'Iceberg' has to offer—constant flowering, cold-hardiness, disease-resistance, a scent of warm, sweet honey, not to mention nearly thornless stems—this "sport" (mutation) of that popular rose is indeed cause for celebration. The sparkling, pretty flowers open to a wide, saucer shape and are suffused with an exciting bright fuchsia pink, with only a bit of cream towards the center.

A bush this easy-going and full of flowers is ideal for borders, edging walkways, or entryway plantings (remember, the low thorn count allows you to plant it in higher-traffic areas if you wish). No matter where you place it, zesty 'Brilliant Pink Iceberg' is sure to bring vibrancy to your landscape.

One of the finest roses to emerge from the late Dr. Griffith Buck's rose-breeding program at Iowa State University. His goal was to develop roses that could weather the vagaries of his Midwest climate, from freezing winters to blazing-hot summers, and still look terrific. Rosy-pink 'Carefree Beauty' fulfills those goals beautifully. It blooms abundantly starting in midseason, and the flowers are really quite lovely, from their plump buds to their splashy opening, when they waft an enticing perfume over your garden.

Smooth, olive-green, disease-resistant leaves cover the moderately thorny plant, making a handsome backdrop. 'Carefree Beauty' becomes a full, substantial bush, so be sure to give it enough room. A row makes an excellent, very tough hedge.

SUBSTITUTIONS/SIMILAR ROSES:
Also available as a tree rose.
Also available as own-root (New Generation®).
'Footloose'
'Greetings'
'Iceberg' (white)

SUBSTITUTIONS/SIMILAR ROSES:
'Applejack' (8 to 10 feet)
'Carefree Wonder'™
'Simplicity'®
'William Baffin'

'Carefree Delight'®
MATURE PLANT HEIGHT: 3 ft.
BLOOM SIZE: 1½ in.
BLOOM TIME: all season
FRAGRANCE: mild, sweet
YEAR INTRODUCED: 1996
AWARDS WON: AARS, 1996

'Carefree Wonder'™
MATURE PLANT HEIGHT: 4 ft. to 5 ft.
BLOOM SIZE: 4 in. to 5 in.
BLOOM TIME: midseason, excellent repeat
FRAGRANCE: mild, fruity
YEAR INTRODUCED: 1990
AWARDS WON: AARS, 1990

Perky pink little blooms, with white eyes, adorn this smaller shrub from late spring to fall—quite a performance! They're single form (just five petals per bloom), and carried in clusters, so the effect is exuberant.

This rose is very dependable and easy-care. It's also disease-resistant, cold hardy and more drought-tolerant than other roses. In short, it's a great landscape rose, one you'll never have to fuss over.

SUBSTITUTIONS/SIMILAR ROSES:
'Ballerina'
'Carefree Wonder'™
'Nearly Wild'
'Wildberry Breeze'

This award-winning rose has it all! The neat, rounded plant exhibits superb disease-resistance. It's very cold hardy (to USDA Zone 4), consistently weathering chilly winters to return in glory the following spring. The bright green foliage is plentiful, yet remains in bounds.

And the flowers...they are fabulous! Bigger than most shrub-rose blossoms, they keeping coming on, stopping only when frost threatens. Their coloration is unique and enchanting: bright pink etched or "hand-painted" in deeper pink, with a white eye and a creamy reverse. This is an exciting, low-maintenance rose for busy gardeners.

SUBSTITUTIONS/SIMILAR ROSES:
'Basye's Blueberry'
'Brilliant Pink Iceberg'
'Footloose'
'Lady of the Dawn'™ (cream pink)
'Mrs. R.M. Finch'
'William Baffin'

'Country Dancer'

MATURE PLANT HEIGHT: 4 ft. to 5 ft.
BLOOM SIZE: 4 in. to 5 in.
BLOOM TIME: all season
FRAGRANCE: moderate, fruity
YEAR INTRODUCED: 1973

Another outstanding Griffith Buck rose (see 'Carefree Beauty'), it is deservedly popular with gardeners in cold climates. Even without winter protection, it comes back every year without fail.

The big, full-petaled, vibrant, watermelon-pink flowers are gorgeous, and they radiate an enchanting, fresh-cut apple scent that is wonderful in the garden—well worth savoring in a home-grown bouquet. The dark green leaves adorn a medium-sized, upright to somewhat spreading bush. Expect a vigorous, long-lasting show.

SUBSTITUTIONS/SIMILAR ROSES:
'Carefree Beauty'™
'Hansa'
'John Davis'
'William Baffin'

'Frau Dagmar Hastrup' ('Frau Dagmar Hartopp')

MATURE PLANT HEIGHT: 3 ft. to 4 ft.
BLOOM SIZE: 3 in. to 3½ in.
BLOOM TIME: all season
FRAGRANCE: intense, clove
YEAR INTRODUCED: circa 1914

An old-time Danish hybrid whose exact origins are lost to history, this deliciously fragrant pink rugosa continues to be popular to this day. It's practically immune to disease and reliably winter-hardy in cold climates.

Its flowers are its main draw. They're big and pretty, open-cupped, and single. The color is beautiful: a soft, elegant, pewter-tinted pink with darker pink veins, almost reminiscent of a geranium petal. Full of rich, glorious, spicy-clove fragrance, they cover the plant all summer long, yielding at last in autumn to big, bright-red hips.

With a tidier, better-mannered habit than some other rugosas, this rose is ideal for a low hedge or property-line planting. Just be warned: It's very thorny.

SUBSTITUTIONS/SIMILAR ROSES:
'Ballerina'
'Nearly Wild'
Rosa carolina (Carolina rose)
Rosa setigera serena (prairie rose, can be a climber,
　3 to 8 feet)
'Sarah Van Fleet' (6 to 8 feet)
'Wildberry Breeze'

'Hansa'

MATURE PLANT HEIGHT: 4 ft. to 5 ft.
BLOOM SIZE: 3 in. to 3½ in.
BLOOM TIME: all season
FRAGRANCE: intense, spicy
YEAR INTRODUCED: 1905

Rich reddish-purple, like a fine Zinfandel wine, is a rare color in roses, but 'Hansa' has it. Everyone who visits your garden will exclaim over its vibrancy and great beauty. Not only that, but the petal-laden flowers (many more petals than the typical rugosa rose) will make you swoon with their heady, clove-like scent.

'Hansa' is an old variety, in commerce since 1905 and still not surpassed. Like all rugosas, it is tough and cold hardy, with disease-proof, quilted foliage, thorny stems, and a rounded, exuberant growth habit. It's often used—spectacularly—in hedges and boundary plantings. But a single plant or two make a dramatic contribution to an informal, cottage-style garden.

SUBSTITUTIONS/SIMILAR ROSES:
'F.J. Grootendorst' (brighter red)
'John Cabot'
'Knock Out'™
'Roseraie de l'Hay'

'Henry Hudson'

MATURE PLANT HEIGHT: 3 ft.
BLOOM SIZE: 3 in. to 4 in.
BLOOM TIME: all season
FRAGRANCE: moderate, spicy
YEAR INTRODUCED: 1976

A relative newcomer to the rugosa class of roses, 'Henry Hudson' was immediately popular with gardeners seeking a truly tough white bloomer. The lovely flowers begin as chubby, deep pink buds and burst open to almost flattened, creamy white blooms with plenty of fluffy petals and a bright center of yellow stamens. Cooler temperatures cause them to flush slightly pink. The fragrance is not as strong as some rugosas, but still has that signature spiciness.

And tough it is. It has survived chilly Zone 4 winters, and even colder ones with ample protection. It is impervious to disease. The crinkled, dark-green leaves are a great stage for the pretty buds and flowers.

Thanks to its smaller size, 'Henry Hudson' is a nice choice for smaller gardens or tighter spaces. No matter where you grow it, you will cherish its pluck as much as its beauty.

SUBSTITUTIONS/SIMILAR ROSES:
'Guinevere' (English style)
'Iceberg'
'Sir Thomas Lipton' (6 to 8 feet)
'Wild Spice' (single)

'John Cabot'
MATURE PLANT HEIGHT: 8 ft.
BLOOM SIZE: 3 in.
BLOOM TIME: midsummer
FRAGRANCE: mild
YEAR INTRODUCED: 1978

Bred in Canada as part of the much-praised cold-hardy Explorer series, 'John Cabot' stands out. Clusters of intense rose-pink blossoms radiate a delicious perfume, while the plant itself is exceptionally tough, disease-resistant, and vigorous.

This plant can be grown as a large shrub or a small climber. Either way, it makes a bright and utterly dependable addition to the garden. It is especially appropriate for cottage-garden schemes with its lush habit and romantic fragrance.

SUBSTITUTIONS/SIMILAR ROSES:
'Alexander MacKenzie'
'Champlain'
'Knock Out'™
'William Baffin'

'Knock Out'™
MATURE PLANT HEIGHT: 3 ft.
BLOOM SIZE: 3 in. to 3½ in.
BLOOM TIME: all season
FRAGRANCE: light, sweet
YEAR INTRODUCED: 2000
AWARDS WON: AARS, 2000; Texas A&M University's Texas
   Superstar Award; Germany's ADR Award

Some rose aficionados are so excited about this rose that they are calling it "the best shrub rose ever" and "the future of shrub roses." It was bred by an American amateur from the Milwaukee area, Bill Radler, and in short order it won top AARS honors and continues to get raves as more gardeners try it. Radler nurtured it from a chance seedling because he was struck by the exceptional disease-resistance of the mossy-green foliage (it appears to be impervious to black spot). The sensational ruby-red, single form blossoms are abundant. These are followed in fall by big, bright orange hips that attract migrating birds to your garden.

Count on 'Knock Out' to weather cold winters (to Zone 4 or 5, at least), and to spend its summers supplying your garden with a constant parade of dashing color. All with no fussing at all on your part.

SUBSTITUTIONS/SIMILAR ROSES:
Also offered as a tree rose.
'Blushing Knock Out' (shell pink)
'Katy Road Pink'
'Pink Knock Out' (bright pink)

'Mlle Cécile Brünner'

MATURE PLANT HEIGHT: 2½ ft. to 3 ft.
BLOOM SIZE: 1½ in.
BLOOM TIME: midsummer, then repeats
FRAGRANCE: light, sweet
YEAR INTRODUCED: 1881

The tiny "sweetheart" pink blossoms of this charming heirloom rose have long been popular as boutonnière or corsage roses. Though small, they have a classic, high-centered, hybrid tea flower form, and are carried in generous sprays. The soft pastel-pink color is consistent and lovely.

Small, dark-green, disease-resistant leaves are in scale with the flowers. The canes are nearly smooth (very few thorns), making the climbing version very appealing for training on a trellis or pergola. The bush is not large, but it does spread outward.

'Mlle Cécile Brünner' is an old favorite that has stood the test of time. It prospers in mild climates and requires protection where winters are cold. Try it in an informal, cottage-garden scheme. It's also very pretty by a low stone wall or cascading over a wooden fence.

SUBSTITUTIONS/SIMILAR ROSES:
An excellent climbing version is available.
'Baby Blanket'
'Bonica'™ (peachy pink)
'China Doll' (rose pink)
'Perle d'Or'
'The Fairy'

'Morden Blush'

MATURE PLANT HEIGHT: 2½ ft. to 4 ft.
BLOOM SIZE: 3 in. to 4 in.
BLOOM TIME: all season
FRAGRANCE: none
YEAR INTRODUCED: 1991

This elegantly beautiful rose is also among the toughest—good news, especially, for gardeners in challenging climates. Bred in Canada, it sails through Zone 3 winters but also tolerates summer heat very well. Not only that, it blooms nonstop; it is not unusual for 'Morden Blush' to produce flowers continuously for a full three months.

And the blossoms are indeed gorgeous. They're full of petals ("double") and a romantic shade of softest peachy pink. They are borne in sprays, so a bush in bloom is a glorious sight. Imagine this rose as a hedge or foundation planting: low maintenance, natural toughness, and all those enchanting flowers!

Because 'Morden Blush' is smaller and more compact than many shrub roses, you might also consider it for a flower border of similarly sized perennials. The color is compatible with so many other hues—from purple and blue to any pastel—and it will carry the show through any lulls with its continuous blooming.

SUBSTITUTIONS/SIMILAR ROSES:
Any in the Morden Series.
'Eglantyne' (English)
'Felicia'
'Lady of the Dawn'™
'Martin Frobisher'

'Morden Centennial'

MATURE PLANT HEIGHT: 3 ft. to 4 ft.
BLOOM SIZE: 3 in.
BLOOM TIME: all season
FRAGRANCE: mild, sweet
YEAR INTRODUCED: 1980

'Morden Fireglow'

MATURE PLANT HEIGHT: 3 ft. to 5 ft.
BLOOM SIZE: 3 in.
BLOOM TIME: all season
FRAGRANCE: none
YEAR INTRODUCED: 1991

Full flowers of pure, satiny pink drape the plant all summer—it has amazing energy! As a sweet bonus, they have a light, lilting perfume that is very appealing. The blooms are nicely complemented by ample, medium-green leaves that resist disease. Fall brings a great show of dark red hips.

Because it hails from the famed Canadian rose-breeding program in Manitoba, you know you can count on 'Morden Centennial' to be rugged (hardy to Zone 4, at least). Indeed, it has pulled through magnificently even without winter protection.

SUBSTITUTIONS/SIMILAR ROSES:
Any in the Morden Series.
'La Marne'
'Pink Rosette'

Another great, winter-hardy rose from the justly famous Canadian rose-breeding program. Like the others, it weathers Zone 3 winters and oppressive heat, and blooms profusely and constantly every summer.

Great clusters of vivacious blooms cover the plant—they're fully double, and rich scarlet underlain with a coral-orange glow.

With an upright, full habit, and plenty of disease-resistant dark green leaves, this is a good, strong plant that requires little care. It makes a splashy hedge, thanks to those fiery flowers. A plant or two, placed towards the back to accommodate its height, adds excitement to a summer flower border.

SUBSTITUTIONS/SIMILAR ROSES:
Any in the Morden Series.
'F.J. Grootendorst' (rugosa, red, larger plant)
'John Franklin' (red)
'Red Rascal' (smaller red flowers)

'Red Meidiland'™
MATURE PLANT HEIGHT: 4 ft.
BLOOM SIZE: 2½ in.
BLOOM TIME: all season
FRAGRANCE: none
YEAR INTRODUCED: 1983

'Simplicity'®
MATURE PLANT HEIGHT: 4 ft. to 5 ft.
BLOOM SIZE: 3 in.
BLOOM TIME: all season
FRAGRANCE: light and sweet
YEAR INTRODUCED: 1978

Bred by France's top rose house, Meilland, this rose is one of their finest, though their other roses are also very good (see below). The single form flowers are a fetching shade of dark red with a neat boss of golden stamens. The attractive bush is studded with clusters of these beauties all summer, and attractive orange-red hips follow in fall.

This is a very easy-going rose. Though its growth habit is dense and vigorous, it remains in bounds and doesn't require much pruning except for an occasional shaping. The foliage has proven to be mildew-free. And the plant prospers in Zones 4 to 9. It makes an excellent, striking hedge or barrier planting.

SUBSTITUTIONS/SIMILAR ROSES:
'Alba Meidiland'™ (white, double)
'Cherry Meidiland'™ (brighter, cherry-red flowers)
'Fire Meidiland'™ (deep red)
'Fuchsia Meidiland'™ (mauve)
'Ice Meidiland'™ (white)

The original in a series of superb hedge roses, pretty pink 'Simplicity' sets the standard. It is touted as "the best-selling rose of all time." Representing years of effort by the late, great, award-winning rose breeder Bill Warriner of Jackson & Perkins, it has proven immensely popular. (Other fine colors have followed—see below.) It offers exceptional resilience (it's grown on its own roots and faithfully returns after a cold winter), tough yet handsome foliage, and lavish clusters of appealing, full flowers that cover the plant and keep coming on, enthusiastically, all summer long. They waft a light, pleasing fragrance.

The intended, and best, use of 'Simplicity' and its kin is as a "living fence." Plant them in a long row below a porch, to outline a garden room or establish a border backdrop, or along a property line—and savor the easy, completely dependable, always-colorful show.

SUBSTITUTIONS/SIMILAR ROSES:
'La Marne'
'Old Blush'
'Purple Simplicity'® (stronger, spicier scent)
'Yellow Simplicity'®
'White Simplicity'®

'Starry Night'™

MATURE PLANT HEIGHT: 3 ft. to 6 ft.
BLOOM SIZE: 2 in. to 3 in.
BLOOM TIME: all season
FRAGRANCE: mild, sweet
YEAR INTRODUCED: 2002
AWARDS WON: AARS, 2002

An exceptional white hedge rose whose flowers don't yellow or turn brown on the bush! They're single form, with crisp texture, and carried in generous clusters; each blossom has a jaunty spray of golden stamens in the middle. The bush is literally draped in brightness all summer long—it's especially thrilling to come home at twilight to the sight of 'Starry Night' twinkling in your landscape.

The AARS judges were impressed with the plant's nonstop blooming, but also raved about its marvelous disease-resistance. All this adds up to an excellent plant, well worth planting where you want plenty of sparkle with minimal effort.

SUBSTITUTIONS/SIMILAR ROSES:
'Crystal Fairy' (double)
'Iceberg' (double)
'Katharina Zeimet' (3 to 4 feet)
'Sir Thomas Lipton' (6 to 8 feet)
'Wild Spice'

'The Fairy'

MATURE PLANT HEIGHT: 2 ft. to 3 ft.
BLOOM SIZE: 1½ in. to 2 in.
BLOOM TIME: midsummer, repeats
FRAGRANCE: none
YEAR INTRODUCED: 1932

Smaller and more compact that most other roses, 'The Fairy' forms a mound of about 3 feet tall and wide. So it fits very well in smaller garden spaces and tucks easily into mixed flower borders—many consider it the perfect perennial-garden rose. It's low-growing and spreading enough to even be used as a groundcover. It also makes a good show as an entryway plant, and it grows beautifully in a large container, such as a half whiskey barrel.

The flowers are small, plush with many petals, and an adorable shade of bright pink. They appear in clusters, so a plant in bloom billows with color! Because of its polyantha background, 'The Fairy' starts blooming a little later than other roses, but once it starts, it doesn't quit until the frosts of fall.

'The Fairy' is grown on its own roots, so it's winter-hardy and will return in glory every summer. It's hardier than many larger roses, surviving well into Zone 4.

SUBSTITUTIONS/SIMILAR ROSES:
There is a climbing version, and it is available as a tree rose as well.
'Caldwell Pink'
'Crystal Fairy' (white aging to soft pink)
'Lovely Fairy' (deep pink blooms, fruity scent)
'Fairy Queen' (ruby red blooms)

'Louise Odier'

MATURE PLANT HEIGHT: 4½ ft. to 5 ft.
BLOOM SIZE: 3 in.
BLOOM TIME: all summer
FRAGRANCE: strong, rich
YEAR INTRODUCED: 1851

'Mme Isaac Pereire'

MATURE PLANT HEIGHT: 5 ft.
BLOOM SIZE: 3½ in. to 4 in.
BLOOM TIME: midsummer, repeats
FRAGRANCE: strong, rich
YEAR INTRODUCED: 1881

Drenched in the most intoxicating, romantic perfume, this old favorite bourbon rose has fabulous, full-petaled flowers of dark, luscious pink—like a Victorian valentine.

The nearly thorn-free canes sometimes bow under the weight of the beautiful blossoms. That quality, coupled with the graceful, upright, vase-like shape (most other bourbons are large shrubs), lend the entire plant a pretty, fountain-of-blooms profile. Feature this old-fashioned classic in a spot with ample elbowroom so it can really show off.

Unlike some other vintage roses, 'Louise Odier' repeat-blooms well into autumn. The plant is vigorous and cold hardy to Zones 4 or 5. It's also disease resistant.

SUBSTITUTIONS/SIMILAR ROSES:
'Gertrude Jekyll'® (English)
'Hénri Martin'
'Mme Isaac Pereire'
'Paul Neyron'
'Rose de Rescht' (damask, 2½ to 3½ feet)

Time and again, fans of vintage roses rave that this Bourbon is "the most heavenly fragrant of all roses!" The aroma is indeed superb—fruity and intoxicating, like sun-warmed berry jam. Raspberry pink blooms, with just a sparkle of golden stamens emerging from their petal-dense form, are equally captivating. And they repeat-bloom until first frost.

This is a big, spreading, billowing bush, with plenty of moderately thorny branches. The leaves are plentiful, dark green, and disease-resistant. 'Mme Isaac Pereire' can also be trained as a climber. Whether shrub or climber, this big plant with its big personality is sure to become a showpiece in your garden.

SUBSTITUTIONS/SIMILAR ROSES:
'Gertrude Jekyll'® (English)
'Great Western' (bourbon)
'Louise Odier'
'Mme Ernest Calvat' (lavender sport of 'Mme Isaac Pereire')
'Paul Neyron'
'Reine des Violettes'

'Maiden's Blush'
MATURE PLANT HEIGHT: 5 ft. to 8 ft.
BLOOM SIZE: 3 in.
BLOOM TIME: once, in early summer
FRAGRANCE: moderate rose perfume
YEAR INTRODUCED: origin unknown, before 1550

The origins of this lovely French alba rose are lost in the mists of time, and even today it is not totally clear what the proper name should be . . . 'Maiden's Blush', 'Great Maiden's Blush', or the racy French name for it, 'Cuisse de Nymphe' ("nymph's thigh").

What is certain is that it is an especially lovely old-fashioned rose. The sweet, blush-pink petals are packed into the full blossom rather imperfectly, which gives it an air of spontaneity. Great clusters adorn a bush of handsome, sage-green foliage—a fetching sight that you'll cherish. As for the wonderful fragrance, it's rich, but not overpowering, sweet but not cloying.

It is also a tough plant. It weathers cold winters, tolerates shade better than most roses, and resists disease. Although it blooms but once a year, its charms are such that it is still a worthy addition to the garden.

SUBSTITUTIONS/SIMILAR ROSES:
'Baronne Prévost'
'Fantin-Latour' (centifolia)
'Geoff Hamilton' (English)
'Marchesa Boccella'
'Small Maiden's Blush' (smaller plant, smaller flowers)
'Souvenir de la Malmaison' (bourbon)

Rosa banksiae 'Lutea'
(Lady Banks' Rose)
MATURE PLANT HEIGHT: 20 ft., or more
BLOOM SIZE: 1½ in.
BLOOM TIME: once, in early summer
FRAGRANCE: mild, sweet
YEAR INTRODUCED: 1824

Not a rose for the faint-hearted, but easy and wonderful in the right spot. The lemon-yellow blossoms are tiny and plush and waft a delicate, sweet scent. They appear in such staggering abundance as to defy belief. (Allegedly someone once actually counted 50,000 blossoms on a single plant.) The annual show starts in late spring or early summer and continues for many weeks—an astounding sight.

As for the foliage, it is in scale with the small flowers and is green and shiny. It is evergreen in the South and deciduous in cooler areas. (This rose is not reliably winter-hardy north of Zone 7.)

This species also has the asset of being virtually thornless, with a naturally vertical growth habit that climbs eagerly. Old stems develop an appealing, exfoliating, cinnamon colored bark. To enjoy this glorious, carefree rose, give it room to roam. Let it cover an old dead tree or give it a sturdy garden shed to scramble up and over.

SUBSTITUTIONS/SIMILAR ROSES:
'Golden Showers' (bright yellow climber)
'Leverkusen'
'Mermaid'
Rosa banksiae var. *alba-plena* (stronger fragrance)
Rosa x *fortuniana* (white)

Rosa gallica 'Versicolor' ('Rosa Mundi')

MATURE PLANT HEIGHT: 3 ft. to 4 ft.
BLOOM SIZE: 3 in. to 3½ in.
BLOOM TIME: once, in early summer
FRAGRANCE: richly perfumed
YEAR INTRODUCED: 12th century (before 1581)

'Rose de Rescht'

MATURE PLANT HEIGHT: 2½ ft. to 3½ ft.
BLOOM SIZE: 3 in.
BLOOM TIME: midseason, repeats well
FRAGRANCE: rich perfume
YEAR INTRODUCED: 1940s

Perhaps the most famous of all old-fashioned roses, this striking rose enchants with its abundant display of peppermint-splashed blossoms. No two are alike; the background is nearly crimson and the markings are creamy white and pink. Bright yellow stamens adorn the centers. The fragrance is delicious.

Legend has it that this rose was named after Fair Rosamund, the mistress of King Henry II of England. The historical timing doesn't quite add up, but it's a romantic thought nonetheless.

This is a rather low-growing, compact bush, with some bristles but no thorns. As such, it's easy to add to a mixed border of other old-fashioned flowers; it also makes a fine hedge. It tolerates some shade, resists disease, and tolerates cold winters well.

SUBSTITUTIONS/SIMILAR ROSES:
'Ferdinand Pichard' (hybrid perpetual)
'Honorine de Brabant' (bourbon)
Rosa gallica 'Officinalis' (light crimson, 'Rosa Mundi' is a sport)

The exotic story behind this Portland rose is that an enterprising young woman explorer named Miss Nancy Lindsay found this rose during the 1940s in a garden in Persia, as Iran was then called, and brought cuttings home to England.

This is a fine rose for modern gardens, thanks to its compact size. The blossoms are unusual and quite beautiful—though small, they're packed with petals and sport a vibrant fuchsia-purple coloration. The ravishing fragrance has been likened to ripe currants. Tidy green foliage is edged in red on young leaves. Fall brings a nice display of distinctive, tubular hips.

SUBSTITUTIONS/SIMILAR ROSES:
'Ards Rover' (hybrid perpetual)
'Louise Odier' (bourbon)
'Mme Isaac Pereire' (bourbon)
'Rose de Roi' (red blushed with purple)

'Souvenir de la Malmaison'
MATURE PLANT HEIGHT: 2 ft. to 3 ft.
BLOOM SIZE: 5 in.
BLOOM TIME: once, in midsummer
FRAGRANCE: strong
YEAR INTRODUCED: 1843

'Tuscany Superb'
MATURE PLANT HEIGHT: 4 ft.
BLOOM SIZE: 3¹/₂ in. to 4 in.
BLOOM TIME: once, early summer
FRAGRANCE: intensely perfumed
YEAR INTRODUCED: 1848

This old-fashioned bourbon beauty maintains its small size, under 3 feet at maturity, so you can fit it in almost anywhere or even grow it in a pretty pot.

The spicily scented blossoms are a gorgeous baby pink, with numerous silky petals. The show starts later than other roses, when many might be entering a lull, and continues on and off till fall.

To reach its full magnificence, this old favorite prefers warm, sunny, dry weather.

SUBSTITUTIONS/SIMILAR ROSES:
There is a climbing version that reaches 6 to 8 feet.
'Clotilde Soupert' (polyantha, 3 to 4 feet)
'Fantin-Latour' (centifolia)
'Geoff Hamilton' (English)
'Red Souvenir de la Malmaison'
'Victorian Spice' (English style shrub)

Elegant, breathtaking! 'Tuscany Superb' wins your heart with its deep crimson blossoms, brushed with black, centered with golden stamens, and boasting a seductive, velvety texture. Their scent is powerful, like a fine red wine. Though it's a once-a-year show, it's well worth the wait. Try planting this gallica with early-flowering perennials so that it will take the stage as they fade.

This easy-going plant is not large, tolerates cold winters, and can take some shade in the garden, prospering where many other roses might not.

SUBSTITUTIONS/SIMILAR ROSES:
'Falstaff' (English)
'Rose de Rescht' (damask)
'The Prince' (English, blooms all season)

'Altissimo'

MATURE PLANT HEIGHT: 8 ft. to 12 ft.
BLOOM SIZE: 4 in. to 5 in.
BLOOM TIME: all season
FRAGRANCE: mild, sweet
YEAR INTRODUCED: 1966

The large, brilliant crimson flowers centered with golden stamens make quite an impact, unusual in that they are single, with five to seven petals each. They offer a stunning display, covering the plant along its full length, not just towards the top. The scent is enticingly sweet but not overpowering.

The lush, dark foliage forms a handsome backdrop and is also disease-resistant. As with all climbers, the canes need to be trained where you want them to go, and on 'Altimissimo' they are nice and pliable.

Show off this lavish bloomer on a pillar, clambering up a porch support, or trained against a wall trellis.

SUBSTITUTIONS/SIMILAR ROSES:
'Blaze' (semi-double)
'Don Juan' (double)
'Dortmund'
'Dynamite'™ (double)
'Stairway to Heaven' (double)

'America'™

MATURE PLANT HEIGHT: 9 ft. to 12 ft.
BLOOM SIZE: 3½ in. to 4½ in.
BLOOM TIME: midseason, repeats
FRAGRANCE: moderate, sweet scent
YEAR INTRODUCED: 1976
AWARDS WON: AARS, 1976

It's rare when the AARS judges bestow top honors on a climber, but to 'America', on the occasion of this nation's bicentennial, they did. And a grand rose it is! The big, full flowers are a warm shade of coral pink and waft a spicy fragrance. Blooming on both old and current-season stems, they make a great show on a large trellis, arbor, pergola, or rambling over a fence.

In addition the having beautiful flowers, the plant itself is top-quality. Plentiful, bright green, disease-resistant foliage covers 'America'. It grows vigorously and is winter-hardy in most areas. This climber is a real champion.

SUBSTITUTIONS/SIMILAR ROSES:
'Dream Weaver'™ (coral pink)
'Fortune's Double Yellow' (apricot yellow)
'Joseph's Coat' (red-yellow blend)
'Warm Welcome' (orange)

'Blaze'

MATURE PLANT HEIGHT: 10 ft. to 15 ft.
BLOOM SIZE: 2 in. to 3 in.
BLOOM TIME: all season
FRAGRANCE: mild, fruity
YEAR INTRODUCED: 1932

In bloom for practically the whole summer, 'Blaze' is hard to beat. The clusters of plush, cherry red flowers that adorn this popular climber, from top to bottom, open all at once. The effect is smashing—so much color!

It's a healthy, vigorous plant with easy-to-manipulate stems. Well-suited to adorning wooden fences or draping over stone walls, 'Blaze' is also a fine choice for backing a mixed flower border with season-long color.

SUBSTITUTIONS/SIMILAR ROSES:

'All Ablaze' (fuller flowers)

'Chevy Chase'

'Don Juan'

'Improved Blaze' (also called 'Blaze Improved', extra disease resistance)

'Nur Mahal' (8 feet)

'Stairway to Heaven'

'Will Scarlet' (10 to 12 feet)

'Don Juan'

MATURE PLANT HEIGHT: 12 ft. to 14 ft.
BLOOM SIZE: 4½ in. to 5 in.
BLOOM TIME: midseason, repeats
FRAGRANCE: intense perfume
YEAR INTRODUCED: 1958

The classic red climber 'Don Juan' has been justly popular for decades, with its velvety crimson blossoms and dark green, leathery, disease-resistant foliage. The flowers have a hybrid-tea form, some appearing singly and others in clusters. In full bloom 'Don Juan' is a truly sensational sight. This rose is also blessed with a heady, almost musky fragrance.

Gardeners in Zone 8 and south will find no finer red climber. Those further north need to give 'Don Juan' winter protection.

SUBSTITUTIONS/SIMILAR ROSES:

'Dublin Bay'

'Dynamite'™

'Stairway to Heaven'

'Thor'

'Dublin Bay'
MATURE PLANT HEIGHT: 8 ft. to 14 ft.
BLOOM SIZE: 4½ in.
BLOOM TIME: midseason, repeats
FRAGRANCE: moderate, spicy
YEAR INTRODUCED: 1975

'Fourth of July'
MATURE PLANT HEIGHT: 10 ft. to 14 ft.
BLOOM SIZE: 4½ in.
BLOOM TIME: all season
FRAGRANCE: strong sweet apple
YEAR INTRODUCED: 1999
AWARDS WON: AARS, 1999

Another wonderful large-flowered climber, this beauty bears its blooms in large, loose clusters. So a plant in full bloom is blanketed with flowers. They are deep, ruby red and double petaled. The effect is exuberant.

Growing vigorously but not rampantly, the stems have large, handsome, disease-resistant leaves and are sparsely thorned. They're easily trained on anything from a tall garden pillar to a trellis.

'Dublin Bay' is a particular favorite of gardeners in the damp Pacific Northwest because its buds and flowers continue to look great even after frequent rains.

SUBSTITUTIONS/SIMILAR ROSES:
'Dortmund' (single flowered)
'Don Juan'
'Stairway to Heaven'
'Thor'

Great sprays of large ruffled blooms, striped and splashed ruby red and bright white—plus a fresh-cut apple scent—there's no other climber like it. The flowers last a long time, on the plant and in a vase.

An excellent repeat-bloomer, 'Fourth of July' has sensational flowers all summer long (even the first year!). Bright green foliage and a tough nature add to its appeal. No wonder it was the first climber to win an AARS award in twenty-three years.

'Fourth of July' looks splendid mounting a pergola, arch, or trellis. If the support is painted white, to match the white petal markings, the show is even more dazzling.

SUBSTITUTIONS/SIMILAR ROSES:
Available as own-root (New Generation®).
'Dortmund' (red with white centers)
'Scentimental' (floribunda)

'Handel'

MATURE PLANT HEIGHT: 12 ft. to 15 ft.
BLOOM SIZE: 3¹/₂ in.
BLOOM TIME: midseason, repeats
FRAGRANCE: slight, fruity
YEAR INTRODUCED: 1965

'Joseph's Coat'

MATURE PLANT HEIGHT: 8 ft. to 10 ft.
BLOOM SIZE: 3 in. to 4 in.
BLOOM TIME: midseason, repeats
FRAGRANCE: mild fragrance
YEAR INTRODUCED: 1964
AWARDS WON: Bagatelle Gold Medal, 1964

Unique among climbers, the vivacious 'Handel' has practically bicolor blossoms. They're cream colored towards the interior and bright pink on the ruffled outer petal edges. The effect is flamboyant, especially when the plant is in its prime in midsummer and the blooms cover it from head to toe. This rose's fragrance is not strong, but on a warm afternoon, you'll find it is undeniably fruity. Glossy, medium olive-green leaves are sometimes susceptible to black spot.

A vigorous grower, 'Handel' is a fine choice for a substantial trellis or even a pergola or gazebo. If you garden in a cold climate, however, it's wise to site this somewhat tender climber in a sheltered location and/or remove it from its support and mulch it for the winter months.

SUBSTITUTIONS/SIMILAR ROSES:
'Berries 'n' Cream'
'Joseph's Coat'
'Shadow Dancer'

Distinctive! This old favorite has jazzy blooms in bright hues of orange, red, yellow and pink, sometimes all of these in one cluster, with a light, fruity scent.

Glossy, bright green foliage accompanies this lively show. It can be susceptible to mildew, but otherwise is quite tough and durable. The stems are thorny, so wear good gloves when training them.

If you have room for only one climbing rose and want a lot of "bang for your buck," 'Joseph's Coat' is ideal. It's also a dashing choice for a boundary or property-line planting. You can be sure that every garden visitor will exclaim over its bright and unique beauty.

SUBSTITUTIONS/SIMILAR ROSES:
'Handel' (pink-and-white bi-colored)
'Seven Sisters' (changes from cream to pink to purple)
'Warm Welcome' (orange with yellow centers)

'New Dawn'

MATURE PLANT HEIGHT: 12 ft. to 20 ft.
BLOOM SIZE: 3 in. to 3½ in.
BLOOM TIME: all season
FRAGRANCE: moderate, fruity
YEAR INTRODUCED: 1930

'Sombreuil'

MATURE PLANT HEIGHT: 12 ft. to 15 ft.
BLOOM SIZE: 3½ in. to 4 in.
BLOOM TIME: early to midseason, repeats
FRAGRANCE: rich perfume
YEAR INTRODUCED: 1850

A soft, almost silvery shade of pink, the fluffy, cupped blossoms gradually age to cream without losing their silky texture. And they're sweetly fragrant—the scent is reminiscent of ripe peaches. These appear in profusion along the entire length of this excellent climber's stems, creating a bountiful display.

Thanks to its long, pliable canes, this rose is easy to train, though look out for its plentiful, big thorns. It looks just beautiful on an arch, cascading over a tall fence, or draping a front porch railing. This was the first plant to receive a plant patent.

SUBSTITUTIONS/SIMILAR ROSES:
'Dr. W. Van Fleet' ('New Dawn' is sport)
'Pinkie' (8 to 12 feet)
'Social Climber'
'White Dawn'

Full, cupped and quartered blossoms laden with up to 100 creamy, vanilla-white petals adorn this vintage climber. The scent is potent and enticing, reminiscent of height-of-summer honeysuckle.

Unlike other old-fashioned roses, 'Sombreuil' does rebloom; there's a big show at the beginning of the season, and then reliable repeat for the rest of the summer. Nice mint-green, disease-resistant leaves provide cool contrast.

This climber is an inspired choice for a pillar or porch railing. It prospers in milder climates (Zone 7 and south).

SUBSTITUTIONS/SIMILAR ROSES:
'Alchymist'
'Felicite et Perpetue'
'Lace Cascade'
'Mme Alfred Carriere'
'White Dawn'

'William Baffin'

MATURE PLANT HEIGHT: 8 ft. to 12 ft.
BLOOM SIZE: 3 in. to 4 in.
BLOOM TIME: midseason, excellent repeat
FRAGRANCE: none
YEAR INTRODUCED: 1983

'Zepherine Drouhin'

MATURE PLANT HEIGHT: 8 ft. to 12 ft.
BLOOM SIZE: 3½ in. to 4 in.
BLOOM TIME: all season
FRAGRANCE: rich, old rose perfume
YEAR INTRODUCED: 1868

Easy, trouble-free, super-hardy, and gorgeous! The splashy blooms have bright, peppermint-pink petals with a dash of white in the centers. They're carried in incredible clusters of up to thirty flowers each. A bush in full bloom can stop traffic.

Exceptionally winter-hardy, 'William Baffin' is a prize for northern gardeners. But it also does well throughout the country. The usual rose diseases never seem to trouble it.

A vigorous grower, it will mount an arch, trellis, or fence and deliver abundant color for many years.

SUBSTITUTIONS/SIMILAR ROSES:
'American Pillar' (smaller, single-form blooms)
'Fourth of July' (red and white splashed)
'Handel' (cream with pink edging)

Beloved by gardeners all over the world, 'Zepherine Drouhin' endears in many ways. Unlike some old-fashioned roses, she repeat-blooms. And what blooms! They're plush with petals, raspberry pink, and laden with a powerful perfume.

Dark green leaves cover the plant well, providing a handsome contrast (in some areas, though, they are subject to black spot and mildew). The canes of this climber are also a real asset—not only are they flexible for easy training and burgundy-hued to add to the plant's beauty, but they are virtually thornless. 'Zepherine Drouhin' is a great bourbon climber for a high-traffic spot, such as draping over a porch or decorating an archway.

SUBSTITUTIONS/SIMILAR ROSES:
'American Beauty'
'High Society'
'Social Climber'
'Veilchenblau'

'Beauty Secret'
MATURE PLANT HEIGHT: 10 in. to 18 in.
BLOOM SIZE: 1½ in.
BLOOM TIME: midseason, repeats
FRAGRANCE: strong rose perfume
YEAR INTRODUCED: 1965
AWARDS WON: ARS Award of Excellence, 1975

'Cupcake'
MATURE PLANT HEIGHT: 12 in. to 16 in.
BLOOM SIZE: 1½ in.
BLOOM TIME: midseason, repeats well
FRAGRANCE: slight
YEAR INTRODUCED: 1981
AWARDS WON: ARS Award of Excellence, 1983

Among miniatures, this is a long-time favorite. It has proven itself to be a reliable bloomer and a tough little plant. It was recognized by the American Rose Society in 1975 with an "Award of Excellence," and continues to be very popular.

Its dark red blooms are not only laden with petals, they have the formal perfection of hybrid tea flowers—in miniature. And they're fragrant as well, wafting a sweet rosy perfume.

Owing to its small size and bright flowers, 'Beauty Secret' would be an outstanding candidate for a traditional perennial border planted with primary colors, either mixed in or as an edging. It also does very well on its own in a pot; expect a beautiful and dependable display all summer long on your deck or patio.

SUBSTITUTIONS/SIMILAR ROSES:
'Crackling Fire' (orange)
'Feisty' (2½ feet)
'Little Artist' (red with white centers)

Borne in small clusters, each dainty little bloom is a consistent, clear, fetching shade of pink. The petals are heavily textured, which means they are especially long lasting on the bush or when snipped for tiny bouquets.

Another nice feature of this particular mini is that its stems are nearly thornless. All the more reason to feature it right where everyone can admire its charms—in pretty pots on the deck or adorning the front steps. 'Cupcake' also makes a terrific addition to a mixed flowerbed with other pastel bloomers.

SUBSTITUTIONS/SIMILAR ROSES:
'Raspberry Punch' (dark pink)
'Winsome' (magenta)

'Gourmet Popcorn'

MATURE PLANT HEIGHT: 1½ ft. to 2 ft.
BLOOM SIZE: 1 in.
BLOOM TIME: all season
FRAGRANCE: strong rose perfume
YEAR INTRODUCED: 1986

'Hot Tamale'

MATURE PLANT HEIGHT: 18 in. to 2 ft.
BLOOM SIZE: 2 in.
BLOOM TIME: midseason, repeats well
FRAGRANCE: none
YEAR INTRODUCED: 1993
AWARDS WON: ARS Award of Excellence, 1994

Charming, small yellow buds pop open to little white blossoms—this miniature rose has a perfect name and lots of spunk! Because they are carried in clusters, the bush is covered in blooms for nearly the entire summer. A sweet, enticing fragrance adds to the appeal.

The plant itself has a round, bushy profile and dark green leaves that are disease resistant. Its small stature makes it ideal for growing in a pot or planter box. It would also be adorable in a mixed flowerbed with spiky purple perennials such as veronica or lavender.

SUBSTITUTIONS/SIMILAR ROSES:
'Crystal Fairy' (shrub, 3 feet tall)
'Green Ice' (8 to 16 inches tall)
'Iceberg' (shrub, 3 feet tall)
'Lindee'
'Snow Shower' (shrub/groundcover, 8 inches to 4 feet)
'White Pet'
'Yvonne Rabier'

Zesty and fun! Perfectly formed, full-petaled flowers open sunny yellow before changing to hot shades of orange, red, and bright pink. It's a color show you don't want to miss, so be sure to plant 'Hot Tamale' where you can admire it daily—in the front yard garden, edging a favorite sunny flower border, or even in pots on a deck or patio.

The upright, bushy plant is a fine stage for these bright blooms, and the dark green, glossy foliage is trouble free.

SUBSTITUTIONS/SIMILAR ROSES:
'Crackling Fire' (copper-orange)
'Rainbow's End' (red and yellow)
'Tropical Twist' (apricot-pink to coral)
'Year 2000' (yellow with red edging)

'Jean Kenneally'
MATURE PLANT HEIGHT: 1½ ft. to 2 ft.
BLOOM SIZE: 1½ in.
BLOOM TIME: midseason, repeats well
FRAGRANCE: soft, mild
YEAR INTRODUCED: 1984
AWARDS WON: ARS Award of Excellence, 1986

'Rainbow's End'
MATURE PLANT HEIGHT: 10 in. to 14 in.
BLOOM SIZE: 1½ in.
BLOOM TIME: midseason, repeats well
FRAGRANCE: none
YEAR INTRODUCED: 1984
AWARDS WON: ARS Award of Excellence, 1986

Unique among miniature roses, 'Jean Kenneally' has sweet, pretty apricot blossoms. They are "exhibition quality," which means that those who grow roses for show consider their form flawless. Indeed, they look like small hybrid tea flowers.

The blossoms are durable and long lasting. They are carried in clusters, which cover the small-sized bush. In a pot, this is a perfect little plant. In the ground, it may grow a bit taller and wider than its peers, with abundant flowers. Tuck some into a pastel-themed perennial border, where they will be a constant source of color.

SUBSTITUTIONS/SIMILAR ROSES:
'Child's Play' (white with pink edging)
'Cupcake' (pink)
'Water Lily'

Classic hybrid-tea-form blooms, in miniature, adorn this perky little plant. And they're gorgeous—a unique blend of strawberry red and buttery yellow. The plant itself is upright, nicely bushy, and well branched. The glossy leaves are attractive and disease-resistant.

This is a perfect mini to grow in pots (you can bring it indoors for the winter if you wish). Tucked into a flower border, it will dependably contribute bright, pretty color.

SUBSTITUTIONS/SIMILAR ROSES:
'Hot Tamale' (orange-red with yellow reverse, 2 feet)
'Tropical Twist' (apricot-pink to coral, 20 inches to 2 feet)
'Year 2000' (yellow with red edging)

'Sun Sprinkles'

MATURE PLANT HEIGHT: 2 ft.
BLOOM SIZE: 2 in.
BLOOM TIME: all season
FRAGRANCE: none
YEAR INTRODUCED: 2001
AWARDS WON: AARS, 2001

'Winsome'

MATURE PLANT HEIGHT: 16 in. to 22 in.
BLOOM SIZE: 2 in.
BLOOM TIME: midseason, repeats
FRAGRANCE: none
YEAR INTRODUCED: 1984
AWARDS WON: ARS Award of Excellence, 1985

Splashy, sunny little yellow flowers cover a compact, rounded bush. They open exuberantly to display lots of petals, which adds to their impact. Best of all, they repeat-bloom all summer long, delivering continuous color you can count on.

'Sun Sprinkles' is the right size for pots, and would be a bright addition to deck or terrace displays with other sun-lovers, including herbs. A row or ribbon of plants can be planted as an edging, or to line a driveway or walkway.

SUBSTITUTIONS/SIMILAR ROSES:
Also available as GardenEase®.
'Lemon Zest' (shrub, 3^1/$_2$ feet)
'Rise 'n' Shine'
'Sun Runner' (groundcover, 1^1/$_2$ to 3 feet, fewer petals)
'Yellow Jacket' (shrub)

In a color not often seen in roses, including miniatures, 'Winsome' delivers big, pointed buds that unfurl to elegant magenta (almost red) blossoms that are a little bigger than its peers. This is a prolific plant, too, with a show that lasts throughout the summer.

The plant is quite bushy, has excellent disease-resistance, and grows vigorously. So this is a good mini for growing in the ground rather than in a container. Its good health and sweetheart blooms would be a welcome addition to a mixed flower border or cutting garden.

SUBSTITUTIONS/SIMILAR ROSES:
'China Doll' (shrub, dark pink)
'Raspberry Punch' (dark pink, 2 feet)
'Sweet Chariot'
'Wild Plum' (lavender, 30 inches)

'Baby Blanket'

MATURE PLANT HEIGHT: 3 ft.
BLOOM SIZE: 3 in.
BLOOM TIME: all season
FRAGRANCE: mild, sweet
YEAR INTRODUCED: 1991

One of the first groundcover roses, and still one of the best. Sweet little pink buds unfurl to small but beautifully formed shell-pink blossoms. Though they may look delicate, they are naturally tough and resilient—they hold up well in summer heat, and repeat-bloom all summer long.

The knee-deep mounds of handsome dark green foliage are vigorous, disease-resistant, and tough. 'Baby Blanket' is an inspired choice for any spot you'd like to blanket with pretty, season-long color.

SUBSTITUTIONS/SIMILAR ROSES:
Also available as a tree rose.
'Bonica'™ (shrub)
'Lovely Fairy' (shrub, dark pink)
'The Fairy' (shrub)

'Electric Blanket'

MATURE PLANT HEIGHT: 1 ft. to 2 ft.
BLOOM SIZE: 2 in. to 3 in.
BLOOM TIME: all season
FRAGRANCE: light, fresh
YEAR INTRODUCED: 2002
AWARDS WON: German Rose Society's top award (ADR)

Hot pink! As if the attention-grabbing color weren't enough, these splendid little flowers are loaded with petals. Great clusters of them decorate this superior new bush. Since it's not as high or spreading as some other groundcover roses, it's a fine choice for smaller gardens and smaller spaces.

'Electric Blanket' was honored by the German Rose Society when it proved, in rigorous trials, its wide adaptability and its valuable ability to resist black spot and other diseases.

SUBSTITUTIONS/SIMILAR ROSES:
Also available as a tree rose.
'China Doll' (shrub)
'Flower Carpet Pink'™
'Foxy Pavement'
'Watermelon Ice' (shrub, lavender pink)

'Footloose'

MATURE PLANT HEIGHT: 3 ft.
BLOOM SIZE: 2½ in.
BLOOM TIME: all season
FRAGRANCE: light and fruity
YEAR INTRODUCED: 1999

'Magic Blanket'

MATURE PLANT HEIGHT: 3 ft.
BLOOM SIZE: 2 in.
BLOOM TIME: all season
FRAGRANCE: light and sweet
YEAR INTRODUCED: 2000

This relative newcomer to the groundcover rose class is a vivacious bright pink. Their small blossoms have lovely ruffled edges. They seem all the more abundant because they are produced in clusters. A light, strawberry-sweet scent radiates from them, charming all who come near.

'Footloose' is a tidy little mounding bush, about as wide as tall. Plant close together to create a mass of lively color. Excellent for beds, edgings, curb-strips, banks—wherever you need season-long, low-care color.

SUBSTITUTIONS/SIMILAR ROSES:
'Flower Carpet Pink'™
'Lovely Fairy' (shrub)
'Scarlet Pavement'

Low growing, with a generous spreading habit (a single plant can grow 6 feet wide!). The creamy white flowers that blanket it are adorable: plump little buds open to fluffy, crisp-white, open blooms. They keep coming all summer, for a generous but carefree show you can count on. 'Magic Blanket' revitalizes any landscape.

SUBSTITUTIONS/SIMILAR ROSES:
Also available as a tree rose.
'Flower Carpet White'™
'Gourmet Popcorn'
'Guinevere' (shrub, English style, soft pink to cream)
'Iceberg' (shrub)
'Snow Pavement'
'Snow Shower' (white, 8 inches to 4 feet)

'Red Ribbons'
MATURE PLANT HEIGHT: 2½ ft.
BLOOM SIZE: 3 in. to 3½ in.
BLOOM TIME: all season
FRAGRANCE: light and sweet
YEAR INTRODUCED: 1990

Plush little cherry-red blossoms, carried in generous clusters, adorn this excellent ground-cover rose all summer long. They're displayed against an attractive backdrop of glossy, dark green leaves.

The plant's habit is nicely symmetrical and naturally mounding, making it an ideal choice for filling a bed or broad area.

SUBSTITUTIONS/SIMILAR ROSES:
Also available as a tree rose.
'Champlain' (shrub, 3 feet)
'Fairy Queen' (shrub, 3 feet)
'Flower Carpet Red'™
'Red Rascal' (shrub, 4 feet)

'Sun Runner'
MATURE PLANT HEIGHT: 1½ ft.
BLOOM SIZE: 1½ in.
BLOOM TIME: all season
FRAGRANCE: light, citrusy
YEAR INTRODUCED: 1998

Bred in Holland, this is a welcome groundcover rose addition—a bright yellow bloomer! A dense, low-growing plant of semi-glossy green leaves produces cheery little single-form flowers continuously. The soft, lemony-sweet scent is a wonderful plus.

'Sun Runner' would be ideal for flanking a walkway to greet visitors, or covering a sunny embankment. Since it is vigorous and fast growing, it will fill in quickly whatever spot you choose.

SUBSTITUTIONS/SIMILAR ROSES:
'Magic Blanket' (creamy white, 3 feet)
'Yellow Jacket' (shrub, 2½ feet)

GROWING ROSES IN THE SOUTHWEST

Bruce and Sharon Asakawa

Introduction

Roses are ubiquitous. There is never a time when the sun isn't shining on roses somewhere in the world. As the sun glides from east to west, its rays continually bathe buds of the world's most popular flower, the rose. Over 100 species of roses and thousands of hybrids can be found flourishing in the wild, in botanical gardens, and in home landscapes.

Rose gardening styles and climatic conditions in America's Southwest can be as varied as the number of varieties available for planting. From Montezuma, New Mexico, east of the Sangre de Cristo Mountains and the hot, dry, and windy climes around Truth or Consequences in the Rio Grande Valley, to the Snowbird retreats of Sedona, and Carefree, Arizona, and Palm Springs and San Diego, California, roses can be found adorning all neighborhoods.

Although they can be found on just about every continent, there is one location in the lower reaches of California's San Joaquin Valley that can be called the "Rose Growing

Capital of the World." Towns with names like Visalia, Wasco, Reedley, del Rey, and Shafter dot the region in the San Joaquin Valley. The rose ranches and research facilities of the area produce millions of roses, on hundreds of acres.

During the winter, in Visalia you can look to the east and see the magnificent snow-capped Sierra Nevada. The ancient Kern River once flowed from these mountains into the San Joaquin Valley between Bakersfield and Oildale. Its flow transported rich soil down to the valley floor and as the water slowed the soil settled, creating an immense alluvial fan. Looking south you can see the rain-shadow side of Southern California's transverse mountain ranges. Turn to the west and you can see the eastern side of California's coastal range. These mountains block the ocean breezes originating along California's central coast. All of these factors have created the perfect area to grow roses and this region is home to millions of roses that eventually find their way into rose gardens around the world.

Weather

Rose gardeners have a love-hate relationship with the weather. Most years the seasons are as they should be, crisp and clear in the spring and fall, warm in the summer, and cold and rainy in the winter. When normalcy prevails, spring and summer are the seasons in which roses, as with most plants, need the most water. Throughout the Southwest region you can find just about every growing zone listed by the USDA and just about every microclimate a plant might experience. The Southwest region is an oasis. We live here and

enjoy our roses by virtue of the water, which in most cases travels hundreds of miles.

There are two events that create obstacles to producing perfect roses. The first event occurs when the Southwest experiences an El Niño, a phenomena that produce exceptionally wet or exceptionally dry weather. When the effect is exceptionally wet and temperatures are mild, roses tend not to go dormant. During an El Niño event, the average winter daytime temperatures can hover around an unseasonably warm 60° to 70° F. If this weather pattern occurs roses don't enter dormancy, so in late December, strip the foliage, winter prune, and spray for diseases and insects. The warm winters will also initiate early growth and early blooming. If this occurs, the first organic rose food application should be in mid-January and distributed in a band along the inside edge of the berm that makes the watering basin. Mulching the soil surface with compost or humus mulch should occur in mid-January.

When an El Niño occurs, anomalies in the weather patterns become fearsome, rainfall becomes either torrential or non-existent, and temperatures are sustained above or below their averages. Southern California's Sonoran Desert, and the "four corners" states of Utah, Colorado, New Mexico, and Arizona are all affected by El Niño. New Mexico's San Juan, Chama, and Rio Grande valleys can be at flood levels during an El Niño. Keep an eye on the weather and the rain gauge and adjust your watering routine accordingly.

The second event occurs in the late summer or early fall, when high-pressure cells build up over the Nevada Mountains and Utah's Great Basin. The pressure differential with the air mass over Southern California generates the "foehn phenomenon," otherwise known as the Santa Ana winds. These are hot, dry, fast moving, northeasterly winds that desiccate all that is in their path. Fortunately the phenomenon is predictable, so roses can be irrigated and protected prior to the event.

Nevada's Mojave Desert has dry, hot weather for near-perfect roses, if sufficient water is provided. Southwestern Arizona's summer monsoon season creates a hot and humid weather pattern as warm, moisture-laden air drifts northward from Mexico, causing flash floods and soil saturation.

Along the Pacific coast, in normal years, Saint Patrick's Day is used as a marker for the last frost day. The further inland your garden is, the further into the year the last frost day moves. In the mountain resorts east of Salt Lake and on either side of the continental divide, the rose growing season is from April to August. Of course when there is an El Niño predicted, all bets are off. Increased rainfall super-saturates the soil, pathogens flourish, and root systems are destroyed. Drought will stress your rose plants, but can be mitigated by frequent watering and mulching. After the winter effects of El Niño subside, and if your roses have survived, there is a rapid flush of new growth indicating spring has arrived.

Designing for Remarkable Roses

It is easy to become overwhelmed by the thousand of roses available for your garden.

Consider the following design criteria to lighten the selection load and to enhance your landscape.

- Solicit lists of recommended roses from your local American Rose Society chapter, your University of California Cooperative Extension advisor's office, or your local garden center.

- Design your rose garden on scaled graph paper. ($1/8$-inch or $1/4$-inch grid). The paper is available at any art supply or blueprint company.

- Some types of roses (hybrid teas in particular) are easiest to maintain when they can be irrigated, pruned, sprayed, fertilized, and deadheaded in a dedicated area.

- Flower beds of roses, annuals, perennials, and shrubs can present a challenge because of the varied maintenance requirements. Choose your rose companion plants carefully and select those that require similar growing conditions.

- Pastel colors recede and can give the illusion of depth when located near an observer.

- Bright colors advance and can give the illusion of proximity when located at a distance.

- Coarse textured foliage creates the illusion of increased nearness.

- Fine textured foliage creates the illusion of increased distance.

- Design your garden with the taller growing roses on the north side of the garden and the lowest growing roses on

the south side. This pattern will provide the most sun exposure as the sun moves from east to west.

- From tallest to shortest the following groups of roses are most available: climbers, grandifloras, hybrid teas, floribundas, polyanthas, shrub, and miniatures.

Rosy Locations

Ideal growing locations in your Southwestern garden should provide sunny springs and summers, cool winters, a plentiful supply of water and nutrients, and rich sandy loam soil. Meeting these conditions will put your roses on the path to becoming a neighborhood showcase. Roses need full sun, at least six hours a day, but some protection from ultra-hot afternoon sun is a good idea. A location that receives a slight breeze will reduce humidity and help keep some diseases and pests under control. Cold weather during fall, winter, and spring seasons will enable your roses to enter and sustain dormancy from late October to late February. But there is a caveat to growing roses where it is cold. If it becomes extremely cold for an extended period of time, damage can occur in the bud or graft union. The bud union should be protected from extreme cold until spring with soil, straw, compost, humus, mulch, or wrapping. The winter protection should be removed when new buds begin to grow.

Rose Soils

Soils are the source of life for your rose plants. Bacteria, fungi, algae, mosses, insects, and critters, both beneficial and pathogenic, share the soil in your rose root zone. Ideal soils for rose gardens are alive and teaming with billions of microorganisms, including bacteria which help complete the nitrogen cycle, making nitrates, the main source of nitrogen, available to your roses. Mycorrhizal fungi, both endotropic (found in a plant's root system) and ectotropic (found on a plant's root system), have a symbiotic relationship with their host rose plants. The fungi, increase by many-fold the rose's ability to absorb water and nutrients and in return the host rose plant provides sustenance to the fungi by manufacturing carbohydrates through the process of photosynthesis. (Note that soils that have had synthetic fertilizers or herbicides applied to them have shown a marked decrease in the mycorrhiza population.) When a rose is being transplanted from one location to another it is imperative that soil, with its beneficial fungi, be moved with the rose from the rose's original location to the new location. If moving the original soil is impractical, using soil amendments with mycorrhizal fungi added will help. In the natural course of becoming established, beneficial microorganisms will re-establish themselves.

Soil texture is defined by the United States Department of Agriculture (USDA) as percentages of silt, sand, and clay. If you just remember that a sandy loam soil is 60 percent sand, 30 percent silt, and 10 percent clay, it will serve as a benchmark for all other soils. In addition to the silt, sand, and clay, 20 to 30 percent of the soil volume should be organic material. The organics will retain moisture, aerate and acidify the soil, and provide fodder for the microorganisms. The organic component can be compost, worm castings, humus mulch, peat moss, or other soil amendments that improve the tilth of your soil.

Soil pH for roses grown in the Southwest should be slightly acidic, in the range of 6 to 6.5 (on a scale of 1 to 14, where 1 is extremely acidic and 14 is extremely alkaline). Many soils that are naturally acidic are derived from decomposing granite. Clay soil derived from sedimentary rock is generally more alkaline and registers higher pH levels. The most important reason for monitoring your soil pH is nutrient availability. If the pH level rises to 8 the availability of nitrates, potassium, iron, zinc, and manganese is negligible. Have your soil tested by an Extension Service office if you suspect your soil is causing a problem with your roses, or have it tested before you install your garden so that you can amend it properly. Many Southwest soils are more alkaline than roses like. Methods to acidify your rose garden soil include:

- Watering to leach out accumulated salts.
- Increasing the organic content.
- Increasing the microorganism activity in the soil.
- Increasing the soil porosity by double digging.
- Applying soil sulfur to lower the pH of a clay soil from 8.0 to 6.5. Begin by applying and blending, to a depth of 8 to 12 inches, soil sulfur at a rate of 46 pounds per 1,000 square feet. Deeply water the soil twice a week, then retest the pH after thirty days.
- Applying gypsum or calcium chloride as per the manufacturers instructions.

Rose Watering

The majority of the plants used in our landscapes, including roses, are dependent on imported water. The natural aquifers in Southern California have never provided sufficient water to meet the expanding demand so it must be brought in from other areas. Unfortunately, although Southern California has access to a bounty of seawater, desalinization is too costly and roses have a low tolerance for saline irrigation water. Adding organic material and active beneficial

Rosa 'Gloire des Rosomanes'

microorganisms to your soil, and occasional deep, thorough watering with non-saline water will mitigate this if you are in a situation in which seawater is being used for irrigation.

Water that flows into Southern California via aqueducts traverses hundreds of miles through valleys, across deserts, and over mountains. One major consequence of moving water across such long distances, is that soluble salts and minerals collect, and become part of the water's chemistry. After irrigating with typical tap water, these dissolved solids remain on the surface of the soil as the water evaporates. For our roses this process can be devastating since this raises the pH of the soil.

In Southern California the water that is used to irrigate roses has registered about 1,000 parts per million (ppm) of total dissolved solids (tds) and a pH of 7.6 to 8.0. This level of tds is so critical that after frequently irrigating our roses, a gray-white crust will form over the soil. These are salts and minerals that have come out of solution, making the soil more alkaline. Garden products that will re-dissolve and leach the salts and minerals, flocculate the soil, and lower the soil pH are available at your local garden center.

Maintaining the moisture content of the soil around your roses is imperative. The ideal moisture level is called "field capacity." This is the condition when all the soil particles are wet, and gravity has moved the water down and through the root zone. You should never let the moisture level decrease to the point where a rose's foliage wilts. Some plants will not survive beyond the wilt point, so water your roses in anticipation of adverse conditions. One of the most frequently asked question about roses is, "In the Southwest, how much and how often should I water my roses?" The simple answer is, "...enough to maintain field capacity."

You can perform your own test to see how well water travels through your soil, called "percolation." Dig a hole 18 inches deep by 18 inches wide, fill it with water once, allow the water to percolate completely through, and then fill it again. This second filling should drain at a rate of 1 inch per hour. In other words, in just under a day the water should have percolated completely. The irrigation frequency should be every second or third day, wetting the soil to a depth of 8 to 12 inches and out as far as the drip line of the plant.

Southern Californians have a unique tool because the City of San Diego's Water Resources Management Program developed an online water calculator. Enter the site at www.sannet.gov, click "departments," click "more," click "water," click "landscape water calculator," click "calculate." Complete the questionnaire and the resulting feedback will suggest a watering schedule for each zone in your landscape. This service is available for all zip codes serviced by the Southern California Metropolitan Water District.

Rose Foods

When you stand in front of 50 feet of shelving loaded with over 100 choices of what to feed your roses, logic should take over and you should tell yourself, choose the one that reads "Rose Food." That narrows it to organic, inorganic, liquid, granular, spikes, tablets, timed released, water soluble, mixed, or prilled. There are sixteen essential elements required for plant growth (H, O, C, N, P, K, S, Ca, Mg, Fe, Zn, Cu, Mn, Mo, Bo, Cl). For the purpose of maintaining beautiful roses we suggest using a granular or liquid organic rose food. Your local garden center carries pre-mixed granular organic rose foods, with 4 percent nitrogen, 6 percent phosphorus, 2 percent potassium (derived from bone, alfalfa, blood, kelp, and feather meals, sunflower hull ash, and dried poultry waste) or a liquid organic plant food, with 12 percent nitrogen, 12 percent phosphorus, and 6 percent potassium. The first application should be made just after the start of growth in the late winter or early spring. Continue applications once a month until the last feeding in August, which should always include potassium for winter hardening off.

Rose Pruning

Roses evolved with beautiful, fragrant flowers to attract pollinators, and thorns to keep foraging animals at bay. If left to their own devices most roses would grow denser and denser as the seasons moved forward. Older branches would become less and less viable and soon flowering would diminish, branches senesce, and new growth become minimal. Pruning balances the plant's structure, opens the canopy, increases flowering, and rejuvenates growth.

Here are a few simple pruning guidelines:

- Head-back the canopy of most roses, before "bud break" in the spring.
- Remove suckers, and dead, diseased, weak, twiggy, and interfering wood.
- Remove wood that is three years or older, leaving four to six healthy canes.
- Remove the lateral branches, opening the center of the plant to sunlight.
- Prune at a downward 45-degree angle, just above a bud that is facing away from the plant's center axis.
- Seal the pruning wounds with pruning paint, or Elmer's glue, if diseases and insects are present.
- Disinfect pruning equipment with Physan if fire blight is present.

Clean up and discard debris from the pruning then apply 2 to 3 inches of mulch over the watering basin.

TASK LIST
for Southwestern Rose Gardeners

Before you read the following task list, take a deep breath, count to ten, and smell the roses. The perfect rose is a rose that you don't have to fret over, but one you just enjoy. Remember, KISS your rose garden, aka: Keep It Simple Seasonally.

An **important note**, when using pesticides, **the label is the law** (read, understand, and follow the label instructions).

Spring

- Plant bareroot roses in the early spring. (Beware that if the bareroot roses have leafed out, a successful planting is questionable.)

- Keep a rose diary. Seasonal events in your rose garden are repetitive. Anticipating changes in your rose garden will save time and effort.

- Prune back your roses approximately five weeks before entering your prize roses at your local rose show.

- Select own-root rose plants if they are available, ensuring sturdy roots and strong growth on most varieties.

- Apply 2 inches of mulch on the ground from the root flare to the drip line. This organic blanket will stabilize soil temperature and soil moisture.

- Monthly apply a complete organic rose and flower food around the inside perimeter of the watering basin.

- Apply a liquid or granular flocculent to the watering basin. This material will loosen the soil, permit better percolation, and help leach salts from the soil.

- Control insect pests by releasing big-eyed bugs, lady beetles, and lacewings. Enlisting natural controls will benefit your entire garden.

- Check the soil pH. Adjusting the soil pH to 6.0 to 6.5 will ensure optimum nutrient availability for your rose plants.

- Control powdery mildew by washing off the foliage, early in the morning, with a strong stream of water. Anti-transpirants also work well to control powdery mildew.

- Remove spent flowers and hips (weekly).

Summer

- Apply monthly, a complete organic rose and flower food around the inside perimeter of the watering basin.

- Remove spent flowers and hips (weekly).

- Control **aphids** by releasing beneficial, voracious predators, such as lady beetles, or wash them off with a strong stream of water and keep ants at bay.

- Control **greenhouse whitefly** by releasing *Encarsia formosa* wasps in the rose garden.

- Control **thrips** by releasing green lacewings and predatory mites. The best time of the day to release is early in the morning.

- Control **caterpillars** by applying *Bacillus thuringiensis* (Bt). Repeated applications are necessary, especially if it rains.

'Blaze'

- Control **two-spotted mites** by releasing predatory mites. They will also control fungus gnats and small thrips
- Control **earwigs** by wetting and rolling up the Sunday newspaper and placing it under your roses—they will move into the cool, humid environment; pick up the roll and discard it.
- Control **brown garden snails** and **slugs** with non-toxic, iron phosphate or predacious decollate snails (where allowed).
- Control **weeds** by top mulching, hand removal, or spot applications of the herbicide glyphosate.
- Control **rust** by avoiding overhead watering and dispose of infected foliage and twigs, applying an anti-transpirant every other week, or spraying with a horticultural oil.
- Control **powdery mildew** by washing the foliage off early in the morning, by maintaining good air circulation, and applying an anti-transpirant.
- Control **black spot** by removing fallen leaves, pruning out diseased twigs, and avoiding wetting the foliage.
- Control the big three rose diseases of rust, powdery mildew, and black spot by applying Triforene.

Autumn

- Remove spent flowers and hips (weekly).
- Decrease the amount and frequency of watering, but maintain "field capacity."
- Check the soil pH.

- Apply a liquid or granular flocculant to the watering basin. This material will loosen the soil, permit better percolation, and help leach salts from the soil.
- Withhold fertilization until early spring except for an application of potassium to help winterize your roses.
- Harvest rose stems for cuttings.
- Collect and prepare hips and seeds for germinating.

Winter

- Rebuild watering basins for your rose plants. The berm that forms the basin should be 4 to 6 inches in height and have a diameter equal to the drip line of the rose plant. The soil surface in the basin should pitch away from the root flare not toward it.
- Remove any old foliage and prune back your rose plants if the weather hasn't triggered dormancy (early January).
- Apply a granular pre-emergent weed control.
- Select additional own-root roses to add to your garden.
- Apply dormant spray, such as a horticultural oil, if insects and diseases were prevalent during the growing season.

ROSE SELECTIONS
for the Southwest

'Fame'

"...our powers, our desires, our food, are really necessary for our existence...But the rose is an extra. Its smell and its colour are an embellishment of life, not a condition of it." (Arthur Conan Doyle, *Memoirs of Sherlock Holmes*, "Adventure X: The Naval Treaty," 1894). Detective extraordinaire Sherlock Holmes realized that the queen of flowers was no "elementary" example of life. Roses enhance our abilities to see, smell, and touch so that it is almost impossible to pass one by without looking, sniffing, and touching.

The first thing most people do when they pass a rosebush is to bend over, cup the blossom in hand, and inhale its fragrance, and if its perfume matches its beauty, the combi-

nation is unforgettable. To encourage the hybridization of more fragrant roses, Dr. James A. Gamble established the James Alexander Gamble Fragrance Medal under the auspices of the American Rose Society with the stipulation that the selection must also have an ARS rating of at least 7.5 on a 1 to 10 scale. Since the first award in 1961, only eleven roses have received this medal, and nine of the eleven have been hybrid teas. Among them are two of our favorite hybrid teas, 'Fragrant Cloud' and 'Double Delight'™.

'Fragrant Cloud' was the 1968 Jackson & Perkins Rose of the Year and the 1970 Gamble Fragrance Medal winner. It not only possesses a magnificent color of vibrant coral-red blossoms offset by dark green leaves, but it also delivers a powerful, sweet honey perfume that scents an entire room. Since my (Sharon's) late mother's favorite coral rose was 'Fragrant Cloud', we planted one amidst our other roses in her memory and are delighted that it blooms so vigorously during the hottest days of summer. It flourishes in drier inland areas and does well under hot, humid conditions, but along the coastal or cooler, humid areas of California, Colorado, Nevada, New Mexico, and Utah, there may be problems with mildew or black spot, a small price to pay because it develops the deepest color under cool conditions.

An AARS winner in 1977, **'Double Delight'**™ became the highest rated (8.6) Gamble champion in 1986. It is the most popular new rose of the last twenty-five years, not only a delight to behold with its huge 5-inch creamy-white flowers edged in strawberry-red, but doubly delightful because one's nose can detect its heady, spicy rose perfume 10 feet away. When Bruce and I owned our own retail garden center, we always set aside one 'Double Delight'™ during bareroot season, but before we could plant it, our entire supply would quickly sell out and we would relinquish our one remaining specimen to a pleading customer. We finally planted a treasured 'Double Delight'™ two years ago, purchased from another retail nursery, because we no longer have a retail business. As in most areas of the Southwest, our 'Double Delight'™ is eager to please, but we find that it shows off the best color and flower size when the days are warm and the nights are cool. Even without its spicy aroma, the beauty of its urn-shaped form, striking bi-colored flowers, and disease-resistant glossy green leaves make 'Double Delight'™ a centerfold that has finally taken its rightful place in our garden.

While many hybrid teas are fragrant, our favorite yellow hybrid tea is not known for its perfume. 'St. Patrick'™ is a slow-opening yellow rose that takes the heat. Its brightly colored flowers are offset by more subtle, grey-green leaves. Normally a true, clear yellow, this 1996 AARS leprechaun can pick up a bit of gold in cool weather, but when the thermometer registers hot, hot, hot in our neighborhood, it produces loads of chartreuse-tinted buds that open to golden-yellow, perfectly formed, fully double flowers with amazing holding power on the plant and as a cut flower. Perhaps the luck of the Irish is the reason for its longevity, because they have lasted as long as two to three weeks in a vase for us.

Dr. Keith Zary, vice president of research for Jackson & Perkins, is one of the world's top rose breeders and it is no accident that under the Jackson & Perkins flagship, he has hybridized seven AARS winners since 1997. Of his prize-winning blooms, 'Gemini'™ is one of his favorites and it has become one of ours too. Named for the twin sign of the zodiac, it is a showy hybrid tea with rich cream flowers edged in coral pink. Best of all, its coral tones intensify, becoming even more beautiful with age. From the moment we planted 'Gemini'™, this two-toned beauty with a light fragrance and dark green, slightly glossy foliage has made herself right at home in our mild-weather garden. We intend for our no-fuss zodiac twin to stay for a long, long time.

Floribundas have a special place in our hearts because true to their designation, they bloom abundantly in upright trusses or sprays of high-centered hybrid tea style flowers on vigorous 3- to 5-foot low-growing plants. 'Angel Face' is a prime example of something old, becoming new again. No one knows why it took thirty-three years before this deliciously perfumed 1969 AARS champion was awarded the Gamble tribute for fragrance in 2001. Perhaps its looks so captivated rosarians that its intense fruity fragrance was considered secondary. Against a backdrop of coppery green leaves, gorgeous buds with petals painted in deep mauve-lavender tones open slowly to reveal fully double, ruffled $3^1/2$- to 4-inch flowers fringed in rich, ruby blushes. Since 'Angel Face' flowers close to the ground, we use it as a colorful border plant and consider it a gift from the angels that this perfect rose also releases a strong, old-fashioned citrus perfume.

Although the 2003 AARS winner, **'Hot Cocoa'**™ is a newcomer to floribunda collectors, we added it to our garden because it displays one of the most mysterious and unique colors among roses. The silk-like blooms have petals that are chocolate-orange with soft, smoky overtones and a rusty orange on the reverse. Depending on the weather, sometimes a purplish haze casts its spell over the blossoms and the color intensity may morph into a dark red. Since it is one of the New Generation Roses® that grows on its own roots, 'Hot Cocoa'™ is more resilient and comes back true to type, even after a harsh winter. The fabulous color of this ruffled,

'Gemini'

moderately fruity-scented flower, combined with its vigor and natural disease-resistance, has proudly earned its place among our other roses. We have the added benefit of a chocolate rose without the calories or cavities.

Often described as the electric lights of the garden, **'Iceberg'** is a rugged floribunda with cool white blooms that open to large double roses. Tough, vigorous and prolific, 'Iceberg' will bloom its heart out all summer long. One of our best landscape roses, with dark green foliage and a mild, honey perfume, its beauty is even more astonishing when planted en masse.

To add color among the mass of white 'Iceberg' roses, we selected another floribunda, **'Purple Tiger'**. Appearing on a hardy, upright plant with matte green foliage, 'Purple Tiger' provides a stunning contrast with bold plum stripes dramatically intermixed with white and pink stripes. Its delicate currant fragrance fills the air with perfume, while providing an eyeful of wild purple among our more sedately colored flowers.

'Queen Elizabeth' was crowned the 1955 AARS grandiflora monarch and it has been a long-time favorite among our roses because of its rich, translucent pink color that becomes a paler blush at the edges. As it matures, candelabras of flowers cover the plant. Grown on its own roots, this rose's elegant beauty and ability to overcome some of the most challenging growing conditions, such as alkaline or poor soil and extremes of heat and cold, make it an ideal choice for the beginning gardener. We have given this monarch plenty of room to expand her realm and she now stands about 6 feet tall, but she can also be pruned back to a more manageable-sized kingdom.

Although grandiflora roses are the offspring of hybrid teas and floribundas, they are taller than either of their parents and have double flower forms of thirty-five to forty petals. Dr. Keith Zary introduced a grandiflora that became a 1998 AARS winner,

'Fame!'™ Gorgeous 4¹/₂-inch, shocking pink flowers with scalloped petals burst forth from lustrous, dark green foliage. Milder temperatures produce the best size and form, but the plant will grow tall, hardy, and bushy in other temperate zones because it is an own-root-grown New Generation Rose®. 'Fame!'™ produces loads of large lightly scented flowers without much care, but it became a must-have rose for our garden because its vase life as a cut flower is two to three times longer than most other rose blossoms.

Just one year after 'Fame!'™ was named the AARS grandiflora, Dr. Keith Zary's 'Candelabra'™ was awarded the same honor by the AARS. Against lush, moss green leaves, 4-inch blooms of coral and orange flowers illuminate the garden. Other orange roses flicker faintly and can't hold a candle to this rose's glowing, free-blooming performance in most regions of the Southwest. It is another New Generation Rose® that stands up to heat and cold. In our garden, its powerful color and hardiness more than compensate for its slightness of fragrance.

'Cherry Parfait'™ is a 5-foot-tall grandiflora that truly deserves its 2003 AARS tribute with its profuse flowering sprays of creamy-white blossoms dipped in lipstick red. Grown on its own roots, it is a good strong grower in all climates with excellent disease resistance. The distinctive bi-colored flowers hold up well in heat and take the spotlight against a backdrop of glossy deep-green leaves. 'Cherry Parfait'™ is a deliciously lovely dessert for the eye, especially since we moved our sweet confection closer to the cool, white flowers of 'Iceberg'.

Climbers provide height and structural interest to our garden with their exuberant blooms cascading over walls, gates, trellises, and pyramidal supports. For elegant cerise-pink flowers with a stunning antique-rose, raspberry fragrance wafting on the summer breeze, 'Zephirine Drouhin' is one of our favorite choices. This bourbon rose was introduced in 1868, and its 15 to 20 foot tall stems grow strong even in alkaline soil, pollution, or shade conditions. We have planted 'Zephirine Drouhin' in an area where we brush up against it, but there have never been any painful encounters because in addition to its beauty and fragrance, it blooms on nearly thornless stems.

'Fourth of July' is the first climbing rose to win the AARS award in twenty-three years. True to its name, this is no wallflower. 'Fourth of July' explodes with a sparkling display of 4-inch, red-striped, ruffled white flowers that start in early summer and don't quit until late fall. This firecracker develops sturdy canes that spread 6 feet and climb as tall as 10 to 15 feet, bearing audacious sprays of irresistible semi-double flowers. As an own-root rose, it has made itself at home in many Southwest gardens. From the first year we planted 'Fourth of July', its vigor and bold looks have started a revolution of fireworks in our landscape and warmed our summer air with the scent of fresh apples.

Another climber to bloom repeatedly throughout the season is 'Joseph's Coat'. Vivid scarlet, yellow, orange, and pink double flowers combine with glossy, apple-green leaves to create climbing 10 to 12 foot tall pillars. Because of its thorny nature, we have effectively used 'Joseph's Coat' as a Technicolor barrier on our property.

'Blaze' (Improved) is one of the most popular climbers since 1932. It is a consistently profuse bloomer with a light, fruity fragrance. Throughout the season, cascades of fiery red blossoms blaze brightly from top to bottom, practically smothering our mailbox stand.

Polyantha roses were predecessors to the modern floribundas and are now making a comeback in popularity because they are strong, compact, 3-foot plants that bear clusters of 1-inch diminutive flowers. Many flower non-stop all season and make excellent border shrubs, such as **'The Fairy'** with pale pink, ruffled, double flowers in large, pyramidal clusters that give off a fruity, apple-like fragrance. When the weather is cool, it shows off its best color, but it is quite hardy and disease resistant. Since 1932 it has been a proven performer and makes an ideal low border or groundcover.

Miniature roses are scaled down versions of modern hybrid teas and floribundas, but our favorite miniature acts more like a bushy shrub. **'Gourmet Popcorn'** is a rounded bush smothered with cascading buds that pop open into fragrant white blooms. The dark green leaves are smooth, like butter, and very disease-resistant. We also use the sprays from 'Gourmet Popcorn' and 'The Fairy' as fillers in flower arrangements. They last longer than your traditional fillers such as baby's breath and add a delicate fragrance and a more unique addition to cut flowers.

For floriferous fencing, **'Simplicity'**® roses grow like hedges or can be pruned low for borders. They bloom freely from early spring through December and because of their hardiness, low maintenance, and vigor, they are one of the best landscape roses in our garden. Although available in rosy pink, sunshine yellow, and snowy white, our favorite is the spicy-perfumed raspberry-colored, **'Purple Simplicity'**®. Our fragrant fence is simply the best.

Since peonies are out of the question in most areas of the Southwest, David Austin English Roses are a welcome substitute in our garden. They not only remind us of peonies, but they possess lavishly petaled and scented blossoms. Along with these traits of long ago, they have been hybridized with equally important attributes such as repeat blooming, hardiness, and reliability. Despite its glamorous appearance, **'Abraham Darby'** is grown on its own roots and stays very hale and hardy amongst our other roses. It is everything an English rose should be—deeply cupped, complexion-perfect, peach-pink flowers with a pastel yellow reverse and a strong, fruity fragrance.

After nearly 35 million years of existence and over 150 species spread across the northern hemisphere from Alaska to Mexico, the question is not if a rose can survive in the Southwest, but how many can fit in your garden. For us, there is always room for one more rose.

ROSE RESOURCES
for the Southwest

American Rose Society. Contact information at P.O. Box 30,000, Shreveport, La. 71130-0030 or visit their website at **www.ars.org.**

Heritage Roses Group (South-West District includes Arizona). Contact information at 100 Bear Oaks Drive, Martinez, Ca. 94553 or visit their website at **www.thefragrantgarden.com.**

National Gardening Association. Contact information at 1100 Dorset Street, South Burlington, Vt. 05403 or visit their website at **www.nationalgardening.com.**

Arizona

Public Rose Displays:

Gene C. Reid Rose Garden features 1080 roses and over 100 species of roses. Newly renovated and re-opened in April 2001, its most impressive displays are in April. Address: 900 South Randolph Way, Tucson 85716.

Heritage Rose Garden is located on the grounds of the University of Arizona's Maricopa County Cooperative Extension office and is maintained by the Heritage Rose Garden Association. It is a demonstration garden with old fashioned rose varieties. Address: 4341 E. Broadway Road, Phoenix 85040-8807.

Mesa Community College Rose Garden is considered the largest rose garden in the Southwest desert with more than 500 bushes and more than 500 varieties. Established in 1996 in partnership with the Mesa-East Valley Rose Society, it is one of only 26 AARS test gardens in the nation. Address: 1833 West Southern Avenue, Mesa 85202.

Historical Sahuaro Ranch Rose Garden was once a historical ranch and is now a regional park. It features over 1,000 rosebushes of over 100 varieties. Address: 9802 North 59th Avenue, Glendale 85302.

Territorial Women's Memorial Rose Garden at the Sharlot Hall Museum is dedicated to Arizona's pioneer women born before 1900 who lived in Arizona prior to 1912 and were part of the state's development. Address: 415 West Gurley Street, Prescott 86301.

Organizations:

Arizona Federation of Garden Clubs. Contact information: 79 Shadow Mountain Drive, Sedona 85366-2730 or visit their website at **www.azgardenclub.org.**

Arizona Master Gardener. Master Gardeners are highly trained volunteers working with the University of Arizona. County programs include Apache, Cochise, Coconino, Gila, Graham, Greenlee, La Paz, Maricopa, Mohave, Navajo, Pima, Pinal, Santa Cruz, Yavapai and Yuma. Contact information at Master Gardeners Program, 4341 E. Broadway Road, Phoenix 85040 or visit their website at **www.cals.arizona.edu/extension/mastergardener.html.**

Federated Garden Clubs of Yuma, Arizona. Contact information at 554 S. 6th Avenue, Yuma 85364-2963.

Mesa-East Valley Rose Society. Local chapter of the ARS. Contact information at Mesa Community College at 1833 W. Southern Avenue, Mesa 85202 or visit their website at **www.roses4az.mevrs.org.**

Pacific Southwest District of the American Rose Society (includes Arizona). Contact information at 25769 Miguel Ct., Valencia, Ca. 91355 or visit their website at **www.pswdistrict.org.**

Rose Society of Tucson. Local chapter of the ARS. Contact information at 1631 E. Calle Altivo, Tucson 85718 or visit their website at **www.tucsonrose.org.**

West Valley Rose Society. Local chapter of the ARS. Contact information at 6130 W. Claremont, Glendale 85308.

Nurseries:

Arizona Nursery Association. Contact information at 1430 W. Broadway, Suite #A-180, Tempe, 85282 or visit their website at **www.azna.org.**

Jackson & Perkins Wholesale, Inc. Contact information at P.O. Box 9100, 2518 S. Pacific Highway, Medford, Or. 97501 or visit their website at **www.jproses.com.**

Southern California

Public Rose Displays:

A. C. Postel Memorial Rose Garden. With about 1,600 roses, this is one of the most popular public gardens in Santa Barbara. Address: 555 Plaza Rubio, Santa Barbara 93103 or go to **www.museumsusa.org/data/museums/CA/9180.htm.**

Descanso Gardens. This oasis of tranquility covers 160 acres of landscape. In addition to 80 acres of flowers such as camellias and lilacs, there is a 5 acre rose garden. Address: 1418 Descanso Drive, La Canada 91011 or visit their website at **www.descanso.com.**

Exposition Park Rose Garden was the first municipally operated public rose garden in the United States. Today, there are 10,000 rosebushes of 100 different varieties as well as 200 currently available cultivars and the annual All-America Selections roses growing on a 7 acre garden. Address: 701 State Drive, Los Angeles 90037 or visit their website at **www.laparks. org/exporosegarden/rosegarden.html**.

Fairmont Park Rose Garden. Address: 2225 Market Street, Riverside 92421.

James J. White Rose Garden. Located in the South Coast Botanic Garden. Address: 26300 Crenshaw Boulevard, Palos Verdes Peninsula 90274 or go to **www.parks.co.la.ca.us/south_coast_botanic.html**.

Huntington Art Gallery and Botanical Gardens. There are 150 acres of gardens including many themed ones such as the rose garden with over 1,500 cultivars arranged historically from the oldest cultivated during Medieval and Renaissance times to roses introduced since 1950. Strolling through this garden is like strolling through the history of the rose. Address: 1151 Oxford Road, San Marino 91108 or visit their website at **www.huntington.org**.

Inez Grant Parker Rose Garden. Located on the east side of Balboa Park, south of the footbridge that crosses Park Boulevard, this is an award-winning, All America Rose Selection display garden. Stroll on three acres filled with over 2,400 rosebushes in 190 varieties. Visit Balboa Park on Park Boulevard, San Diego 92101 or go to **www.balboapark.org/aboutgardens.html**.

Mission Historical Park Rose Garden. Visit at Upper Laguna and Los Olivos, Santa Barbara 93103.

Pageant of Roses Garden. This is the official display garden for the ARS and AARS as well as a test site for the ARS. Over the years, the 3.5 acre garden has expanded to include 7,000 rosebushes and more than 600 varieties. In 1984, the All-America Rose Selections designated the Pageant of Roses Garden as the most outstanding public rose garden in the United States. Address: Rose Hills Memorial Park and Mortuary, 3888 Workman Mill Road, Whittier 90601 or visit their website at **www.rosehills.com**.

Rogers Gardens. This 7$^{1}/_{2}$-acre retail nursery has numerous demonstration gardens including a rose garden. Address: 2301 San Joaquin Hills Road, Corona Del Mar 92625 or visit their website at **www.rogersgardens.com**.

South Coast Botanic Gardens. See how plants can transform a former landfill site into a garden of beauty. One of their many display gardens is an English rose garden. Address: 26300 Crenshaw Boulevard, Palos Verdes Peninsula 90274 or visit their website at **www.palosverdes.com/botanicgardens**.

The Flower Fields® at Carlsbad. Famous for its 50 acre field of blooming Giant Tecolote ranunculus in the spring, it also is known as an AARS test and display garden of 50 different varieties of roses, plus the Christopher W. Greenwood Walk of Fame Garden that features every AARS winning rose since 1940. Address: 5704 Paseo Del Norte, Carlsbad or visit their website at **www.theflowerfields.com**.

The Richard Nixon Library and Birthplace. In addition to the Nixon Library Museum and restored birthplace, it is also the largest public rose garden in Orange County with over 1,400 rosebushes. Address: 18001 Yorba Linda Road, Yorba Linda or visit their website at **www.nixonfoundation.org**.

The Rose Haven/Johnson Community Rose Garden. There are about 75 varieties of roses and 1,000 rosebushes on an acre of land. Address: 30592 Jedediah Road, Temecula.

Tournament of Roses Wrigley Garden. Surrounding the Wrigley mansion are many varieties of roses including the All-America Rose Selections, 'Tournament of Roses' rose. Address: 391 S. Orange Grove Boulevard, Pasadena 91184 or visit their website at **www.tournamentofroses.com**.

Victoria Rose Garden. Part of the Arboretum of Los Angeles County and refurbished in the 1950s by Los Volantarias, this garden features old garden roses, turn-of-the-20th-century roses, and David Austin roses amidst perennial color beds. Address: 301 N. Baldwin Avenue, Arcadia 91007 or visit their website at **www.arboretum.org**.

Virginia Robinson Gardens. Located on 6.2 acres of opulent gardens and terraces, it includes an impressive rose garden. The only Beverly Hills residential garden open to the public, reservations must be made before a visit. Address: 1008 Eden Way, Beverly Hills 90210 or visit their website at **www.parks.co.la.ca.us/Virginia_Gardens.html**.

Watts Senior Citizen Rose Garden. A gazebo surrounded by an award-winning rose garden. Address: 1657 E. Century Boulevard, Los Angeles 90002 or go to **www.laparks.org/dos/horticulture/watts.htm**.

Westminster Civic Center Rose Garden. There are 43 varieties and approximately 120 rosebushes, planted and labeled around the Civic Center area. Address: 8200 Westminster Boulevard, Westminster 92683.

Organizations:

Local societies of the ARS are California Coastal (Carlsbad), East County (El Cajon), Fair Friends of Roses (Ventura), Los Angeles, Orange County, Pacific Rose (Arcadia), Rose Society of Saddleback Mountain, San Diego, San Fernando Valley, Santa Clarita Valley, and Ventura County.

Master Gardeners of California. Contact information at the University of California Cooperative Extension, 700 Emery Way, San Jose 95128 or visit their website at www.mastergardeners.org, or contact the local University of California Cooperative Extension office (such as Los Angeles, Orange, San Diego, Santa Barbara and Ventura) to find out if your county has a Master Gardener Program.

Pacific Southwest District of the American Rose Society (includes Southern California). Contact information at 25769 Miguel Ct., Valencia 91355 or visit their website at www.pswdistrict.org.

Southern California Garden Clubs. Contact information at 512 Newton Street, San Fernando 91340 or visit their website at www.CaliforniaGardenClubs.org.

Southern California Horticultural Society. Contact information at P.O. Box 41080, Los Angeles 90041-0080 or visit their website at www.socalhort.org.

Nurseries:

California Association of Nurserymen. Contact information at 4620 Northgate Blvd., #155, Sacramento, 95834.

Jackson & Perkins Wholesale, Inc. Contact information at P.O. Box 9100, 2518 S. Pacific Highway, Medford, Or. 97501 or visit their website at www.jproses.com.

Colorado

Public Rose Displays:

Boulder-Dushanbe Teahouse Rose Garden is maintained by the Boulder Valley Rose Society and demonstrates types of roses that do well in Colorado. Address: 1770 13th Street, Boulder or visit their website at www.boulderrose.org.

Denver Botanic Gardens' newest display is a Monet Garden that replicates the plants and design elements of the artist's garden at Giverny. Address: 1005 York Street, Denver 80206 or visit their website at www.botanicgardens.org.

Hudson Gardens is a thirty acre outdoor regional display garden that includes a rose garden. Address: 6115 South Santa Fe Drive, Littleton.

Jefferson County Sheriff's Complex Rose Garden features an All-America Rose Selections accredited garden. Address: 200 Jefferson County Parkway, Golden 80401-2697.

Longmont Memorial Rose Garden is dedicated to veterans of all wars and became an All-America Rose Selection Public Garden in 1952. It now has over 1,400 rosebushes. Address: Roosevelt Park, 700 Longs Peak, Longmont 80501.

Mesa County Office (Colorado State Cooperative Education) Demonstration Gardens includes a rose garden. Address: 2775 U.S. Highway 50 Orchard Mesa, Grand Junction 81502-5028.

War Memorial Rose Garden is maintained by the Arapaho Rose Society and displays over one thousand roses on two acres of formal rose beds. Address: 5804 S. Bemis Street, Littleton.

Western Colorado Botanical Gardens has a rose garden as well as native, Japanese, sensory, and children's gardens. Address: 641 Struthers Avenue, Grand Junction 81501.

Organizations:

Local ARS chapters in Colorado: Arapaho Rose Society, Boulder Valley Rose Society, Denver Rose Society, Four Corners Rose Society in Durango, Loveland Rose Society in Loveland, Pikes Peak Rose Society in Colorado Springs, St. Vrain Rose Society in Longmont.

Master Gardeners. Contact information at Cooperative Extension, 1 Administration Building, Colorado State University, Fort Collins 805023-4040 or visit their website at www.colostate.edu/Depts/CoopExt.

Rocky Mountain District of the ARS (includes Colorado). Contact information at 14450 Rankin Road, Elbert 80106-9068.

Nurseries:

Colorado Nursery Association. Contact information at 5290 East Yale Circle, Denver 80222 or visit their website at www.info@colorado-nursery-assn.org.

Jackson & Perkins Wholesale, in Inc. Contact information at P.O. Box 9100, 2518 S. Pacific Highway, Medford, Or. 97501 or visit their website at **www.jproses.com**.

Public Rose Displays:

Desert Demonstration Gardens. In cooperation with the Kiwanis Club, the Las Vegas Valley Water District donated over two acres of land to create a series of water efficient landscapes that includes a rose garden with over 65 rosebushes and a rose hedge composed of fifteen Simplicity® rose plants. Address: 3701 W. Alta Drive, Las Vegas 89153 or visit their website at **www.lvspgardens.org**.

Elko County Rose Garden. A community garden containing winter-hardy, easy-care roses for USDA Zone 5. Located within the high desert of northeastern Nevada, there are over 73 Dr. Buck roses of 63 varieties. Visit the garden behind the Elko County Courthouse at the corner of 6th and Pine Street in Elko 89801 or go to **www.elkrose.com**.

Fred Galloway Reno Municipal Garden. This city park features an accredited All-America Rose Selections garden. Address: 1900 Idlewild Drive, Reno 89509.

Organizations:

Elko Rose Garden Association. Contact information at **www.elkrose.com**.

Las Vegas Rose Society is a local chapter of the ARS. Contact information at the Nevada Garden Club Center, 3533 W. Washington Boulevard, Las Vegas.

Master Gardener Programs of Nevada. Contact information at University of Nevada Cooperative Extension, P.O. Box 11130, Reno 89520-0027 or visit their website at **www.mastergardeners.com/ MasterGardenersNevada/htm**.

NCNH District of the American Rose Society (includes Nevada, except Las Vegas). Contact information at **www.ncnhdistrict.org**.

Nevada Garden Clubs, Inc. Contact information at P.O. Box 27624, Las Vegas 89126.

Pacific Southwest District of the American Rose Society (includes Southern Nevada) Contact information at 25769 Miguel Ct., Valencia, Ca. 91355 or visit their website at **www.pswdistrict.org**.

Nurseries:

Jackson & Perkins. Contact information at P.O. Box 9100, 2518 S. Pacific Highway, Medford, Or. 97501 or visit their website at **www.jproses.com**.

Public Rose Display:

Albuquerque Rose Garden. Maintained by the Albuquerque Rose Society, this garden displays over 1,200 bushes, including 433 cultivars from 26 classes of roses. Located near the Wyoming Regional Library. Address: 8203 Apache Ave. NE, Albuquerque 87110 or visit their website at **www.albuquerquerose.com**.

Organizations:

Albuquerque Rose Society is the local chapter of the ARS. Contact information at Albuquerque Rose Society, 9200 Flushing Meadows Drive NE, Albuquerque 87111 or visit their website at **www.albuquerquerose.com**.

Master Gardener Program of New Mexico. Local cities or counties include Albuquerque, Sandoval, Santa Fe and Valencia. Contact information at New Mexico State University, 9301 Indian School Road, Suite 201, Albuquerque 87112 or visit their website at **www.mastergardeners.com/MasterGardeners NewMexico.htm**.

Moriarty Garden Club. Contact information at P.O. Box 1626, Moriarty 87035 or e-mail at **kd5bp@lobo.net**.

Pacific Southwest District of the American Rose Society (includes New Mexico). Contact information at 25769 Miguel Ct., Valencia, Ca. 91355 or visit their website at **www.pswdistrict.org**.

Uptown Garden Club is located in Albuquerque, New Mexico. Contact information at **www.angelfire.com/ nm/UptownGardenClub**.

Nurseries:

New Mexico Association of Nursery Industries. Contact information at P.O. Box 667, Estancia 87016.

Jackson & Perkins Wholesale, Inc. Contact information at P.O. Box 9100, 2518 S. Pacific Highway, Medford, Or. 97501 or visit their website at **www.jproses.com**.

Utah

Public Rose Displays:

Murray Rose Garden-Garden of Freedom. This rose garden honors the men and women who served their country. Address: 5150 South Street, Murray 84157-0520 or visit their website at **www.ci.murray.utah.us/recfac/parkspools/RoseGarden.html**.

Nephi Federated Women's Club Memorial Rose Garden. This lovely garden is an All-America Rose Selections garden. Address: 100 E. North Street, Nephi 84648.

Red Butte Garden and State Arboretum of Utah. There are 13 acres of display gardens including the Fragrance Garden, the Floral Garden, and the Rose Garden. Another special area on campus is the Faculty Women's Club Rose Garden. Address: University of Utah, 300 Wakara Way, Salt Lake City 84108 or visit their website at **www.redbuttegarden.org**.

Territorial Statehouse State Park Rose Garden. Besides being Utah's oldest existing governmental building, it also boasts an All-America Rose Selections garden. Address: 50 West Capitol Ave., Fillmore 84631 or visit their website at **www.stateparks.utah.gov**.

Thanksgiving Gardens. Within this family entertainment park are numerous gardens including an English garden and a rose garden with over 2,000 rosebushes. Address: 2095 Thanksgiving Way, Lehi 84043 or visit their website at **www.thanksgivingpoint.com**.

Organizations:

Rocky Mountain District of the ARS (includes Utah). Contact information at 14450 Rankin Road, Elbert, Co. 80106-9068.

UNLA-Utah Green Association (Utah Nursery and Landscape Association). Contact information at P.O. Box 526314, Salt Lake City 84152-6314 or visit their website at **www.utahgreen.org**.

Utah Master Gardeners. Contact information at 28 East State Street, Farmington 84025 or visit their website at **www.extensionusu.edu/UMG/flash/home/home.htm** or contact the Utah State University Extension Offices in your county for local Master Gardener information.

'Candelabra'

Utah Rose Society. Local society of the ARS. Contact information at 1602 E. 2100 South, Salt Lake City or visit their website at **www.utahroses.tripod.com**.

Nurseries:

Jackson & Perkins Wholesale, Inc. Contact information at P.O. Box 9100, 2518 S. Pacific Highway, Medford, Or. 97501 or visit their website at **www.jproses.com**.

UNLA-Utah Green Association (Utah Nursery and Landscape Association). Contact information at P.O. Box 526314, Salt Lake City 84152-6314 or visit their website at **www.utahgreen.org**.

USDA HARDINESS ZONES
for the Southwest

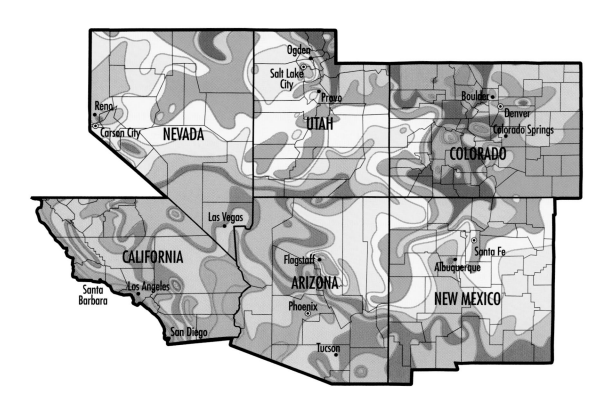

ZONE	Average Minimum Temperature °F	ZONE	Average Minimum Temperature °F
2b	-40 to -45	7a	5 to 0
3a	-35 to -40	7b	10 to 5
3b	-30 to -35	8a	15 to 10
4a	-25 to -30	8b	20 to 15
4b	-20 to -25	9a	25 to 20
5a	-15 to -20	9b	30 to 25
5b	-10 to -15	10a	35 to 30
6a	-5 to -10	10b	40 to 35
6b	0 to -5	11	40 and Above

PRECIPITATION
for the Southwest

January 1 to December 31
Averaged from 1961 to 1990

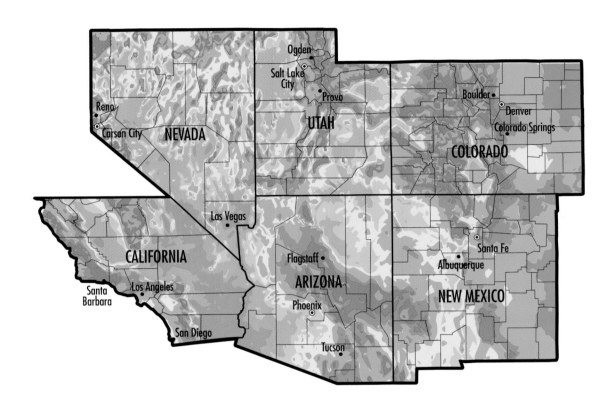

Inches

2   5   8   10   12   16   20   30   40   60

INDEX

MEET THE AUTHORS

Teri Dunn

Teri Dunn is a freelance writer and editor. She is a former Senior Copy Writer for Jackson & Perkins. Her articles on roses, perennials, waterlilies, wildflowers, and other topics have appeared in *Horticulture* magazine, for which she worked for many years as an Associate Editor. Teri is the author of numerous other gardening titles, including the acclaimed *Potting Places: Creative Ideas for Practical Gardening Workplaces, Cottage Gardens, 600 Essential Plants,* and several books in the popular *100 Favorites Series* on roses, perennials, herbs, shade plants, and others. She resides on Cape Ann, Massachusetts, with her husband Shawn and sons Wes and Tristan.

Bruce and Sharon Asakawa are co-authors of *Bruce and Sharon Asakawa's California Gardener's Guide* and co-hosts of the popular syndicated California television program "Garden Compass." Bruce is a landscape architect and educator who has taught horticulture for many years through the University of California San Diego Extension program. He has also chaired the California Certified Nurseryman's program. Sharon began working in the family garden center business after she and Bruce married. Sharon and Bruce have also shared their knowledge of gardening and other subjects in numerous magazine articles and through *Garden Compass Magazine.*

Bruce and Sharon Asakawa